Saga Hillbom

CITY OF BRONZE, CITY OF SILVER

ISBN: 978-91-519-3830-1

To Robin, for always offering her invaluable advice and an honest opinion

To my parents, for their constant support and encouragement

"What you leave behind is not what is engraved in stone but what is woven into the life of others."

Pericles

GLOSSARY

Aeropagus – The part of the Athenian law courts where cases of intentional homicide were tried

Agōgá – The Spartan education regime which was mandatory for male citizens and included harsh physical trials and military training as well as *musíca*

Agorá – A city's centre of commerce and trade, generally a large square

Amphora – A container for liquids, grains, etc.

Apella – The Spartan assembly

Arete – The concept of excellence in any field, including knowledge, moral virtue, and athletic perfection

Artos – Bread

Asphodel Meadows – The "standard" part of the underworld in Greek mythology where ordinary souls are sent

Bacchoi – Branches carried by the initiates at the Eleusinian Mysteries

Bibliotheca – Library

Khitōn – A garment consisting of a single rectangular piece of cloth, often linen or wool, which was draped over the body and fastened by the shoulders with *fibulae*

Collytus – One of Athens' richer demes

Chorēgos – A wealthy Athenian citizen who sponsors a playwright at the *Dionysia*

Dionysia – A festival held in spring in honour of Dionysus, the main festival for Greek drama

Dipylon Gate – The main gate in Athens' city walls

Drachma – Currency corresponding to six obols, the average daily wage for a *hoplite* or a skilled worker

Ecclesia – The Athenian people's assembly, open to all male citizens over the age of eighteen

Elysium – Paradise in Greek mythology, where great heroes and those chosen by the gods are sent

Engysis – Engagement or marriage contract

Éphoroi – An annually elected council of five who ruled Sparta together with its two kings

Fibula – A pin or brooch used to fasten clothes by the shoulders, often decorative as well

Gerousia – The Spartan council of elders

Gymnasium – A training facility as well as a place for socializing and intellectual discussions

Hellas – The ancient Greek name for Greece

Heílotes – An enslaved population group, under Spartan rule, who worked to support Spartan economy and society, and were often extremely badly treated

Hetaira – A courtesan offering entertainment and companionship as well as sexual services

Hēbōntes – A section of the *agōgá* where the members were roughly 20 years old

Himation – A mantle or cloak usually worn over a *khitōn* or *peplos*

Hippies – Cavalry

Hómoioi – Male Spartan citizens, meaning "equals"

Hoplite – Heavily armed infantry

Hoplon – A circular, convex shield carried by a *hoplite*

Hyacinthia – A Spartan festival honouring Apollo and his mortal lover Hyacinthus

Kerameikos – The potters' quarters in Athens, the site for an important cemetery

Khaíre – Greeting phrase

Kline – A sofa or bed

Klismos – A chair with curved legs and curved backrest

Kottabos – A popular drinking game

Kratēr – A large vessel used for mixing wine and water

Krupteía – Spartan secret police whose main purpose was to terrorize the *heílote* population

Kybernētēs – The commander on a *trireme*

Kykeon – A drink used at the mystery rites at Eleusis to induce hallucinations and other symptoms associated with substance use

Kylix – A broad, shallow drinking cup

Kyrios – Guardian

Melas zomos – The infamous Spartan black soup consisting mainly of pig's blood, salt, and vinegar

Mina – Currency corresponding to seventy *drachmae*

Miasma – Contagious pollution thought to follow bloodshed or similar crimes

Mora – Military unit composed of roughly 600 men

Musíca – Education in music, poetry, dancing, and singing

Obol – Currency corresponding to one sixth of a *drachma*

Oikos – A household and/or family

Orchestra – The flat area in the centre of a theatre where plays were performed

Palestra – An open-air, square area for exercising

Pentēkostys – Military unit composed of 128 men during the time of the Peloponnesian War according to Thucydides

Peplos – A female garment similar to *khitōn*, folded vertically and fastened by the shoulders, which in Sparta was sometimes knee-length and open on one side

Philtatos – Meaning "most beloved"

Pnynx Hill – The hill in central Athens where the *ecclesia* convened

Polis – City state

Pornai – Prostitutes, often sex slaves

Satyr play – A promiscuous play in which were based on mythology and featured choruses dressed as satyrs, supposed to lighten the audience's mood after tragedies had been performed

Stadion – A unit of length corresponding to approximately 180 meters

Stoa – A roofed walkway lined with colonnades, common in the *agorá*

Strategos – Military general and statesman, a public office to which ten men were elected annually by vote in Athens

Symposiarch – The "drinking master" at a *symposion*, the man who dictated how much each guest was to drink

Symposion – A banquet followed by a drinking party, often including entertainment

Syssitia – A Spartan mess hall with obligatory daily meals

Talent – Currency corresponding to sixty *minae*

Tártaros – The part of the underworld in Greek mythology where gave sinners are punished

Thranitai – The top rowers on a *trireme*

Thyrorós – A person who, symbolically, guards the door to the bridal chamber during a couple's wedding night

Triērarchos – The sponsor of a *trireme*, one of the most expensive liturgies in Athens

Trireme – A long, thin warship with three rows of oars

Xiphos – A short sword

Zither – A type of string instrument

Zoster – A type of belt

PROLOGUE

THE HIGH, OLIVE-GREEN grass whisked against Alethea's palms as she ran across the plain, the sharp straws prickling her tender skin. She was barefoot, as usual, and she hardly noticed the sharp little stones cutting into her pink soles.

A rippling laughter—melodious rather than the high-pitched sound one might expect to hear from a girl of six years—left her lips. 'You will never catch me! You're too slow!'

The boy behind her, Apolonio, offered no answer but sprinted faster, desperate not to let his sister win the race. True, she was only a year younger than him, and had been a natural runner ever since her feet had abandoned the waddling steps of toddlers—but Apolonio was every bit as competitive. The faint wind ruffled the thick locks of hair that surrounded his face like a frame of ebony, tousling them in a way that would make his mother sigh loudly when she caught sight of him. It would merely be a sigh for show, though, because Myrrene secretly relished the playful vitality of her children.

As Alethea turned her head to flash her brother a gleeful smile, a moment of inattention made her stumble on a protruding root, and she stooped face-first into the grass. This was enough to allow

Apolonio to catch up, and he soon tumbled down on top of her with a cry of victorious delight. There, on Sparta's sun-baked eastern plain, they remained for some time, listening to the crickets and waiting for their breaths to return to normal.

'I'll miss you when you go away. I don't think you will like it either—the *agōgá*.' Alethea kept her gaze on the sky above.

'I thought you envied me.'

'I do! I just hope you're tough enough. Did you hear about the boy with the fox?' Alethea almost whispered the last sentence, her eyes glittering with excitement.

Apolonio rolled over onto his stomach and rested his chin on his arms, peach-coloured lips pouting then twisting in a grimace. 'I hope I'll be that good. If it's true.'

The subject of the children's speculation—the boy with the fox—was a well-spread rumour among the Spartan youths, so well-spread that it had become a sort of truth, especially to those too young to think critically of it. The tale was that one of the older boys, after catching a fox to supplement the meagre diet customary in the military barracks, had been forced to hide it underneath his cloak to avoid being found out during the daily inspection. The fox, frantic to escape, had begun to gnaw at the boy's torso. Eventually, the fox had eaten its way to the bone—or, rather, to the vital organs—after which the boy had dropped dead in his attempt to prevent the inspector from discovering his violation of the strict rules. Alethea was certain that such discipline and pain-endurance could only be viewed with awe.

'I hope so too.' She brushed off a dragonfly that landed on her brow. 'I wish I could go.'

'I know.' Apolonio glowed. 'But we'll see each other often.'

'Yes.' It was true; while her brother was raised in the *agōgá*, Alethea would undergo her own education. They would both be drilled in obedience, *musíca*, hunting, and a moderate dose of literacy. Naturally, Apolonio would learn the art of war to a further extent, but girls and boys would exercise together: racing, riding, throwing the discus. Unlike the rest of Hellas' offspring, Spartan youths could expect to interact on several occasions despite the segregation which the boys' admission to the *agōgá* signified.

Even if the city had not been safely ensconced in the mountainous landscape, a secret jewel hidden in the Eurotas valley, Sparta would have had little to fear. Its soldiers were its city walls, and they would fight for their home until their blood dyed the earth scarlet, just as they had done in the battles of Thermopylae and Marathon against the Persians. When she thought about it, Alethea felt only pride— she knew it was the rest of Hellas who had reason to be afraid.

CHAPTER ONE

Thirteen years later

I T'S TIME YOU were married,' Myrrene stated, pacing the room, massaging her cheeks with freshly churned olive oil and fragrant herbs to give them a lustrous appearance and smooth the skin stretching tight over her high cheekbones. Despite the brackets of wrinkles that had begun to emerge around her eyes, Myrrene did not look her forty-five years; there was something timeless about the way she carried herself, and her eyes were as sharp as a hawk's.

'Yes.' Alethea lingered two steps behind her mother, unwilling to let her curiosity show.

'What say you—' Myrrene turned around, her eyes pinning Alethea's grey ones. '—what say you of Crysanthos? Chrysanthos son of Teleki. His family is respected, and I should think you'd count yourself fortunate to be wed to a man so close to you in age.'

Alethea suppressed the urge to crinkle her nose. 'Is he not a little...lacking in spirit?'

Myrrene chortled at the look on her daughter's face. 'Lacking in spirit? Chrysanthos is well-known for his endurance, for lasting days without sleep or food—whether there are men who face battle with more eagerness is irrelevant, as long as he faces it. You are too fussy, my dear.'

Chrysanthos with the cascading mass of blond, sun-kissed hair which he stubbornly refused to braid back, rose-petal lips, and skin dappled with no more than two or three faded scars. Crysanthos who, had he lived anywhere in the world but in Sparta, might have indulged in his vanity like a cat licking its glossy fur-coat. Crysanthos who fought only beca

se he had to, who fought as good as his kinsman but still preferred the idle game of flirtation. *Too soft. Will he make an honourable husband? Prettiness won't win any victories in battle.*

'I believe I haven't seen him in months, perhaps years. Is he still the same?'

'You'll have to find that out for yourself.' Myrrene proceeded to rub her forehead furiously with the scented oil, as if trying to erase every shadow of a crease. Alethea felt a sting of irritation at her otherwise so pragmatic mother's fear of an aging face. 'And if you can't find solace in his looks—which I think you will, if you're human—then take some satisfaction knowing you'll have what most young women and men in this *polis* would cut off a finger to have.'

Alethea's cheeks burned and she cursed the blush. 'And you honestly think Crysanthos will be content with me, when he could have all those finger-less youths if he wished?'

Myrrene shrugged, plugging the flask of oil with a piece of cork, and arched a dark eyebrow. 'I'm certain you will find a way to please your husband, Alethea. You're light on your feet, both in dancing and racing, and your eyes aren't displeasing to look at. That will have to do.'

Always the matchmaker. Alethea had no doubt that it was her mother, not her father, who had suggested the union; Myrrene was skilled in making each party see only the best in the other. *If she wished, she could have convinced a king to marry a beggar, or a snake to befriend a goat.*

Once they had parted, and Alethea had ventured to the garden to clear her thoughts, she caught herself reconciling with her fate quicker than the stubborn part of her might have wished. Though he was not the man she would have picked, her fate could have been far more unpleasant, and there were worse men to be tied to. Her mother was right in one thing: Crysanthos was enduring, and famous for it. That was some comfort.

Summer was budding, fresh in its cradle. The fig trees had begun to bear fruit, although the figs would not be ripe for almost another month. Now they were small and hard under the lush green leaves. Behind them, Mount Taygetus dominated the skyline. Streams trickled from the rocky mountainside, pouring out in the Eurotas.

Alethea cocked her head, squinting at the sun bleeding through a thin veil of clouds, bathing the grass beneath her feet in white gold. The day was yet young, but the sun would soon rise to its full height as Helios drove his chariot across the sky, and the heat would blaze down on her scalp.

Helios...Apollo...her thoughts immediately carried to Apolonio; he was never more than a heartbeat away in her mind, pulled into the light at every chance. It had been thus since they were born—Alethea could not remember further back than their fifth year, but she could not fathom a time when her mind had been hers and hers alone. Always, always there had been a fragment belonging to him. Like a splinter, it would not go away, but Alethea only took pleasure knowing there was someone so deeply entwined with herself that not even the Gods themselves could undo the knot if they tried. It was strange to think that he had existed a whole year without her, that they were not the twins she so often imagined.

He already knows about my marriage, of course. Mother and father would have spoken to him first, or sent a messenger. Would Apolonio be pleased? There was no telling, but she had often seen him lingering by Crysanthos' side. Where there was a sun there was bound to be a dark-haired shadow, and Apolonio appeared to have accepted this role long ago.

He can tell me whether I shall be happy, whether I ought to dance or weep. He knows the man who is to be my fate better than I do.

The dusk lay heavy over the military barracks as Alethea strode towards them, the brown cloak swept tightly around her shoulders in an attempt to make herself scarce. Although women were no rare sight in the dark of night at the barracks, this provided no comfort, for it was equally common that they fared badly at the hands of the soldiers. Alethea had no intentions of being one of those who came with longing in her eyes to visit a husband or a son, and left with torn clothes and bruised thighs after stumbling across one of his comrades. *I'd rather slit the brute's throat—but that would be inconvenient. For the army, for myself.*

She mumbled a prayer to Artemis under her breath, and it seemed that the chaste goddess of the wild and moon was feeling charitable, because no hands sticky from wine sought to grab her wrist as she sneaked through the network of barracks as quiet as a mountain lion hunting. Halting outside one of the buildings, she pressed against the wall and waited.

A few minutes passed before a familiar figure emerged from the barrack and closed the distance between them with long steps, gathering her into the warm harbour of his arms. Alethea made no resistance; she knew his ebony locks, she knew the scent of cloves and leather; she would have known him in pitch dark and in the Asphodel Meadows. Moments later, as they withdrew from the clinging embrace, she caught a glint of unease in her brother's cat eyes.

Apolonio chewed on his lower lip before speaking. 'You are well?'

'Well enough. And you, brother?'

'Yes. I would have a word with you—it concerns your marriage.'

Alethea's brows knitted. 'What can be said of it? It's a fine match.' She frowned harder as she watched the unmistakable blush rise on Apolonio's cheeks, the same blush she so often found herself trying to disguise regardless of the emotion that caused it. The sun had not yet risen, but the dusk was lifting and she could discern every contour in his face.

'You know he's my comrade in arms. You know my affections sometimes...sometimes take the upper hand of me?'

'I did not.' Alethea folded her arms across her chest, more puzzled with every passing second. 'For all I know, and may the gods help me if I can't tell my own brother's sentiments, for all I know you're more sensible than that. But cease this...this talking in riddles!'

Apolonio mirrored her arms. 'I'll tell you bluntly then, since you're dear to me, that his love exceeds that of women, and he has no desire to wed you. His eyes are fixed on another.' As he spoke, the blush changed from pale peach to burning crimson.

Alethea swallowed several times, frozen to the spot. *His eyes are fixed on another. Another.* 'You?' she pressed forth, almost choking.

'I wish fate hadn't had it so.'

'But it is, isn't it? Crysanthos enjoys the fruits of our family to the fullest, doesn't he? Me he takes for a suitable façade, and you he takes to warm his bedroll!' Alethea hissed. Apolonio's lips parted, but she proceeded before he had a chance to speak. 'I thought you'd left pederasty and such relations behind you two, three years ago!'

'I did! This is different, this is…haven't you known love?'

'I doubt I *will* know it, now that my husband-to-be is certain never to love me. I would have doubted even if he *had* loved me.' She shook her head. 'You can't carry on, unless you wish my honour damaged.'

Pain flashed in Apolonio's face. His lips twitched and he caught her hands in his, holding them steady. Despite the shock and humiliation rumbling inside her, Alethea could not help but marvel at how warm they were in contrast to the crisp chill in the air, and hated herself for it.

'I would never wish for such a thing—don't you know me better? This will be the end of it, I swear by Zeus, and no one need ever know. I had to tell you, though. I couldn't bear it if you discovered the true nature of his love by some slip of his tongue.' His hands clutched hers tighter. 'I hate to see you so dismayed.'

Alethea tilted her head to meet his eyes. Though they had been of the same height for most of their youth, Apolonio had grown a half head higher than her the past couple of years, his squared shoulders had broadened while hers had remained slim. *At least I'm still the fastest one.* 'You do dismay me,' she whispered. 'We all have a role to play, for the good of the *polis*, but I can't play mine properly if my husband drools after another. You swear this will be the end of it?'

'I swear.'

'Good.'

Once the promise had been pronounced, the conversation lightened, and the cramped feeling in Alethea's chest eased as if someone had loosened the screws on bars of iron locked around her ribs. A small crisis had been averted. Apolonio had regained his senses, and with some luck, there would be no gossip to pass around.

Alethea retrieved a small loaf of olive-specked bread from the deep pockets of her cloak and tore it in two, offering half to her brother, 'I thought you might be hungry.'

'Always,' he rewarded her with that familiar half-smile, then took a generous bite of the bread. 'We stole a chicken from a *heílote* yesterday, but it was too bony to feed more than one man.'

'Perhaps they should feed themselves a little less and their chickens a little more.'

'One can always dream. You ought to return home—morning is approaching.'

Alethea nodded. The birds had begun to chirp where they sat on the branches of olive trees and cypresses. The entirety of the *hēbōntes* would be summoned for morning drills within the hour. She reached up and gave Apolonio a peck on the lips. 'Take care, brother. And remember what you swore to me.'

'I will.' Then he turned and was gone once more.

Like every time she laid eyes on her sister, Alethea involuntarily recalled the day she had last seen Delina in their home, the day before the younger girl was taken to the temple of Artemis to serve the goddess of the moon and the hunt, the goddess of the young and their purity. Almost seven years had come to pass, and with each year, Alethea's relief grew like a flower no longer barred from the sun. She rarely gave voice to it, yet she could not doubt Delina's painful awareness of how her presence had cast a shroud of gloom over the *oikos*. The dreams, the hallucinations, the screams. The odd turns of speech and the ever-present burden of caution—these were the burdens lifted from her family's shoulders when she accepted the cloak of a venerated priestess. She had done it willingly, though, and the temple was not only a sanctuary to Artemis but a sanctuary for her own dwindling thoughts.

Alethea took another step forward, lips curved. 'How is my little sister?'

'Well, thank you.' Delina plucked at the flowers heaped in her lap, spreading them out as if to prepare the crafting of a flower crown. 'What brings you?'

'I suppose you've heard of my impending wedding?' *Even you must know by now. It's been half a month.*

Delina sat silent for a moment. The roundness of her cheeks, the soft jawline, the slightly up-turned nose, and her short stature made her appear younger still than her sixteen years. Only her eyes, which bore a striking resemblance to Myrrene's hawk globes, testified to the sharp knowledge held in her head.

'She's displeased to lose another virgin to matrimony.' Delina's voice was as faint as a breeze, as if there was no air in her lungs to give it force. Yet she spoke with such austere certainty that the most seasoned war lord would not have dared question a single word. Her mouth was puckered as if sucking on an olive, lips pricked red. Alethea remembered how her sister used to pinch her lip with the tip of her nails whenever the voices in her head became too loud—perhaps she still did.

'Artemis? She has more precious ones than me, I'm sure.'

A flicker of coldness crossed Delina's face. 'You will not be wed, for there are obstacles. Bloodshed.'

Curiosity rippled through Alethea's body. 'Because of me?'

'No. Because fate wills it. Because hostilities among men never truly die, but spark again and again until all their sons have bled out in the plains.'

'You mean Athens is growing too powerful, reaching for what is not theirs.'

Delina gave no answer. She had returned her attention to the garlands of flowers in her lap, entwining them with her thin, bony fingers. A few moments passed in silence before her frail voice cut through the air again like a brittle blade about to snap in two. 'You ought to make yourself pretty for the festival. You still make yourself pretty?'

Alethea pursed her lips. 'Not as often as our mother would like, and still they have a match for me. Perhaps Artemis will make me hideous, if she wishes to keep me in her realm.' Such words were dangerously close to slandering the gods, and she regretted them the second they left her lips. 'Forgive me. Will you come, too?'

Delina showed her teeth in a rare smile. 'No. If people want to hear what I have to say—what the gods have to say—they can come here and I'll receive them. They would think I spoiled their fun if I came to their feasts.'

'You always say *they*.'

'If I were one of them, I wouldn't be here.'

No, no I suppose you wouldn't. But many envy your lot, many want to be closer to the deities.

Alethea left her sister thus. As she walked back to the *oikos*, she tinged at Delina's foreboding. Athens was hoarding wealth from her allies like a rat hoarding food, and Sparta's soldiers were weary from training. A war would be a time of leisure in comparison.

The Hyacinthia was a festival to marvel at. The legend told the tragic story of Hyacinth, a prince of Sparta, whose beauty could have made the gods envious, or worse, could make them fall in love with him, a mere mortal. The young prince chose to give his affection to Apollo, and visited his sacred lands, indulging in everything the god would show him: the flowers, the magnificent cattle, the wide-stretched grounds. This brought the wrath of the western wind Zephyros, who also desired Hyacinth's love. Hence, as Apollo threw a discus, Zephyros changed its course so that it struck Hyacinth's temple, wounding him fatally. Though Apollo used all his powers of healing, the god could do nothing to save his lover, but transformed him into a flower, so that he might live on in another shape: the hyacinth.

The story was one of Alethea's favourites; there was something utterly captivating about the infatuation of one divine with one earthly, and how something so trivial as a gust of wind could wreck every chance of happiness.

The festival lasted for three whole days. The first and the third were solemn in spirit, dedicated to mourning the death of the hero and making sacrifices to family members who were dead also. The second day, however, was like the golden yolk of the egg, so brimming with music and dancing that one had no choice but surrender to the mirth. This was no day for sorrow, but for singing the glory of the gods and the passion that was the heart of the myth.

There were horse races, also, and Alethea's stomach fluttered with delight as she watched the four-legged creatures surge forward with dangerous strength. The chariots they pulled were simple, two-wheeled constructions, providing no safety. Muscles tensed under the horses' sweat-soaked, shiny furs. Whites of their eyes showing, they galloped faster and faster each time the charioteer allowed the reins to slip between his fingers. The chariots barely touched the ground except for when the wheels bumped against a protruding stone. *Careful now.* Alethea slammed her palms against the wooden rail in pure exasperation as the horses drew close to the sharp turning-point. She had seen several vehicles overturned through the years, the drivers crushed to bone splinters and flesh beneath the animals' hammering hooves. No such accident occurred this time, though, and the competitors crossed the finishing line unharmed.

'Kreon should have allowed them to run their full speed! If he had, they might have won,' Alethea said, her face still flushed from the heat of the race.

Myrrene shook her head. 'You would be wise to pick another team to cheer for, daughter. Kreon may be a brave charioteer, but only a fool would let his horses run wild.'

'He's been overturned before and lived.'

The man of whom they were speaking—a stout figure with calloused hands and knobby scars like worms underneath his tanned skin—had stepped down from his chariot and was talking quietly to the distraught horses. Indeed, he had been overturned many times, or even pushed from his chariot by another competitor, and it showed.

After the horseraces, the people flocked towards the enormous tents where the evening banquet took place. Men and women alike were welcome, as long as they were free and honourable.

Alethea cast a sideways glance at her intended husband and her brother. Crysanthos and Apolonio were seated with their military comrades at another table, grins spread across their faces, dice rolling from their hands. With his golden locks and cheeks smoother than cream, Crysanthos certainly attracted the gaze of numerous girls and boys. *They can't help it, I suppose, but they know it just as well as I do: he doesn't possess the qualities they* really *value. If one were to place a bow in his hand and a lyre in the other, they'd drop to their knees, mistaking him for Apollo come down from the skies.*

Apolonio did not bear any striking resemblance to Hyacinthus, yet it was impossible to look at them together, knowing what she now knew, without noticing the familiar way their hands brushed against one another. *Perhaps it's not over after all. Or perhaps it's just habit.* It did not matter, Alethea concluded, for there was nothing she could do but pray that the other guests were too distracted by the festivities to notice.

She returned her attention to the plate in front of her as *heílotes* began bringing in the food. Roasted lamb and oxen dripping with grease, bread soaked in honey, olives, dried fruit to sweeten their tongues and wine to muddle their minds. Goats had been slaughtered; the blood had poured out, and now the flesh had been roasted on spits, the best parts sacrificed to and the rest served to the humans. Such elaborate dining was everything but customary in Sparta, and Alethea wondered how she would manage to eat it all.

The wine was pure and rich, undiluted, the bitterness of the grapes prominent on her tongue. Athenians would have furrowed their brows, claiming it to be a savage habit. One who drank wine without stirring it with water risked illness or even madness, they said. This was a small oddity of the Spartans, though, compared to their women: lithe and lustrous, their bodies as well-fed as those of their male counterparts, they drank and talked freely, knowing their rightful place was at the banquet and not hidden from public sight. The girls were brought up under similar conditions to the boys. They exercised and danced together, hunted and sang, breathed the fresh Laconian air. The women's purpose was clear: to bear healthy, thriving children and thus contribute to the state and the army. A man's battle was behind a shield, a woman's was on a birthing chair, but they were equal in importance and prestige, and thriving children required thriving mothers.

Naturally, it would be no real festivity without dancing. Alethea's limbs itched, yearning to begin. She had spent the hour before the banquet begun carefully arranging long bronze pins—one of them a gift from Apolonio, the top shaped like a mountain cat—so that they would keep the obsidian garlands of hair in place on her head, and had draped herself in the purest white cloth fastened by the shoulders with large *fibulae*. She had tied a string of leather a finger's width above her waist, making the fabric fold thickly, and proceeded to massage her feet with a salve made from goat's fat and herbs to soften the muscles. However, the fine *peplos* and the leather string were only intended for the rest of the celebrations, because the dance itself would be executed almost in the nude, as was custom.

Eight other girls had also been chosen to perform the dance. Their hair was arranged in a manner identical to Alethea's, and their eyes shone amber in the firelight. When the musicians picked up their lyres, running their slender fingers across the strings, Alethea took her place among them. At first, the music was slow and harmonic, then hands slapped drums and the rhythm quickened. The pink soles of the girls' feet beat against the grass—which was still warm from the sun—synchronized like one being, and Alethea felt the music pump through her veins. The musicians sang of legends and myths, heroes and monsters, returning to names like Hercules, Perseus, Jason, Theseus, and Achilles. She knew their stories by heart, but never tired of hearing them told in intricate verse where the words entwined like lovers' hands. Of course, Hyacinthus and Apollo were the main objects of the song.

When night had cast its dark veil over the sky and the moon became visible like a bright chip of bone, the music and the dancing subsided. The other girls and women had already retired, though the men remained to boast and talk long into the night, and Alethea had to return to the *oikos*. In spite of the freedom she had savoured during the celebrations, there was a certain line of decency which could not be crossed, and she was dangerously close by remaining at this hour.

Gripping one of the long, sharp pins that kept her curls in place but could serve as a weapon, Alethea treaded across the field sheathed in shadows.

'I asked to sit at your table.' Apolonio's steps became apparent behind her, perfectly steady despite the slippery, dew-drenched grass.

Alethea offered a slight smile, though he could not see it. 'Don't you every year? And every year they say "no, you shall sit with your comrades".'

'So they do, but what kind of brother would I be if I didn't ask?' His steps grew longer until he had caught up on her pace and was walking beside her. Alethea inhaled his faint scent.

'How is my betrothed?' Her eyes sought his in the dark, exchanging a glance.

Apolonio snickered. 'Enjoying life's pleasures to the fullest, as is his nature. You mustn't despair—he knows his place and will take it once the time comes.'

'Yes, I know.' *At least I hope I know.* 'Delina said something a few days ago, something I'm eager to learn the truth of. That there will be bloodshed.'

'Ah. Isn't there *always* bloodshed somewhere or other?'

Alethea gave him a shove with her shoulder. 'You know what I mean. What she meant. Bloodshed involving our people.'

'I should think that's not so much a prophecy from Artemis as it is plain truth. The gods speak in riddles, as you well know, but war is unavoidable. Any child could give that foreboding.'

'You think Athens will give cause for reprimanding.' Alethea's lips twitched in a smile at the last word, and from the corner of her eye she could see Apolonio's do the same. The cool moonlight danced on his hair, painting every glossy patch white as if it was chiselled from the finest marble.

'I think they already have. I think our thirty years will be cut short to fifteen, or perhaps sixteen.'

Thirty years: that was the amount of time the peace treaty had promised, but the number had never truly been intended to keep both parties at bay, and the cracks in the treaty became more obvious every passing day. Like a thin sheath of linen wrapped around a wound where a blade had torn flesh from bone, it could not stem the old hostilities between the two *poleis*. The linen was soaked-through with blood now, and perhaps the only way to avoid death was to sever the limb and burn the stump.

'The Megarians will demand it.'

'Others, too.'

When the news of the Megarian Decree had reached Sparta some time ago, citizens had raised their voices and named it a catalyst of the war they had been waiting for. Megara had fought against Athens at the naval Battle of Sybota the previous year; Athens' revenge took the shape of a decree banning Megara from the *agorá* and the Athenian ports. They had claimed other, less provocative reasons, but no one in their right mind believed it. Now, the Megarians, devastated by the trade embargo, were seeking the help of their allies in the

Peloponnesian League, which, of course, sat under Sparta's leadership.

They had reached the winding path leading up to the *oikos*—a frugal building of mud bricks in two stories and with red clay tiles for roof, framed by the small garden terrace where thyme and figs grew—and Apolonio's steps ceased.

'Yes,' Alethea said before her brother had the chance. 'You must go back, or they'll start looking. Promise me something, though.'

'Another thing?' His eyes twinkled with both amusement and caution.

'Another thing, but not about Crysanthos. Promise me you'll bring news of the war if there is any. Tell me what they say in the barracks but won't say to their wives and older kinsmen. I would be prepared.'

'That I can promise. Goodnight, sister, and give our mother my greetings. She'd do well to eat a bit more on a day of celebration such as this.'

CHAPTER TWO

LATER THAT SAME summer, a formal declaration of war was issued against Athens and its allies known as the Delian League. Embassies from the members of the Peloponnesian League had assembled in Sparta, such as distressed Megarians and their sea-sprayed neighbours from the renowned Corinth, to present their complaints to the *éphoroi* and King Archidamus.

An Athenian envoy—uninvited, of course—had joined them, resulting in a heated debate between Athens and Corinth, whose hostile relations had grown worse following the Battles of Sybota and Potidaea, and the issuing of the Megarian Decree. However, Athens had not been the sole target of the Corinthians' criticism; Sparta, they said, was far too passive while their allies suffered. If the *polis* did not come to the aid of those city states so dependent on it, the Peloponnesian League itself would begin to crumble. No accusation could have stung more in the eyes of the *éphoroi*, nor injured the common citizen's sense of pride more fundamentally. *Passive.* The word was almost synonymous with *cowardly*, which in turn was a word more dreaded than plague. The Athenians' threats, which were plain reminders of their own military prowess in the Persian wars, were not quite as daunting.

During the spring and summer that year, the number of Spartans who viewed a war with the Delian League as not only a necessary measure against Athens' expanding power, but another sweet opportunity to assert their own dominance, had grown. Hence, there were no gasps of surprise when a clear majority of the Spartan assembly voted in favour of combat. The ambassadors from the other *poleis* had not been in unison, yet the result was clear enough: there now existed a state of war between the Peloponnesian and the Delian Leagues, one headed by Sparta and the other by Athens.

Word reached Alethea with the speed of Apolonio's messenger. *So, it is official, then. I knew it would be—I know the end, too. We'll cut away their confidence, if they have any, and those cultivated manners won't do them any good. Perhaps this time Attica shall be rid of blabbering, faint-hearted Athenian oppressors.* The Spartans' own enslavement of the *heílotes*, or their lording over the throng of city states who dared not object, did not alter her feelings. She knew, of course, but just as she knew, she was certain that there was a distinct line between greedy tyranny and rightful supremacy, a line defined by who the perpetrator and the victim happened to be.

Delina's eyes rolled back in her skull, showing only the milky whites, and her throat bulged as the cramps rode her frail body. Once her limbs relaxed, strands of hair lay glued to her sticky forehead, her cheeks drained of all colour.

Alethea watched with a sour taste on her tongue. *Those visions must hurt horribly. I wonder why they take such a physical shape.* Though she did not know why, she had never dared to ask. Another question sprung to her mind instead. 'What did you see? Tell me.'

Delina's eyes had rolled back again, but she stared in front of her like a deer gazing at a hunter about to launch an arrow, pupils small as peppercorn. 'No.'

'Why not?'

'No. I shan't.' Delina turned around and began walking towards the temple without another word, but Alethea latched onto her wrist. Pulling harder than she had intended, she forced her sister to meet her eyes once more.

Delina made no attempt to escape but her face froze like a cruel statue, lips pressed in a thin line. The coldness, as always, provided an odd contrast to her youthfully soft cheeks. 'You cannot command me, sister.'

'I know it—' Alethea loosened her grip on Delina's wrist. '—but whatever it is you won't tell me must be of great importance. And I'm curious to learn.'

'You have only yourself to blame, then. Apolonio is doomed if he goes. He won't live a long life.'

Alethea grappled for words. It was as if someone had wound a rope with tiny knives around her chest over and over again, the blades cutting her and the tightness of the rope forcing her heart to shrink. *You lie. You only say that because I was harsh. That's not what you saw.* 'No,' was all she could bring herself to say.

'You asked me, and I told you.' Delina's lips curled in a strange smile and her eyes remained sharp. 'Goodnight, Alethea.' She then retreated behind the great stone pillars that constituted her sanctuary as well as the goddess', enveloped in the shadows they cast.

Alethea stood astounded, clutching the folds of her *peplos* until the bone in her knuckles showed through the skin and her nails left deep, reddening marks in her palms. It could not be, it simply could not. Delina was not always correct in her sights—after all, they were meant to be riddles of sort, as was every message or sign the gods sent—but neither was she entirely wrong very often. In fact, Alethea could count on one hand the times when there had been no truth whatsoever in what her sister told. Furthermore, Apolonio's death was in no way an unlikely scenario, since even the strongest soldiers could easily be struck down by a well-aimed arrow or spear. It was an respectable death, but Alethea preferred Apolonio alive. To try and prevent a man's death on the battle field... It went against everything she had been taught, everything a true Spartan was supposed to do. And yet, in some strange way, she had never pondered the possibility of losing the one closest to her, but had thought of him as invincible. It was just a thought, she realised, and not in her nature, but nevertheless it had always been there. Now, grotesque images of what this war might bring flooded her mind: not only honour and excitement but gruesome death.

I have to watch over him. I must try.

The sunlight turned Crysanthos' hair to a bright halo, giving the illusion of a deity, which Alethea noted was one of his most annoying traits. His voice, however, was not the thunder of a god but high-pitched and jittery, like a lyre whose strings had begun to snap.

Alethea took a deep breath to conclude what she had been telling him. 'So you see, then, that you must bring me with you, with the army.'

Crysanthos shrugged. 'I don't see it. What could you do to protect him, anyhow?'

'You don't trust my abilities? You, with more enthusiasm for staring at your own reflection than standing behind a shield?' She thrust a pointy finger in his chest. Flattery might be smoother than insults in the game of persuasion, but the latter was a thousand times more satisfying, and had worked in her favour surprisingly often.

Crysanthos did not burst into a fit of rage; he merely twitched and tucked a strand of hair behind his ear. 'I'm a competent soldier, *wife*.'

Alethea scoffed. *Half-witted boy*. 'You may call me that in due time. Do you want children, Crysanthos? And do you want your wife to be the one to carry them?'

The deity-imitation in front of her looked as if he had been asked whether the moon would continue to travel across the sky as it had done since the dawning of time. The answer was too obvious to utter.

Maybe you'll have something to say to this, then. 'I will give you a string of healthy sons. Or, if I find myself terribly vexed, they might be still-born. There are means to which a woman can turn—our secrets, you might say—draughts and so forth.'

'Would you...would you do such a thing?'

'Do you want to find out?'

'I could...could marry another girl.'

'And I would be none the poorer. But I think you'd find it inconvenient, considering your grandfather agreed to the betrothal already and Artemis have given her rare blessing. My sister said so. I think you know who she is.' Alethea held her breath. She could not remember the last time she had given such a lengthy statement.

'Apolonio is less cruel than you, yes, that's the difference between the two of you.' A hint of offense had snuck into Crysanthos' voice, making every word a whine.

'I'm not cruel, only pragmatic. The difference between my brother and I is that he chose to show you our best traits, and I the most useful.' Alethea watched her future husband push the same strand of hair back again and marvelled at the nature of their relationship. *What an odd little threesome we make, Crysanthos, Apolonio, and I. The couple and the in-between... But who's really who?*

Their time was running short seeing as the afternoon's sizzling heat was quickly subsiding into the lukewarm softness of the evening. The sky was no longer bright blue, but the colour of withering lavender, and a faint breeze whisked the olive trees' branches back and forth.

Crysanthos stole a glance over his shoulder at the barracks. 'What would you have me do, then? Sneak you into a cart when the troops leave?'

'No.' She ran her tongue over her teeth. 'I won't defy the *éphoroi*, so we'll have to convince them. I know your grandfather is a member of the *Gerousia*, and the *éphoroi* will listen to him.'

The authorities she spoke of were not to be taken lightly. The *Gerousia*, the council of elders, were held in high esteem by the citizenry; the *éphoroi*, a council of five with great legal authority, did not even have to kneel before kings. Involving them in such a petty matter as one's personal desires or ambitions was not customary—certainly not in times of war, when the *polis* as a whole held greater importance than ever—but Alethea could think of no other option that did not involve disobeying their rule.

The bulge on Crysanthos' throat bobbed several times. 'I'll do what I can, as long as you promise to be a good wife to me once this is over.'

'Of course,' Alethea did her best to make her voice as smooth as honey and cream, but it had never been her greatest talent. 'I shall be the loveliest woman you'll find in Sparta, and your *oikos* will be filled with more healthy children than you can count. And if I don't please you, then you won't see much of me anyways.'

This appeared to satisfy him, because he nodded and began walking back to the barracks.

Except there's no guarantee you'll be alive once this is over. I hope you will be, for the sake of Apolonio's heart, but I just might find myself married to someone of better character. That's all in the hands of the gods. Alethea crossed her arms and clutched herself, watching Crysanthos' shimmering halo disappear in the distance. Her stomach fluttered with anticipation, though some of it was plain hunger, she realised. She had no sundial at hand to tell the time, but the colour of the sky and the growling of her belly were signs certain enough to send her on her way back to the house.

Persuading the cause for her concern to cooperate proved a more difficult task than convincing Crysanthos had been, since Apolonio would not be so easily swayed by threats and insults. Moreover, Alethea could not bring herself to heap them on him.

She caught her brother practicing with his spear, his entire body plunging the weapon forward in an impressive arch, muscles dancing under the skin on his back, dust rising around his sandals. The thin streaks of white running across his scapula were the fading scars from an old rite of passage, in which the boys in the *agōgá* were brutally whipped at the altar of Artemis. He was alone on the exercise grounds save for four or five other young men, all of whom were occupied with discuses. Such a moment of relative solitude, in comparison to the usual mass of soldiers, was rare, and the opportunity must be seized. *Perhaps the others are on some quest, or training elsewhere.*

With utmost care, Alethea approached Apolonio from behind, treading with light steps. When she was a hand's width behind him, she gave his arm a hard pinch.

Apolonio spun around, the hand which had plunged the spear now gripping after his knife. 'Sister!' His face relaxed and a gleam of mutual mischief entered his cat's eyes as he rubbed the red mark on his arm. 'Do you come bearing news, or merely to mock?'

'Both, I suppose.' She smiled. 'Although you throw better each time I see it—soon, I won't have reason to mock.'

'I should hope not. I doubt you can throw at all.'

'Spears are not my weapon of choice. You know that. They're not very convenient to carry around for a woman.'

'I know. And the news?' Apolonio tilted his head,

Alethea braced herself for his reaction. *He's too correct, if there is such a thing, just like I would have been at any other time, but he must know eventually.* 'It appears your *mora* won't solely consist of men this time. I intent to go with you on campaign.' There was no simpler way to put it, yet she cringed at how foolish it sounded when she said it out loud.

Apolonio frowned. 'You're serious. There is that look on your face.'

'Yes.'

'Why? And how...how, by Zeus, would you do such a thing?'

With as much calm as she could summon, Alethea retold Delina's prophecy, her stomach twisting. Every word was like a dagger puncturing her entrails, because repeating them felt like confirming their truth. She watched Apolonio's jaw clench.

'If I could, I would make you stay here with me, but I can't, can I?'

'No, and never say such things!'

'Don't you see? It's for *your* sake!'

'That's the very root of my objection. You would put your own and mine interests above Sparta? You would deprive the army of a soldier for fear of losing a brother?'

Alethea chipped for air, so strong was the shame that flooded her, and felt her face flame red. 'Only in this matter. Only this exception.'

'Is not every man an exception to someone?' Apolonio retorted, failing to harden his voice enough to give credibility to his words. The scent of cloves and leather blended with sweat, droplets of which crowned his temples. His fingers were still closed in a tight grip around the knife shaft. Alethea knew their palms were covered in callouses from years of pressure on the same spots. *I would miss those hands.*

'I'm going.'

Apolonio shook his head. 'If my death is fated, then there is nothing you can do to change it.'

'I said I'm going—the fates *will* have to change,' she replied, blind with emotion. The other soldiers' eyes had begun to stray from their weapons to the heated spectacle, and she flashed them the most admonishing stare she could muster, which filled its purpose. *You'd do better to practise. Athenian's won't be struck down by curious peeping.*

Apolonio grabbed her by the shoulders, shaking her until her teeth clattered. The gesture might have appeared harsh in the eyes of an observer, yet Alethea hardly felt it. 'And what if you should die?' he said.

'I would not resent a death on campaign any more than a death in childbirth.'

'A death in childbirth would be more useful.'

'Don't chide me any longer, brother. In every other matter I will do what's expected, and you know it. I've spoken to Crysanthos—his grandfather will bring this about.'

'But you still need my aid in convincing them.'

'I need your aid in many things.'

The sun beat down on the siblings where they stood, their faces set in stone. Around them, the Peloponnesian plain, crowded with trees bearing figs and olives, extended as far as the mountains allowed. Alethea craned her neck to get a better view of Apolonio, and was cruelly reminded of how she loathed having to look up at the few men in her life, despite her own tall stature.

News arrived from Crysanthos mere days later. The *éphoroi* had initially been hesitant to say the least, but the reverence that the members of the *gerousia* employed, by old age alone as well as by the office they held, had been enough to persuade them. If the beloved grandson of one of Sparta's most respected citizens was anxious to bring his new wife on campaign, well, they had more urgent issues to solve than thwarting him. The wife in question would have to make herself scarce, of course, remaining in the camp to avoid placing herself in danger or, worse, infringing on the soldiers' space and resources.

Alethea accepted the conditions with a hint of dissatisfaction. Foolishly, she had not fully anticipated the diminutive role she would have to play, but had pictured herself the protector scuttling from one side of the battlefield to the other, magically sending every dangerous arrow flying in the opposite direction. *I won't even come near the field, not like that. What did I expect?* And yet, it was a small miracle in itself to have obtained permission to go at all. A small miracle would have to suffice.

There was something which needed to be done first, since Crysanthos' appeal largely depended on the word *wife*. If the *éphoroi* learned that he had not yet entered any binding contract—only private promises between family members—with the woman for whom they had made an exception, there was no telling what measures they would take. The remedy was obvious: the marriage had to take place without further delay. Thus, the flickering possibility of another match being made was effectively smothered.

Alethea reminded herself, for the hundredth time, it seemed, of what her mother had said the day she had first revealed the intended union to her daughter. Crysanthos was sought-after by many, known for his endurance and as easy on the eyes as if he was the offspring of Aphrodite. True, he was neither the brightest nor the most fearless, but that was a price Alethea would have to pay. *I'd rather be annoyed than treated poorly, rather married to Apolonio's vain confidant than to a scoundrel. I could refuse, but who would then bring me? And we won't see much of one another once we return from the war.*

The marriage would not be apparent in the eyes of the public for quite some time. Crysanthos would come to her occasionally, cloaked in the dark of night, and though babies might result, they would not share a domestic life for almost another decade, when he reached his thirtieth year and she her twenty-ninth. Then, having completed his military training, her husband would be allowed to leave the barracks in order to live with her and any children they might have produced through the years—the only proof of their union as well as the only true purpose—while still dining each night in the *syssitia*, the mess hall, with his comrades. Even at this point, he would spend a significant amount of time either at war or on the exercise grounds. Furthermore, if the arrangement was fruitless, it could easily be broken.

The razor cut her hair close to the scalp, ringlets of black falling to the floor like writhing snakes. Alethea watched with new-found pleasure at how much lighter her head felt. Once the marriage was a fact, she would be forbidden to wear her hair long like that of an unmarried girl, reach no longer than her collarbone. She draped herself in the coarse man's garments intended for the ceremony, then strapped on the equally mannish sandals. The sight would have caused a foreigner to choke on his wine, but Alethea had known ever since she was a clucking girl what a Spartan wedding meant. The ritual of disguising oneself as a boy was thought to ease the groom's transitioning from pederasty to marital duty, although Alethea suspected many soldiers had already spend the night with a woman by the time they took a wife. *But rituals are rituals. Tradition must be observed.*

For what felt like an eternity but might have been mere minutes, she waited in the gloomy bedchamber set aside for her wedding night. Then, a sudden crack in the door, and a familiar silhouette slipped inside. Crysanthos caught sight of his bride, and with irritating ease, lifted her from her feet and slung her across one shoulder to carry her to the bed. The symbolic abduction could take various forms, depending on the bride's willingness, but Alethea chose to make little resistance. *We ought to get it over with.* She could not see her capturer's face clearly even as he put her down on the bed; Crysanthos made no effort to muddle the encounter with empty kisses or caresses. He had come directly from the *syssitia* and would return there shortly. Alethea realised with a twinge of remorse that he would probably seat himself next to her brother, acting as if he had never been gone, and perhaps wish it had been Apolonio waiting for him in the dark. She quashed the image in her mind. She could not allow Crysanthos' preference for another put a thorn in her pride, when her warmest feelings for him were tolerance.

His hands were surprisingly gentle; despite his indifference for her person, he was experienced, and it did not lie in his character to employ roughness. They did not speak until they had once more dressed.

'Will you bring me instructions before we depart, so that I can prepare?' Alethea asked, fastening the last strip on her sandals.

'Of course, but they will send envoys first.'

'I know. But you'll arrange things once the time comes.'

Crysanthos nodded, yawning, and slipped out of the room. Alethea clenched her jaw. *He better keep that promise.*

Just as her new husband had said—and as anyone with more intelligence than a hen might have predicted—envoys soon sped across the peninsula, passing Corinth and Megara, to that renowned place called Athens. They were to bring bargains of peace, bargains to which the Athenian government could hardly agree. Thereby, Sparta could formally claim to have reached out a hand in peace, and any doubt of Athens' aggressions would be wiped out as they refused the offer.

The Spartans in favour of war perceived it as a strategy and an opportunity to mock, while some reluctant souls clung to the hope that a half-hearted new treaty could yet be reached. Among them was the ruling king, Archidamus, or at least that was what Alethea had heard. Her stomach churned as she pictured the supposedly great leader looming in his throne hall, perhaps thinking with fondness of his old friend Pericles while the men in his army gritted their teeth at the very same thought. *He's not a stupid man. Far from it. But if he allows nostalgic memories to make him too complacent...then the gods only know where Hellas will end up.* Archidamus' co-regent, King Pleistoanax, was still in exile, having been accused of receiving bribes from the Athenian leader during the previous war over a decade earlier.

The first envoy departed in late summer, after the heat had passed its peak but before the olives had ripened. Alethea watched the small retinue on the horizon, standing up to her knees in the sun-warmed Eurotas river.

Her mother waded next to her, hands cupped and brimming with glinting sea shells. Myrrene sighed. 'You have barely collected any shells, Alethea. Is the river bed plain where you stand?'

'No, mother.' Alethea scooped down to retrieve a single pale pink chip from the clay around her toes. 'What do you think they will reply?'

'Our northern adversary?'

'Yes.'

'I think they have enough sense not to let our men inside their city.'

'Does the common labourer of Athens have any sense? They're allowed to rule, aren't they?'

'The common labourer is governed by others—he may have a vote, but his thoughts are not unfiltered.'

Alethea dropped the seashell in her mother's palm with the rest. 'This is pointless.'

Myrrene arched a brow, her hawk-eyes peering, inspecting. 'You always enjoyed our little sessions, or at least the result. I remember when you were younger, I had to insist you take the necklaces off when you went to bed so that you wouldn't strangle yourself in your sleep.'

'I'm not so young anymore. They're pretty—'

Her mother gave up a snort of derision. 'If you're no longer young, then I must be an old crone. Cease this nonsense and help me instead.'

Alethea obeyed, though her thoughts kept straying from the envoy and to the impending reply which would decide the course of events, decide the future of more *poleis* than she could count on her fingers. If they were unsuccessful in reaching a conclusion, Sparta might continue to send embassies throughout the autumn and into wintertime.

She slowly accumulated the shells in her palms and then in the scoop she created by stretching out the hem of her *peplos*. Once mother and daughter were content with the idle work—or, rather, when Myrrene was content and Alethea was feverous to escape to the racing tracks—they returned to the *oikos*, leaving the finger-aching task of carefully piercing every shell with a needle to the *heílotes*.

Alethea did not bother to change her clothes but simply kept the wet hem in a knot above her knees, because it was similar enough to the short garment worn by girls and women when racing. To her delight, she found the tracks almost empty, and the wind in her ears and her feet pounding against the ground were all she could hear as she ran. Pearls of sweat erupted on her temples and the back of her neck, her breath strained, yet her legs refused to give in even as she accelerated. With sturdier sandals, she could have continued beyond the tracks and south for several hours until she reached the ocean if she had wanted to.

Alethea had seen the ocean once when she was nine: her father had had a rare errand in the city of Gytheion and decided to bring his wide-eyed daughter with him so as to teach her the ways of the world. That was in the days when he had still visited home occasionally, instead of spending all his time in the army quarters, only involving himself with his wife when necessary. Those were the days before Myrrene had disgraced him by birthing the misshapen boy no one in the family dared speak of. The *gerousia* had rejected the lumpy little creature without a second glance since he would never make a competent soldier, and his parents' shame had been buried with him. The practice of disposing of weak or disabled babies was deemed vital to prevent the state from growing equally weak. Providing for and raising a boy who could never contribute to the army was synonymous with wasting resources.

Alethea shook her thoughts from the little brother she might have had, returning them to the ocean she remembered. The water had been the brightest turquoise by the beach, specks of sun like silver on the waves, the colour deepening into dark blue further out. There was something about that seemingly infinite open space Alethea found frightening. The rollicking of the waves against the sharp-cropped black rocks sounded just like the familiar Eurotas river, yet there was an uncertainty as to what lay at the other side of the vast space. She had been raised between mountains, a safely enclosed place, and like any Spartan she could not imagine calling another piece of land home.

CHAPTER 3

THE *ECCLESIA*, THE Athenian people's assembly, was swarming with men draped in thick *himation* over their *khitōns* against the cold, the wind ruffling the elders' greying beards and the youths' crowns of luscious hair. Some rubbed their hands frantically, trying to keep warm, while others merely clenched their jaws and endured. They were there to discuss matters of great importance, and those who fussed about the weather were soon silenced by their companions.

Although the men sprung from every trade and background, all earned enough money to afford sacrificing a day's wages in order to attend the meeting. Furthermore, they were equal under the law and possessed the same rights, being Athenian citizens and urban dwellers. Hence, the six thousand blended together like one buzzing mass, a bubble of privilege in contrast to the slaves, women, children, and non-citizens.

This was what Eucleides saw when he looked upon the *ecclesia*. Every time, he had the itching feeling that something was not quite right with the constitution of this democracy—but he saw neither the issue clearly, nor a solution.

'Cousin! Stop this futile daydreaming,' Cosimo said and yanked at Eucleides' *khitōn*.

Eucleides nodded and sat down on the bare rock, becoming another keg in the machinery on the Pnynx Hill.

The *strategoi*, the generals, spoke first, and Pericles was the foremost of the *strategoi*. Despite his respectable age, he climbed the elevated platform with ease, and the crowd fell silent before he so much as raised his hand.

'Athenians! We are assembled today to debate urgent matters, namely that of war. Another Spartan envoy arrived the day before yesterday.' His voice carried like the deep chiming of a bell. 'They claim there need be no war if the Megarian Decree is revoked.'

A wave of whispers swept through the crowd. If the Spartans were genuine this time, they had been offered the chance to escape the conflict with their lives, saving their sons and brothers as well from the perils of warfare. It would sting, of course, but perhaps revoking the Decree would be worth the embarrassment of following Sparta's whims.

'He better take the chance,' Cosimo hissed in Eucleides' ear. 'I have no inclination to spend my days on a trireme's deck.'

'Me neither.' Eucleides grimaced. 'I'd rather be a common *hoplite* than a captain at sea.'

'You'd rather not fight at all.' The statement was a matter of fact. Neither of the cousins had been bred for battle—they were too fine-limbed, too nimble-minded–but at least Cosimo had some experience as a *triērarchos*. The two years of military training, which was mandatory for all Athenian young men, had done little to harden Eucleides' disposition. However, military offices were closely entwined with those of the state; thus, this lack of enthusiasm for the battlefield was starting to turn into a disadvantage on the political scene. If there was indeed a war, he would likely be neither *hoplite* nor on a *trireme*, but on a horseback as part of the cavalry, where most men of his status ended up.

Pericles is wise. He will do what is best. Yes, he must see reason... Eucleides swallowed and listened to the remnant of the oration. Once Pericles was finished and the other *strategoi* wishing to speak had done so, the turn passed to citizens above the age of fifty, and finally to the younger attendants of the *ecclesia*.

Cosimo was one of them. With the audacity of a prince, he rose and climbed the platform, chin pointing skyward. Then, to the delight of some and the horror of others, he began launching his counterarguments. 'Will you send your children, your nephews, to be slaughtered by savages? They may be brave men, but the brutality of the Peloponnese is well known.' He spoke to the older men, before turning to a patch in the crowd where those his own age had gathered. 'And you! Will you gladly have your throats slit by a Spartan sword, when this petty dilemma can be solved easily, if Pericles will only act in favour of every citizen and put aside his own pride.'

Eucleides' stomach fluttered. *Those are not just empty words. Though our foremost politician shouldn't be slandered like that... Cosimo is right.* It was their habit that Eucleides spoke after his cousin, or the reverse, enhancing what the other had just said and furthering the agenda they had agreed on before the *ecclesia* assembled. For almost a year now, the two of them had combined Cosimo's relentless tactics and gifts of insult sometimes disguised as flattery with Eucleides' cordial charm and education, to acquire a reputation as promising politicians. Hence, Eucleides gathered the folds of his cream-white *khitōn* around his ankles and strode forth. In the corner of his eye, he caught a glimpse of Pericles and his fellow *strategoi*, grim-mouthed and with eyes as unyielding as stone. Regardless of their political views, every ambitious youth with the gift of speech and the face of a sculpture was a threat.

'What better signifies greatness than lenience? What better way to demonstrate the wisdom of Athens than to choose the path of peace? We can afford to revoke the Decree, for our influence extends far beyond Megara. The Megarians were foolish, it's true, but shall we Athenians follow in those tracks? The savage Spartans are willing to negotiate. If we seize this rare opportunity, we can be the saviours of thousands of lives and inspire all of Hellas to conduct themselves in a similar manner. We must never let stubborn pride hinder us—stubborn pride belongs to the Peloponnese.'

Ultimately, it was decided that the Megarian Decree would not be revoked. Pericles sent an Athenian messenger to the Spartan *apella* claiming that an archaic law forbade the taking down of the tablet issuing the decree. The Spartans, Eucleides heard, replied in their laconic manner that he should simply turn the tablet around so that it faced the wall, because there was no law against *that*. These twists and turns were nothing more; it was clear for everyone to see that there would be no real peace negotiations. Moreover, it was decided the country-dwellers would be gathered like a flock of sheep and put in safety within the Long Walls, protecting them from the raids that would doubtlessly follow.

All this was announced at yet another meeting of the *ecclesia*. Sighs of frustration and murmurs of concern spread up the rows of men seated on the steps, as was the general response whenever the impending war was brought up.

How many months now before the hoplites march into Attica? How long before they ravage the countryside and try to breech our walls? Maybe a mere month... The thought chilled Eucleides to the bone.

He nudged Cosimo in the side. 'Do you think my father can pull some strings? Surely we can be of more use in state business than...than out there?'

Cosimo's lips twitched in a smile, the cold sunlight like a pool on his prominent cheekbones. 'A rare thing, to hear you say something so superbly clever. It *would* be a pity if they beat your brains out.' His voice was as if soaked in honey, skilfully hiding the slight.

'Thank you, I think.'

As they walked through the filthy streets back to the *oikos*, the subject of Cosimo's bride bubbled to the surface, as it so often did.

'And who will it be?' Eucleides said.

'That depends on whose father pays me the most.'

'You're much too insensitive. A dowry is a fine thing, but the twinkle of love in a woman's eye...'

Cosimo's only reply was a snort. The question of marriage was not one of passion, nor affection, but one of status and financial stability. His cousin's soft heart was naught but an inconvenience, an odd fish in a pond of sensible sharks.

Eucleides knew it, so he made no further attempt at the time being. Instead, he approached the aspects of the choice he knew Cosimo would better understand. 'To my comprehension, a union with my father's half-niece would strengthen the family.'

'She's all of seventeen, though.'

'I would choose her, then, if I were you. You would be more compatible.'

Cosimo's lips twitched in a grimace. 'There must be something wrong with her if she hasn't been married yet. Perhaps she doesn't know how to keep quiet.'

'Is that so horrible?'

'I think I'll put my effort into the other one—Efigenia, daughter of Thaddeus.'

They had reached the Acropolis and walked in line with the elevated, cropped rock. Upon it towered the Parthenon, freshly sculpted and finished the previous year. The fine-grained Pentelic marble was the purest white, while the oldest parts of the temple were beginning to shift in the lightest amber nuance because of the oxidised iron in the stone. Dedicated to the city's patron deity, Athena, it had quickly become the unrivalled pearl of Athens.

Eucleides gave a nod towards the temple. 'You must agree with me, when I say Pericles made a wise investment.'

'If I must, I do.' Cosimo squinted for the sun. 'That man is old and obstinate like a goat, but even a goat can have a bright idea once in a while, I suppose.'

They continued through the narrow streets south-westward of the Acropolis, entering the district of the Collytus deme. It was one of the wealthier districts; although the houses still sat as tight as teeth, they were both larger and of better quality than most in the city, and almost all had several small windows.

A knock from the inside of one of the doors they passed made Eucleides and Cosimo both leap past it to avoid been knocked down as it opened and a man emerged into the street. The practice of knocking before one opened one's front door was a necessity considering the city's layout and the constant stream of people.

'And you? How is *your* future bride?' Cosimo asked.

How would I know, when I've never laid eyes on her? 'She's well, I assume. She just turned six.' He had to count in his head—yes, the little girl his father had chosen from one of his old friends' families to be his daughter-in-law someday was still playing with dolls.

Cosimo slapped Eucleides' back. 'Then you both have almost a decade to ripen. The best alliances are made well in advance.'

'Perhaps.' Eucleides attempted a smile. 'Let's hope father is not bothered by his aching legs this evening,' he continued as they entered the *oikos*: a two-story house with walls of limestone.

The two young men stepped into an oasis of calm compared to the bustling city outside the door. Slaves slipped along the walls like cats trying to avoid notice, carrying out their daily chores, but other than that the house was completely still. *Then father isn't well after all.* Eucleides sighed. Whenever the head of the *oikos* was tormented by his legs and the heat in his head, he remained in bed. When he was not, he gladly strolled from room to room seemingly without purpose, hands clasped idly behind his back and a low humming continuously on his swollen lips.

The fourth resident of the *oikos*, Cosimo's mother, was quite the opposite of her older brother. As long as Eucleides could remember, no illness had ever ailed her, yet she was all but idle and her lips too thin, too shrivelled, for that kind of humming.

'I will see to him,' Eucleides announced, unlacing his winter sandals. 'Don't expect me until dinner.'

He found the older man, Achaikos, just as he had expected to find him: half-lying, half-sitting on the *kline* in his bedchamber, leaning his ample body mass on the backrest. At first, the slow heaving of his chest indicated sleep, but his eyes twinkled open as his son entered, and his lips formed a vague smile. 'Is that you, Eucleides?'

'Yes, father.' Eucleides returned the smile and knelt by the *kline*. 'How are your legs this afternoon?'

Achaikos grunted. 'Stiff as a sheep's arse.'

Eucleides nodded. 'Have you had some fresh air? It does wonders, I'm sure you know.'

'I...I can't remember. Maybe...no...'

'We've been to the Pnynx. There's news—I shall tell you later, if you wish.'

'Yes...yes. News. You can tell me later. Now, get off your knees and to your scrolls.'

'Yes, father. I will send a slave or two to assist you to the table.' Eucleides rose from his kneeling position and departed the bedchamber.

The scrolls his father had spoken of were indeed calling his name. Tight rolls of papyrus—some new and bright, others archaic and flaxen—filled seven sturdy chests in the *bibliotheca* on the second floor. The collection ranged from the *Iliad* to the *Oresteia*, containing every significant literary work and drama Achaikos had managed to get hold of.

Eucleides selected one of the most recent scrolls, Sophocles' *Antigone*, and sat down by the desk which dominated the room. *Just for today. Tomorrow I can continue with Solon's reforms.* Escaping his supposed studies in favour of a favourite drama, which would be of little use to his carrier, had become a guilty pleasure. Antigone's despair to have her brother buried properly, Creon's cruel judgement, the series of suicides as a result of love. A comedy might be more easily digested, but Eucleides eagerly absorbed the tragedy. It had always struck a chord inside him, though he had only been a child of ten when it was first performed at the Dionysia festival. His father had used to bring him to every tragedy, every comedy, and certainly every satyr play worth seeing, and together they had spent hundreds of hours in the theatre. The Dionysia was the unchallenged theatrical highlight of every year, and of father and son's year as well. By the end of every performance, Eucleides' bottom had ached from sitting and his belly had hurt from eating too many honey-roasted nuts, but the memories of those days held the innermost place in his heart.

By nightfall, the slaves filled the table with a variety of dishes large enough to satisfy every taste yet modest enough for what was in no way a banquet: legumes in a sauce of crushed tomatoes and garlic, wheat bread and olive oil, goat's cheese, pork, figs drizzled with sticky honey for dessert, and diluted wine to drink.

Eucleides eyed his father as they ate. Achaikos fumbled with the food, honey and wine dripping down his chin. One of the slaves—a broad-shouldered man with skin like polished ebony and clean-shaven scalp—had to aid his master with a damp linen cloth. The man was usually occupied with heavier labour, and Eucleides pitied him where he stood, looking bizarrely out of place. *If I could only remember his name... He's rather new.*

Cosimo placed a slice of goat cheese on a piece of bread, inspected the mouthful in his hand, then returned it to his plate with a look of distaste. 'Has your son informed you yet on the day's proceedings, uncle?' he asked. 'The thought of it takes away my appetite.'

'The day's proceedings?' A flicker of confusion crossed Achaikos' face for a moment. 'Ah, yes. He said he would.'

Eucleides exchanged a glance with Cosimo. *Does he need to be troubled? Yes? Do I tell him or will you? You.* The silent exchange was almost as clear as if they had spoken it, the result of fifteen years of companionship.

Cosimo pushed the leftovers on his plate neatly to the side before speaking. 'Pericles refused another envoy offering peace in exchange for the revocation of the Megarian Decree. We voted to take the offer, naturally, but there's no doubt he swayed the general opinion. The Spartans will hardly give another chance to negotiate.'

'Our votes were in favour of peace,' Eucleides added to clarify. 'Not the degradation of Athens' standing, just peace.'

Achaikos' puffed-up, reddening face brought his son's thoughts to a blushing bumblebee. A protruding vein pulsated on the older man's temple, showing through the few strands of grey hair he had left. 'They think they can send my boys to war? They... You voted against it? You would shame our city?'

Eucleides did not answer, for it would be of little use. Achaikos was quick to anger but equally quick to joy, and constantly what Eucleides was convinced was the fog in his mind made his speech too ambivalent to interpret correctly. Often, both anger and joy were lavished on everyone in general rather than directed at a specific target.

'We felt you ought to know, uncle, being the head of the *oikos*. Nevertheless, you shouldn't be agitated, because through your wise speech and your well-renowned friends, you could spare us both from being called upon.' Cosimo had applied the familiar honey-glaze to his voice.

Eucleides smiled as his father's face returned to its normal colour and the idleness, which so often seemed to possess him when untroubled by politics and the like, once more settled in his eyes.

'Cosimo's wedding plans are proceeding nicely— aren't they?'

'I'm still trying to make my pick, but yes.' Achaikos chewed for what must have been a whole minute before swallowing, his teeth few and decayed. 'Who...who are the candidates?'

Poor, dear man. A man who has forgotten his chief authority: to decide who to welcome into the oikos *and who to refuse.*

'Your orphaned half-niece, the pretty one. If not her, then there's the daughter of Thaddeus, who is younger.'

'Efigenia,' Eucleides said. 'That's her name.'

'Yes. I shall meet with her father shortly.'

Achaikos grunted and shifted his considerable weight. 'Have you no rivals, then?'

Cosimo's eyes flashed hard as marble, the expression disappearing before his uncle could take notice. 'Perhaps. But none with as respectable a family lineage.'

In that manner, the evening grew old and the air crisp. Each man retired to his choice of pastime: Eucleides to his scrolls, Cosimo to his beloved dogs, and Achaikos to an early sleep.

CHAPTER FOUR

T HE SOPHIST SPREAD his hands in a wondering gesture, his wavy beard and hair fluttering in the breeze like an unfinished tapestry the colour of almonds blending with the white strings on the loom. Though he must be in his sixtieth year, these streaks of white were still tenuous, and the lines presiding on his forehead scarce. Now, he snivelled deeply as if afflicted by a clogged nose—this was usually a sign that he was about to make a poignant statement to the cluster of students forming a half-circle by his feet—and spoke. 'Man is the measure of all things: of the things that are, that they are, of the things that are not, that they are not.'

A moment passed; Eucleides could almost smell the other young aristocrats' fervent brain activity. Each draped in a *himation*, they gazed at Protagoras with twinkling eyes and nails bitten down to the skin.

'Then there is no objective truth?' Eucleides asked.

The sophist's glance darted to him for a second before returning to the group. 'That's a subjective matter.' His maggot-like mouth, overshadowed by a moustache, curved in a wily smile. 'Every man's perception of a matter is a truth of sorts. If you consider this theory of mine to be false, you are right, for your perception must be true. However, the perception of a man who believes in the theory is equally true, thus, it does not matter what your opinion is, because if you think I'm wrong, you have proven me right.'

The twists and turns of his tongue would have made the cleverest of audiences scratch their scalps and knit their brows in frustration. It was a difficult task to argue against Protagoras regardless of the subject and regardless of the opinion you held; this was very much a skill he had acquired and intended for his pupils to learn.

Eucleides recalled numerous sessions in the gymnasium, such as this, or on the sun-basted sandstone of the Acropolis, where they had been drilled to pleasant exhaustion in the art of rhetoric as well as the lustrous concept of *arete*: excellence or virtue. *They say only those with noble blood in their veins can possess it. But I would bet a hundred* talents *that even the most impoverished could learn, if he listened to the likes of this man.*

In spite of the intriguing monologue, Eucleides' glance strayed to the middle of the open area in the gymnasium, where his cousin was brushing grains of sand off his oiled limbs gleaming in the cool sunlight. The cold rarely if ever discouraged the naked men as they wrestled, raced, or hauled the javelin and discus. With muscles rippling and hair flinging about their ears, they practiced the long jump. The entire gymnasia reeked of fresh sweat mingling with olive oil and the roasted broad beans which a comically short man—a poorer citizen judging by his tattered clothes—had started selling to the athletes.

A tug at Eucleides arm made him return his attention to Protagoras.

'To you, the money that man there—' Protagoras gestured to the man selling broad beans. '—earns selling eatables is likely a poor wage. To him, however, it must be a grand sum. Which of these two is true?'

'But by claiming this, any tyrant could excuse his savage actions!' one of the young men exclaimed, a bewildered look on his spotty face.

'Isn't that what they already do? Haven't all tyrants painted themselves as heroes, promoting their own truth?' The subject of the discussion passed from relativism to mathematics, though their teacher's own lack of enthusiasm for numbers and formulas was well-known. 'The subject matter is unknowable and the terminology distasteful,' he said, then loudly crunched a roasted bean between his teeth, as if to emphasis his aversion.

Once Protagoras assessed that the young men had had their beliefs questioned enough for one day, he took his leave with a demonstrative snivel, his *himation* flapping as he strode away.

Eucleides found Cosimo, who had finished his own practice of *arete* long before, dressing himself and drinking for refreshment. The diluted wine disappeared down his throat in a scant trickle until, eventually, the cup was empty.

'Doesn't he teach you mathematics, then?'

'Not to any great extent—although I've no doubt he could tell us anything and have us believe it was about geometry simply by placing the right words in the right places. How is your wrestling? You looked sandy earlier.' Eucleides' smile held jest in it, but he took care not to let it escalate to mockery.

Cosimo adjusted the folds of his *khitōn*. 'Sand can be brushed off. Protagoras' teachings must be intriguing, or you would have seen my opponent far filthier than I.'

Arete could be achieved in many ways: by expanding the horizon of one's mind, by cultivating one's speech, by sculpting one's body. While Eucleides did the former by soaking up wise men's words like bread soaking up wine, Cosimo had chosen to engage in the latter. *'I'm already years ahead of you in politics and the like, cousin'*, he would sometimes say. *'Why then should I not spend my time wrestling?'* However, Eucleides suspected there was little more to Cosimo's relentless visits to the gymnasium than the prospect of locating uncorrupted youths whom he might snare with his honeyed tongue until they swore to vote in his favour the next time they attended the *ecclesia*.

'I'll put my name forth in the Olympic Games, Eucleides.' Cosimo's smile could have melted marble. 'The *pentathlon*...a good choice, don't you think?'

Eucleides gave a little laugh. 'A good choice indeed. I'll enjoy seeing you in a laurel circlet.'

'Gods willing.'

I never know if you're serious when you say those things.

The *andron*, the designated men's quarters of the house, was lit up with a myriad of small terracotta lamps, illuminating the polished stone floor and the crimson-painted plaster covering the walls. Eight *klinai* lined three of the dining room's walls, leaving the door free, the simple wooden structures almost succumbing under the piles of plush pillows assemble for the guests' comfort. Slave boys were arranging bowls and plates on the small tables placed in front of each *kline*, filling every bit of bare surface with dishes of grilled meats and soups, oysters and bread.

Three resolute knocks sounded through the door connecting the *andron* with the street. Eucleides and Cosimo exchanged a glance. *I believe that's our call.*

Fourteen men were invited to the *symposion*, fourteen men of which some leaped with the vigour of youth while others walked crippled by old age, but of which all were citizens of considerable wealth who brought both wits and a certain glamour to the occasion. Polykleitos, the sculptor, was among them, wearing his favourite sandals. The most unruly and sought-after guest, however, Eucleides expected would not arrive a minute sooner than the banquet was over and the drinking games in full flourish.

Each man removed his footwear and proceeded to have his feet washed by one of the slave boys.

Eucleides placed circlets of bright green vines entwined with silvery olive leaves on their heads. 'Welcome. Consider yourself crowned devotees of Dionysus in all his glory.' This was met with a series of cheers and acclamation. He flashed them a smile. 'But first something for our stomachs.' *And please let it be substantial enough... Devotees or not, too much to drink on an empty belly can make any man unpleasant.*

Cosimo appeared to be of similar sentiments, because he gave Eucleides a nudge with his pointy elbow as they followed the guests into the dining room of the *andron*. 'It's a mystery to me how they enjoy drunkenness so—the loss of restraint.'

'Don't you cherish a high-spirited *symposion* just as they do?'

'I cherish seeing *them* without restraint. Rather fascinating.' Cosimo's teeth gleamed like white chips of ivory in the obscure passage. 'And the other entertainments, of course.'

'I convinced Xenia to attend the latter part of the evening.' *At least those four sets of pearl-earrings did.*

Cosimo's eyebrows arched, a hint of genuine approval sweeping across his face, but he had no opportunity to reply, as the guests had now taken their seats on the *klinai* and were reclining against the small mountains of pillows.

The dining was little more than a formality, an excuse for the aftermath. Nevertheless, the men ate with hearty appetite, certainly fulfilling Eucleides' unspoken hope.

Polykleitos, whose nimble sculptor's hands skilfully separated the shell from a clam, was beginning to creep out of his own shell sooner than expected. 'It's a strange thing, don't you think, to marry,' he said when the subject of Cosimo's impending wedding briefly caught the group's attention.

'How so?' one of the other men replied.

'Surely, it is not in human nature to tie oneself to a single person.'

'Human nature or not, dear Polykleitos, I think my cousin looks foremost to the practical benefits of such a union.' Eucleides looked at Cosimo. *Don't think I don't listen to your rambling about dowries.*

Polykleitos was not convinced. 'I don't doubt it compromises one's free spirit.'

Theodoros, a man of thirty-four with twitching feet and a good dash of humour, spoke next, 'I think I heard Socrates say something of marriage: if you get a bad wife, you become a breeder of hens...or if you get a good wife, you shall have good weather—'

'You've lost yourself in a labyrinth of words.' Eucleides laughed and wiped stew off his fingers on a piece of bread. 'He said "If you get a good wife, you become happy, and if you get a bad wife you become a philosopher." Yet I wonder if wives really can be inherently bad. It all depends on whether you grow to love each other.'

Cosimo crinkled his nose. 'Socrates has the face of a grumpy cat and willingly walks barefoot in the filth of the street.'

'Better a bright mind than a bright appearance,' Polykleitos said. 'But the possibility of becoming a philosopher isn't enough to make me consider marriage in a favourable light—on the contrary.'

The other guests had effortlessly fallen into the rhythm of affable conversation, musing together about everything from unruly slaves to the latest fashion of *fibulae*, to the terms of man's existence. No one spoke a word of politics, nor of the corrosive conflict with the Peloponnesian League; these subjects might on another occasion have dominated the room, but this was an evening designated to frivolous leisure unspoilt by dire discussions.

The *symposiarch* was elected by lottery. The man would be the master of the *symposion*, tasked with deciding the strength of the diluted wine as well as how many cups each member of the group would drink. He thereby presided over the nature of the evening: whether it would be a civilised gathering filled with speculation and displays of intelligence, or merely a drunken fog.

Eucleides bit his lip as the name drawn from the pot was that of Gennadios, who was infamous for his bravado in drinking. Once Gennadios had finished grinning, the time had come to make libations to the gods. Hence, they sprinkled a handful of wine on the floor—slaves would have to scrub their fingers bloody during the early morning hours to remove the crimson stains as well as the scattered food which the dogs had not devoured after their masters had gone to rest—and joined their voices in a hymn dedicated to Dionysus. Other deities and mythical figures were praised as well, as was the habit at any banquet when the guests felt the need to give thanks for their good fortunes.

Eventually came the entertainment. Two flute girls with swarthy complexions and limber wrists positioned themselves in the middle of the room, each beginning to pluck the strings of her *barbiton*. No more than a few seconds passed before they had to shuffle to the corner, though, as an adolescent boy and girl entered the scene, naked save for flimsy loincloths and gold bracelets. Together they performed an erotic dance depicting Dionysus' passion for Ariadne when he found her sleeping on the island of Naxos, abandoned by Theseus. The youths' every movement was brimming with fervour, limbs entwining like serpents and feet twirling, the dance was chaos itself yet coherent like Ariadne's string of red yarn. Eucleides watched wide-eyed and lull-minded. *Such perfection... No, not perfection. Passion is marvellous, but love is perfection...*

The group had worked their way through the first two *kratērs* and a good deal of the third. Eucleides felt a quiver of dread at how quickly the guests drank and therefor expected their hosts to drink as well. The wine felt thicker and sweeter with every drip that landed on his tongue, adding to the intoxication. He did not mind the merry debauchery nor the sweet state of oblivion that tended to follow, on the contrary, it lay in his nature to seek pleasure for himself and those around him. What had sowed the grain of reluctance always making itself known when a *symposion* crept closer to its pinnacle was a sticky cluster of memories perhaps fifteen years old. *The flick of a clumsy hand spilling a pool of wine on his silky boy's hair, harsh words sounding gentle as lullabies compared to the hands that came after. A chorus of disorder, splinters of broken furniture.*

Eucleides was jerked from the flashes of memories by no less than five unevenly bangs on the door to the *andron*. The men on the *klinai* exchanged a series of amused glances, eyebrows flitting towards hairlines. Like lazy cats disturbed in a pleasant slumber by an adventurous mouse tripping over their paws, they pushed themselves up against the pillows and waited with anticipation gleaming in their wine-glazed eyes for the slaves to show the last guest inside.

A *khitōn* the colour of eggplant with hems embroidered in gold and the equally shiny *zoster* tied almost below the hipbones, a tousled mass of glossy dark coils crowned with what appeared to be a woman's veil twisted to a circlet, a bewildered face with rosy cheeks. As Pericles' young protégée walked through the dining room with wobbly steps, his garments began slipping and he had to bundle the cloth in his hand to prevent it from dropping entirely, revealing what was expected in a gymnasium but not at a banquet.

'I heard you were indulging without me. Ah, see there! Already three *kratērs* gone.'

One of the older men, a sophist of lesser renown than Protagoras, gestured for Alcibiades to have a seat on the *kline* he occupied, while he himself shuffled to an already crowded one.

'Welcome,' Cosimo said, applying a thick layer of sticky flattery to his voice. 'Just in time for *kottabos*.'

The *symposiarch* raised a hand in protest. 'First, the fourth *kratēr*. We shall not make the game an easy one.'

With muffled complaints—no one had any desire to suffer the humiliating punishments which resulted if one disobeyed the *symposiarch*—the men emptied cup after cup. Eucleides' grain of reluctance had now been ploughed too deep into obscurity to make itself known; even Cosimo's frosty attitude towards the liquid seemed to have warmed up since Alcibiades' entry. *The two of them are like a swan and a rooster. But apparently even the swan must adapt to the rooster sometimes, at least if he wishes to remain in the right circles.*

The adolescents performing the dance of Ariadne and Dionysus resumed the show, and when finished, were hastily replaced by a throng of *hetairai* decked in exquisite jewellery and with clothes as loosely fastened as Alcibiades'.

Xenia, who was more sought after among the elite of Athens than Egyptian glass beads, swaggered at the end of the small procession, tossing her mane of copper-red hair over her bare shoulders to allow the terracotta lamps' light to reflect in it. Indeed, Xenia knew her tricks: she knew how to laugh or cry at the right whim, she knew how to attract every eye in the room, and she certainly knew one or two reputable tactics between the sheets. As with any rare commodity desired by many, the value of her company only rose with every man who offered to pay, and many of them had begun to drool in her tracks merely because they wanted to have something which their friends had failed in obtaining. Eucleides could not help but succumb to the same fatal longing, but he knew all too well it was only a glowing surface he yearned for. *Hetairai*—much less *pornai* or slave girls—could not afford to be genuine in their love; it was all naught but a spectacle put together with the utmost precision to attract customers, or else they would likely suffer an even worse fate at the mercy of poverty.

'How is your dear guardian?' Cosimo asked Alcibiades, paler than the Parthenon from forcing the wine down his throat. Eucleides offered him the bowl of chestnuts in an attempt to resurrect his wellbeing.

'As good-humoured as can be,' Alcibiades replied, pulling one of the younger *hetairai* onto his lap with one hand. 'This war business is really taking its toll, though. Where—' his eyes darted around the room. '—where is the old crook anyhow?'

Eucleides marvelled at him. 'Your revered guardian would never attend an occasion such as this. I'm sure you know it. I'm afraid we're far too humble.'

'He's a bore, that's all. Never feasts. Ah, let's play something!'

Kottabos was the most popular drinking game in Athens, perhaps in all Hellas. The contestants poured wine in a broad, shallow cup, a *kylix*, then hooked their right index finger through one of the handles and leaned the *kylix* against the back of their wrist by bending the hand upwards. Leaning on one's left elbow, one made a flick of the wrist to send a spurt of wine through the air with the goal of hitting a small bronze statuette placed on the top of a rod of the same material. If one succeeded in knocking down the statuette in such a way that it fell against the platter fastened half-way up the rod, it caused a distinctive sound, and the man who made the most noise was declared winner. Of course, a great deal of *kottabos* was pure luck, but the players rarely admitted this. Instead, they spent many hours teaching their sons and nephews the precise angle with which to flick the wrist and the right amount of wine to pour in the *kylix*.

Cosimo was the first to try his hand in the game. He reached up to tuck a strand of chestnut richness behind his ear under the vine-and olive-circlet, fixed his gaze on the statuette, and sent the wine flying in a graceful bow without blinking. Despite the liquor's elegant spurt and the young man's equally elegant execution, the statuette only obtained the slightest stain and remained firmly on its pedestal.

Let's hope Xenia makes him merry again. A miss like that could dampen anyone's mood.

Neither Eucleides nor Cosimo had yet perfected the art, although Eucleides secretly prided himself on having been declared winner at the last *symposion* they had attended. It appeared that fortune had decided to stay. When the turn passed to him, the statuette fell in a perfectly straight line, clashing with the platter and giving rise to a serenade of clatter. A spontaneous scatter of applause followed, while Eucleides studied his wrist, puzzled as to where he had acquired any skill—because fortune was not endless—in a game which his father had been too bawdily drunken to teach him in his early boyhood.

'Quite nicely done,' Cosimo said, his voice lacking the malice which likely would have been there if any of the other men had succeeded.

As the turn passed from one guest to another, it became increasingly difficult to discern who made the most noise, and the slaves had to return the statuette to its place many times over. In the end, no winner could be declared.

The lewd battle over Xenia's all-consuming gaze begun properly once *kottabos* had been ticked off the list and the slaves had begun preparing the fifth *kratēr* as well as another refill of chestnuts. At this stage, Cosimo's skin had shifted to a sickly, almost transparent nuance comparable to the inside of a dosina shell. Eucleides tried to meet his cousin's misty eyes but could not concentrate on any one object, since everything he saw doubled and quivered. However, he could see that the other men lounging around the room were showing signs of approaching their own limits.

One of the few exceptions was Alcibiades, which could have surprised no-one. Nineteen years old and the youngest man present, he was infamous for his drunken behaviour: the opulent and sometimes even non-existing clothes, the outstandingly late arrivals, the promiscuous language and the reckless escapades. Rumour held it that he and a friend of his had once stolen a goat from a renowned citizen and tied the animal to a pole in the middle of the *agorá*, adorned in a crimson cape and with a laurel of pure gold around its horns. Naturally, the goat had caused its fair share of commotion upon discovery. What resulted in greater clamour, though, was the tablet by its hooves stating that it had ventured out for a breath of fresh air and lost its way.

Cold beams of morning light trickled in through the small window, painting the slumbering devotees of Dionysus with strokes of white and marbled blues. Not everyone had retired home the night before; four or five guests still lay slumped on the *klinai*, as did two olive-skinned *hetairai* and a slave girl with nothing but a sheer piece of cloth slung over her tawny body.

Eucleides squeezed his eyes shut, then blinked several times, the light impossibly sharp and impossibly merciless. *By Aphrodite...was the wine so strong? That man, the* symposiarch, *was he out for revenge of some sort?* He closed his eyes again, sinking back into the softly pounding, red lull of his head, trying to recall the events that had transpired.

One image was clearer than the rest: Alcibiades flashing his bare thighs under the ludicrous *himation* before sauntering off to yet another gathering, arm hooked through Xenia's and a grin smeared on his face.

'Why, it seems to me our young shooting star has taken the prize,' Polykleitos had remarked before returning to his rambling about the gold and ivory statue of Hera he had crafted.

The rest of night's darkest hours were dim in Eucleides' memory, a blurred series of pictures and snippets of dialogue, words better left unsaid. *And that's the awful part about it all, the dark counterpart to the lovely rapture and those mirthful games. You never know what you might have said or done.*

Cosimo's voice—a strange, hollow echo reserved for mornings such as this—pulled Eucleides once more into the light. 'Cousin? Is it dawn, or midday?'

'How would I know?'

'Of course. Well, let's disperse of these...lice.' He gestured vaguely towards the men on the *klinai*, blue veins sashing across his slender arm.

'Must you call them that?'

Cosimo arched an eyebrow. 'Not if *you* remember their names.'

'I only barely remember my own name,' Eucleides said miserably. 'I do remember Alcibiades and Xenia leaving—that happened, didn't it?'

'Unfortunately. That spoiled boy always gets *everything*.'

'She doesn't love him, you know. She has little choice, when he can pay more than you.'

'You think I care whom that woman loves? If the cream of society competed for a shiny trinket, you would yearn to have it also.'

CHAPTER FIVE

T HE GIRL WAS fourteen years old, yet she moved with a rare sophistication, gliding across the floor with the calm grace of a matured woman. The veil hid her eyes so that Eucleides could only see the contours of her face behind the fabric. The fullness in her well-shaped limbs, however, made her pleasant to look at, and the golden bracelets that clad her wrists witnessed of sufficient wealth. Strands of hair the colour of wheat showed where the veil ended. Eucleides had never seen such hair before; it was a rare pearl in a riverbed of pebbles, enough to make Aphrodite jealous. *Perhaps that was part of why he chose her, aside from the alliance and the dowry. Six* talents*!*

The sum the bride's father, her *kyrios*, had paid was impressive, though Cosimo had accepted the offer with a straight face, as if he had expected nothing less. Eucleides recalled the firm handshake his cousin had exchanged with his future father-in-law to seal the contract of the *engysis* after speaking the ritual phrases. They had made a trade of sorts: Cosimo would provide for the girl, Efigenia, and in return he would receive the six *talents* as well as the right to sire legitimate children by her.

The groom, who was dressed in his finest clothes, inspected the young bride as if she was cattle being sold in the *agorá*. Would she be a worthy investment? Would she provide children to the state and the *oikos*? Eucleides sent a quick prayer to Hera that it would be so, for he knew well enough how Cosimo could turn to unpleasant manners when something—or someone—did not live up to his expectations. Mistresses and prostitutes could attend to his every need, but only a wife could give his sons Athenian citizenship and elevate his own status. A barren wife was nothing but a sore rash, and would be sent back to her *kyrios* in disgrace.

The wedding ceremony began with the premarital sacrifices to the gods. Then, Efigenia's garlands of hair was cut from her scalp to signify the approaching loss of her virginity. Eucleides watched them fall heavily to the ground, a wasted treasure. *It will grow back, and with it her beauty. I hope she's not mourning it... Beauty is such a transient thing, it should always be revered.* It did not occur to him that if the girl was mourning something, it was likely to be her childhood and family home as well, not solely her hair.

After the customary rituals had been conducted, the wedding feast followed; the guests took their places, men on one side of the room and women on the other. The bride and groom sat too far apart to hear what the other said, but no one had intended for a conversation to take place.

Cosimo ate sparely from every dish, picking at the oxen and the vegetables. Cakes baked with honey, wheat bread, and goat's cheese all sat on his plate, but most of it remained there.

'Have you no appetite? I should think you'd be in good spirits, with such a lovely bride.. I thought you'd be joyous,' Eucleides said.

Cosimo sucked on his fingers, one by one, before answering. 'The dowry pleases me. I don't know about her so-called loveliness. What is it you see that I don't?'

Eucleides laughed. 'I see as little as you do, and curse the veil! But surely, her hair was wonderful, and her manners very graceful.'

'If she wasn't graceful, she would have been poorly trained.'

'I wish you'd speak kindlier sometimes.' Eucleides attempted a smile and begun to heap gleaming white and pink sea food onto his plate. 'Pericles believes—'

'Cousin. Eucleides.' Cosimo's voice had taken on the mentor-like tone he so often used when correcting his younger companion. He smiled. 'Don't take the wisdoms of men who aren't wise to begin with. Now, cease this talk of my wife.'

'Alright then. Do you think Pericles' tactics will be successful?'

'To cram everyone inside Athens' walls? It's ridiculous. It's not our fault that the country-dwellers chose to live unsheltered in their farms, and now they're allowed to move in here with us?'

'But if we can spare their lives—'

'By compromising our own? Pericles be damned.'

The guests devoured the luxurious dishes one by one and the wine poured in a seemingly never-ending stream. Voices grew louder, and boastful stories told by members of both families escalated until the heroic deeds they claimed to have done were enough to compare with Heracles'. When the feast eventually came to an end and the lavish gifts had been presented, Cosimo and Efigenia climbed onto the carriage that would take them from her *oikos* to his. The oxen pulled it forward slowly enough for the guests to walk on the side, accompanied by music. The bright ripple of flutes mingled with the deeper notes of the *zither*,

entwined like yarn on a loom, and though Eucleides
had always preferred the spoken word to melodies,
the sound spread a warm feeling in his body. He
tilted his head too look at the pitch-black sky, where
the full moon hung low, signifying this was a good
time for a marriage. *We could use some good luck
however small it may be. These are turbulent times.*

The hope he nurtured during the procession to
his father's house was soon squashed. Eucleides had
been appointed *thyrorós* a few days ago, and
accepted the task of guarding the bridal chamber.
The guests sang their hymns to ward off malevolent
spirits, as was customary, yet he could clearly hear
the bride's whimpers through the door. She did not
scream—she was too strictly brought up, too
precisely moulded to dare—but the sounds
contained no less misery than those of a poorly
slaughtered animal. Eucleides swallowed several
times, knowing he could not leave his post in
accordance with tradition, grasping after a thought
to comfort himself. *Perhaps she's unhappy over
something else—her hair—or just confused. He
wouldn't hurt her so.* Creating illusions had been one
of his most useful skills for as long as he could recall,
whether it was in the shape of pretty words spoken
to the members of the *ecclesia* or persuasion
directed at himself.

When both the whimpers and the hymns had
died down, all that was left was the lulling chatter of
tired guests longing to collapse on their own beds
and sleep away the intoxication the wine and the
merriment had brought on.

Efigenia pinned a blank expression to her face and
put her hands to work weaving in the women's
quarters, using the scarlet yarn she had received as a
bridal gift from her older sister. Unless she made a

misstep and ended up with a tapestry full of bumpy knots, it would bring some colour to the walls. There was no true need for precaution, though, as she had not made any visible mistake in her weaving for several years. Even if she *had* received education in arithmetic, Efigenia could not have counted the hours she had spent this way, seated at a wooden loom made by Athens' most distinguished craftsmen. She knew the clusters of white threads kept straight by the weights tied to their ends a thousand times better than she knew her husband's face—, nd despite the process being dull, she secretly preferred it to Cosimo's rare company.

Efigenia was almost surprised when no one slapped her exposed fingers, then remembered she had not uttered a word of this preference out loud. She managed to smooth over the slightest itch of displeasure before her own thoughts went too far. It became easier every time she did it. *He's not at fault, no, no. It must be tiring, performing all those duties, attending stately business. No wonder he's too tired to talk much when he gets home. Silly girl. It's not my place to judge, just as it's not a mouse's place to judge a sacred bull.* The tapestry was beginning to take shape: a thin, red line on the white threads, like a single pencil stroke on a marble tablet, growing wider by the minute.

'What is that?'

It was as if she had summoned him by mere thought. Efigenia's head snapped up from the loom. 'A tapestry, husband. I'm weaving.'

'I can see that.' Cosimo's eyes wandered over the scarlet yarn, his lips pressed tightly together. 'I meant the colour. It's ghastly.'

'I...I will remove it and start anew.'

Cosimo frowned and gave the tiniest shake of his head, as if he could not imagine why she would bother him with the matter. 'I will come to you tonight. Be quiet this time.'

'Yes.' She lowered her eyes until the whiteness of the floor began to burn. She then raised her glance slightly, only to watch Cosimo through a shield of eyelashes as he departed from the *gynaikeion,* sandals clicking against stone and the dark blue *himation* swaying as he walked.

He will come tonight. Her stomach tightened to a knot. They had not performed their marital duties since the wedding night six days ago, and she had no disillusions about why; she had seen the distaste written on Cosimo's face when he left her in the bedchamber. He might as well have been looking at a rotting fish, or perhaps dog's faeces on the street. She knew he had married her for her dowry, and the fact now remained that she would be a nuisance regardless of how scarce she made herself, because she would cost him both money and time. *I should have kept silent.* For as long as she could remember, Efigenia had been taught to swallow her words and follow the whims of those around her, yet she had failed in this most crucial situation. Her husband had not acted with considerable violence, but the steadfast grip around her wrists, the smell of his breath... It was one thing to know oneself a pawn in a greater game, another to feel the panic of a captive animal spring upon oneself without warning.

Efigenia gave herself a light slap, straightened her back and squared her shoulders. Dawdling was a poor pastime, as was thinking about the inevitable nightly encounter. She pulled the loose end of the red yarn and continued pulling until the strip of tapestry was completely unravelled. *Perhaps blue is better... Surely, he must like blue, dressing in it and all.*

As it turned out, Cosimo's distaste for the colour red extended to tomatoes, cherries, wine—indeed, everything eatable or drinkable seemed to turn his stomach, except for the clearest of spring water and the most expensive dishes. Wine he did drink when the occasion required it, but never for pleasure. It was as if the luxuries lined up on the table were there with the sole purpose of demonstrating wealth and decorating the room.

Efigenia observed all this in her husband through a slit in the door. The women of the *oikos* never dined with the men, but the curiosity had taken the better of her in a brief moment of weakness. In a matter of seconds, she took two quick steps away from the door, ashamed. *Spying on your husband! Is that the manners of a good wife? You silly girl.* Cosimo's ways puzzled her, yet her brain reasoned in the matter with a velocity she did not know she possessed. *Of course, how stupid of me. Of course a man of such high morals, with such great* arete, *must not overindulge in base things like food or fornication.* That also explained his icy, business-like behaviour in the bedchamber, which had begun to replace the distaste from their wedding night.

Efigenia later glanced at her own plate, which suddenly looked overfull, vulgar even. Without giving it any further thought, she flipped her knife and discarded half of the fish to the floor where the dogs tripping under the table might finish it.

Lady Milos, Cosimo's mother, did not notice, for she was far too caught up in the household accounts she had brought with her to the table and was now scanning. The cost of bracelets and rings for herself, *khitōns* and papyrus for her son and her nephew, yarn and beauty concoctions for her young daughter-in-law—and nothing of great value for her brother, who owned the land and the silver mine paying for all these things. This distribution of expenses was not out of meanness, Efigenia reckoned, but simply the result of an ageing man past his years of both vanity and socialising, who was now either too fog-headed or too content to require much in the way of expensive goods.

Efigenia could not detect any similarities between Lady Milos and Cosimo except for their pale complexion and their desire to accumulate wealth. Certainly, the older woman's appearance was nothing like her slender son. Folds of fat spilled over where her clothes and jewellery cut into her limbs, her garments looked garish to say the least, and she had a comic habit of waddling forth like a large, white goose, yet cared greatly about her dignity. At first glance, Efigenia had been seized by longing for an embrace from this stout woman, but when she had received it, her ribs had nearly cracked.

'Is everything in its order?' Efigenia asked.

Lady Milos snapped up from the scrolls. 'Oh, yes.' Her nose began drooping again, but Efigenia was determined to keep her mother-in-law's attention.

'I wish I was as clever as you, Lady. I'm afraid I cannot make much sense of numbers and letters.'

'No, dear, I suppose you can't. You were not taught reading and writing?'

'My Lady Mother always said literacy is not necessary for a girl in my position. My father said I would have a headache for a month.' Efigenia kept her eyes on her hands, then allowed a spoonful of chickpeas to fall to the floor, leaving unfortunate oily stains on her sandals.

Lady Milos reached for another sesame cookie. 'Your mother was quite right. When you become mistress of your own *oikos*, though, and have to balance the income and output, you shall learn a thing or two.'

'I thought...I thought Cosimo would decide those things.'

Lady Milo's mouth shrivelled for a moment as if she had chewed on a lemon, her cheeks flaring red. 'He will. But don't make the mistake of thinking he will be able to do it all.'

Efigenia's eyes darted as she fervently tried to think of a reply to satisfy her mother-in-law while still displaying respect for her husband, but found none. Instead, she turned to the ever-present subject of war to rescue her from the awkward situation.

'Are you frightened of the Spartans, Lady?'

'What good would that do me? No, my girl, those savage peoples won't be stopped by our fear. You mustn't let it show.'

'What if...what if they invade Attica? What if they sack Athens?' Efigenia barely dared hear the answer, and nothing could have prepared her for the brash honesty from the older woman's sesame-crumbed lips.

'Then we'll be evacuated, left to wander the waste-laid country, raped or killed, if it all happens in a haste.' Lady Milos might just as well have been speaking about a war taken place hundreds of years ago in a far-off land, so dry and matter-of-fact was her voice.

CHAPTER SIX

THE SPARTAN ARMY marched toward the Isthmus of Corinth like one rhythmic body, boots beating the dusty soil as dictated by the hymns deeply ingrained in the soldiers, which they now gave voice to: a deadly chorus rehearsing melodious battle cries.

Despite this unity, the army was divided into six *morae*; each *mora* consisted of some six hundred men. The *hómoioi* flanked the cargo mules and *heílotes* carrying provisions—the former ambling with twinkling black eyes, the latter with shoulders sloping under the weight of the baggage—none of whom shared the Spartans' zealous spirits.

Each man was fully decked in armour: greaves, cuirasses of stiffened linen glued together with animal fat and strengthened by a thin layer of bronze, and the imposing Corinthian helmet, which impaired one's vision and hearing but served its purpose superbly. In addition to this, they were equipped with a circular, convex *hoplon* shield of wood and bronze, a spear, and a short sword.

Alethea walked at the end of Apolonio's and Crysanthos' *mora*, accompanied by two *heílotes* not only to carry her few belongings but to act as guards, though she suspected this arrangement was a mere formality. If an unexpected danger approached, both she and the thousands of *hómoioi* were perfectly sufficient as defence. Moreover, the troops of the Delian League were still a long march away, and lions were seen in myth rather than in reality these days.

Filling her lungs with the crisp spring air infused with cypress and sweat, she relished in the pleasantly mild temperature. The men, naturally, were well-versed in walking rapidly carrying heavy armour in every imaginable weather, but Alethea highly doubted they were as comfortable as she in her knee-length *peplos* and lack of both shield and helmet. *But comfort is not for us. They should have made me a little more useful. Well, at least I'm here.* She still could not quite grasp that she, a woman, was accompanying the army at her own request, by her own persuasion. Of course, a great deal of her triumph was the result of Crysanthos' relations, but she chose to look past that. The prickling displeasure from breaking convention was thoroughly overridden by the joy from being close to Apolonio as well as from beholding the magnificent war machine that was the Spartan military.

A few days passed monotonously. When dawn broke, they sacrificed cattle to the gods, during the day they walked, and when darkness fell, they halted to rest and dine. Alethea preferred the evenings by far, for it was then she could sometimes steal an hour or two of her brother's company.

'Don't you think this open landscape is a little too...*open?*' she asked one of those times as they sat leaning against a poplar tree, the rest of the *mora* slumbering under the night sky's deep-blue canvas.

Apolonio gave a short laugh, toying with her fingers as if studying every curve and bend. 'You're used to the Eurotas valley and towering Taygetus, sister.'

'Yes,' Alethea mumbled. 'I don't see how anyone could willingly live in such an exposed place as this.'

'They don't see the world as we do.'

'I know. Will you tell me a story?'

Apolonio shrugged, one shoulder scraping against the poplar's coarse bark. 'Which one?'

Not the one of Medusa, Polyxena, Cassandra, Daphne, Europa, Leda... Not one of all those poor women, at least not today. 'Tell me of Circe,' she finally decided.

'You know it better than I.'

'That's not the point.'

Apolonio gave her foot an annoyed little kick but obliged, painting the picture of Helios' witch daughter on her island in impressively vivid colours considering the sparse words he used.

'You've grown soft-hearted. Almost like a sponge.' Alethea ran her tongue over her teeth trying to remove the last grains of rye and the taste of salted meat which lingered from the rustic evening meal she had ingested an hour earlier with the equally rustic men. Brushing dust off their Corinthian helmets, some braiding their hair, the soldiers had gathered in small clusters around flickering fires reflecting flashes of gold in their eyes. Each man— and one woman—had received their share of the provisions. Afterward, they had sung hymns by Tyrtaeus.

'Is that so? I think not,' Apolonio replied.

'Oh, yes. I'm the newly-wed and you're the one with that strange glow in your eyes.'

'I wish you wouldn't muse over it. You only pain yourself.' He stretched out an arm so that she could rest her head upon it instead of on the poplar trunk. 'It's nothing.'

Alethea sighed. 'It's not *nothing*. Such unions are all very well in youth, but then? Then you marry and fulfil your duty of begetting children. Sparta is already weak in numbers.'

'And I will. He will. Emotions need not interfere with procreation, you know.'

'You promised me there would be no blabbering tongues, no dishonour on me or on yourself,' Alethea said in a low voice, meeting his eyes.

Apolonio gazed back, the soft lavender nuances of dusk painting his face. 'I know. There has been none, though. And when this is over—' He cast a glance around the distant camp. '—when this is over and we return to Sparta, *that* will be over, too.'

'Are you still encouraging it?'

'No. It just has to...wear off.'

None of them spoke further on the subject. There was little more that could be said, and Alethea saw no use in spoiling the otherwise sublime evening as it was where they sat on the plain, wrapped in crimson cloaks against the cooling air. *We really shouldn't speak at all.*

'Any plans on great heroism in your first *real* battle?' she whispered, slightly teasing.

'Hm. Heroism as a unit, perhaps.'

It was true. The days of single-combat, one legendary man against another while the undistinguishable masses cheered on, belonged to the Trojan War and the Centauromachy. These days it seemed practicalities had caught up with Hellas, replacing individual greatness with tactics dependent on the unit as such. If one man dropped his shield and broke the phalanx formation, the gap in the defensive wall made everything crumble until one side stood as victors and the other as fleeing cockroaches lacking the required willpower.

'I've no doubt,' Alethea mumbled, then placed a quick kiss on her brother's temple and drifted off to Morpheus' realm.

Alethea did not get more than a few hours of fluttering sleep that night, but the sight which met them at the Isthmus of Corinth the following day was enough to revive even the most exhausted of spectators.

The Spartan soldiers were indeed the fraction of the Peloponnese troops who would strike the greatest chill in the league's opponents, but they were just that: a fraction. Alethea did not know the exact numeric as she gazed out over the masses of men assembled at the Isthmus, yet she estimated they must be at least thirty thousand in total. Proud Boeotians, jittery Corinthians, and bitter Megarians, among others, flocked to the Spartan leader.

The speech King Archidamus held was reserved for the generals and officers of the allied *poleis'* armies, hence Alethea's account of it was less than second-hand. Nevertheless, the message was clear. Archidamus urged for caution and vigilance, imposing upon his fellow generals the possibility that the war might still be nipped in its bud before any bloody battles broke out. In addition, he showed no signs of leaving the Isthmus of Corinth to march on Attica yet, but loitered.

The soldiers, in particular the Spartans and the Corinthians, rumbled with puzzled impatience. Had not those long autumn and winter months that had passed since the declaration of war last summer been sufficient agony? Had they not bided their time enough already? Furthermore, each hour they dawdled away was an hour for the Athenians to prepare, to mass their forces and seek protection within the Long Walls.

Alethea's entire body sizzled with frustration. *How can our leader still favour placidity over battle? Of course, one should never rush into these things, but we took a vote, we considered the matter through and through. The soldiers did.*

Apolonio was equally distraught, if not more. 'If only to ravage their land, to provoke, we should be on the march,' he said for the third time in one day as he sat polishing the edge of his shield with a soiled woollen rag. 'Apollo have mercy...'

'I know. I can just imagine them fleeing inside their city walls, scrambling away with wooden shutters tucked under their arms to save prized possessions,' Alethea replied with a sharp half-smile which her brother mirrored instantly.

'Farmers made *hoplites* during a month or two of the year.'

'I don't think their thick heads can contain both skills at once.'

Apolonio scoffed, discarding the rag and holding up his work to reflect the sunlight in the bronze. 'They only contain the skills of farmers, really.'

'Good.'

'Good for us.'

Good for us if we catch them in time... If not, we can hardly climb their walls. They're as solid as the walls of Troy. While this was perhaps an overstatement, it was not a considerable one. Regardless, none of the Hellenes were particularity drilled in siege warfare; there were methods one might apply, but there was no habit of doing so, and Sparta rarely broke its habits.

Eventually, King Archidamus had no choice but to marshal the two-thirds of the combined Peloponnesian troops he had been tasked to lead and depart from the Isthmus. At the same time, however, a messenger was sent speeding to Athens to inquire whether they would not relent, now that they could see for themselves the size of the army they would have to face.

Shabby-looking and embittered, his red tunic stained from his travels, the man returned to the army. 'I wasn't permitted to speak, to enter the *ecclesia* or even their cursed city, where the beggars are many and the streets reek. They instead escorted me to the Attic frontier and gave me the answer, that the next time you wish to negotiate, you must first withdraw your soldiers from the field,' he told his king. 'This day will be the beginning of great evils for the Hellenes.'

Once they reached the Megarid, yet another realisation dawned on the Peloponnese like a bucket of scorching water: they were to continue north to Oinói, an Athenian fortress near the Attic-Boeotian border, not southeast to Eleusis, which would have been the fastest rout to Athens. Like a stray dog not daring to approach the juiciest bone for fear of being kicked, Archidamus traipsed around searching for sinewy scraps.

I can't see the point. To besiege a walled little city now *hardly offers much strategical advance, does it?* Alethea asked herself as they marched. Since she was unable to voice these thoughts to anyone but the *heílote* carrying her provision, she kept silent, wondering if perhaps she was not the only one to question their course. No Spartan would openly object to his orders, but even the most drilled of minds must have doubts.

For two whole days they marched, first east following the coastline with its endless silver-flecked water, then north through the countryside.

Oinói was nothing remarkable in the way of architecture nor in size. A modest site without great renown, it melted into the bushy landscape. The inhabitants were prepared; they knew the target practice they would be to the attackers from the southwest if they allowed so much as the tiniest crack in their defence.

The mission proved as fruitless as an olive grove in winter. Days piled up as the army camped outside the walls of Oinói, attempting half-hearted besiegement tactics. The arrows carrying licking flames either bounced back, fell flat, or extinguished in the air before they reached their target. The thick tree trunk the men used for battering ram was not strong enough, and the time was not sufficient to starve the city out.

Eventually, Archidamus surrendered to his allies and his own soldiers' tensed whispers, abandoning the siege to continue towards Athens. Time continued to seep away rapidly as it tends to do, spilling onto the soil they marched over. The crops were ripe—this the army saw proof of every time they burnt a farm to its foundation or cut down a fruit-bearing tree—and soon each man would be needed in his own *polis* to tend to the harvest.

When they reached Eleusis, situated on the plain northwest of Athens, they set up camp in order for the proper raids might begin.

Each time a group of soldiers were dispatched from the camp, Alethea remained in the small tent she had been designated, sometimes making little excursions through the endless rows of similar tents to stretch her legs and cure boredom. Apolonio and Crysanthos both went off frequently but returned with little more than bruises, their stories as monotonous as their bodies were unscathed.

'Don't expect any epic battles, sister. There's hardly any resistance worth mentioning,' Apolonio said one night by the campfire.

'Do you wish there was?'

'It would be more worthy of the effort if they dared face us. But I like living.'

Alethea drew a sharp breath and the cheese she held between her fingers suddenly lost all appeal. 'You will live regardless. I promise.'

'You're very confident in that.' Apolonio smiled, drawing her close in one rough movement.

I have to be, just to stay sane. She settled into his arms and searched for another subject. 'I'm not sure I like this place. Do you know of the Eleusinian mysteries?'

'Only a little. They're *mysteries.*'

A man sitting on the opposite side of the crackling fire raised his voice, the golden light animating his close-cropped beard and dark eyes. 'I hear they involve a piglet, and a basket filled with unknown objects. Some say it contains one of Demeter's toes, or the breast of an Amazon.'

Alethea and Apolonio stared in unison. *And they say* we *are the savage and bizarre ones.*

Crysanthos spread a piece of cloth on the ground—presumably to avoid spoiling his spotless tunic—and joined the group. His eyes wandered to Apolonio, but to Alethea's relief, that was all.

'What do they do with the...piglet?' yet another man asked.

'Who knows? Those who reveal anything risk death.'

'Then it must be truly morbid.'

Alethea reached for another piece of cheese, her appetite revived. *And what might the rites be for? Glory, health, pleasure, superstition?*

She received no satisfactory answers that night. The Eleusinian mysteries were soon forgotten, pressed aside by sleep's temptation.

Two pair of hands fumbled in the dark: one pair wandering across her arm and leg, the other tugging impatiently at her cloak. Then, the distinct pressure of fingertips digging into her flesh and a gust of cold air brushing against her now exposed collar bone.

Do something. Do something. A knife, a pin, anything... Just do *something!* Despite the volume rising in her head, Alethea remained frozen as if she had met Medusa's fatal gaze, unable to lift so much as a finger. *Scream then.* But no, not a single note managed to escape her lips. Instead, she began counting every shallow breath, trying to distract herself from the repulsive blend of whispers and rustling clothes.

Just as she reached seven, footsteps approached, vaguely familiar in the way every third step was quicker than the rest. Alethea caught a glimpse of hair that was bright despite night's shade.

'Archidamus himself will hear of your misconduct, not to speak of the *éphoroi*. And the *gerousia*. My grandfather—'

The weight of men pressing against her body lightened, hands withdrew and someone cursed under his breath, and the attackers disappeared in the dark. No Spartan would risk being publicly scolded by his commanders on the accusation of lacking in discipline and distracting himself from his military purposes. This was the only reason why few had bothered Alethea with so much as a saucy glance: they knew the unwritten rule strictly limiting their activities to those of war. Furthermore, the humiliation of being caught was worse than the act itself—Alethea recalled the tale of the boy who had allowed a fox to gnaw him to the bone rather than confessing to having stolen it.

A moment passed before she regained a shred of mobility and could push herself up on her elbows, the metallic taste of blood on her tongue.

Crysanthos stood towering over her, though he remained one of the least frightening men she knew. With that face, second only to Helen on the tally of Spartan beauty, he could have smeared pig's blood on his cheeks and bared his teeth while still being a treat for the eye. *Why you? Why does it have to be you who saves me, who sees me like this?*

'So you do care, then, about your wife's virtue,' Alethea said, concealing the tremble in her voice under a thick sheet of scorn.

Crysanthos jerked his head to the side, tossing his curls in place. 'Apolonio loves you.' The words came hesitantly of his lips. 'And—'

'And you love him.' Alethea's cheeks flamed with regret and humiliation both. *He means no harm, yet I taunt him. He means no harm, yet he makes me feel as redundant as a warm blanket on a summer afternoon. It's all for Apolonio. Not me.*

'Do you know where he is?' Crysanthos inquired after a short silence.

'If he was here, none of this would have happened. And if I knew, I'd be with him.'

'Then...' her husband's eyes darted as if he was trying to solve a complicated riddle. 'Then you don't know?'

'No.' *Stupid man. Husband. Rescuer. Obstacle. Resource.*

Crysanthos' face at once became a mask of disinterest and he turned on his heel, embarking on a quest to find their mutual heartthrob.

'Thank you,' Alethea squeezed forth, jaw clenched, refusing to look at his crimson-clad back. 'Get him for me.'

When left in solace again, a thousand indictments hit her like searing blades. *What's the matter with me? Why didn't I... Why did I leave it to him to stop them? And next time, what then?* To her own fury, she realised her legs were still locked in the same position, and tears stung behind her nasal bone. *But it's not my fault—that I do know. It's their shortcomings, their vile...*

The encounter was far from the first of that nature she had found herself in during the past six or seven years, but she knew they would have been more common had she grown up anywhere else. No *polis*, indeed no place in the world where humans presided, was entirely sheltered from this kind of perversions, and most were infested with it.

Apolonio returned shortly thereafter, panting and dishevelled, face set in stone but a dangerous twinkle in his eyes. Alethea knew the look well. Many times, her own misery disguised with anger had showed itself in identical ways.

Crysanthos trailed behind her brother but did not remain for long, leaving them to sit quietly for the rest of the night, arms wrapped around their knees, back to back. There was a peculiar but immense comfort in sitting thus, without the need to speak more than a scattered word or two, while dawn slowly bled through the clouds.

CHAPTER SEVEN

A VOICE, RISING high pitched before plummeting and then rising again like the yelps and howls of a scalded pig, erupted from the crowd. Its source was a man of robust stature with hair like black wool and cheeks ruddy where the blood vessels had burst. The man was robed in a simple *khitōn*, though his wealth was apparent in the ivy-green *himation* and the superfluous gold details decorating both his sandals and the *fibulae* pinning his clothes in place by the shoulders.

'The savages may be laying waste to Attic land in this very moment,' he said, the tanned skin on his forehead in deep folds, nostrils flaring like those of a bull prepared to fight. 'But will they touch the property of this man?'

Every eye in the *ecclesia* followed his pointing finger. Pericles' jaw clenched noticeably, but he remained silent.

Cleon hitched up his *khitōn* to his knees so that he might move about freely while speaking, revealing hairy, muscular calves. 'I doubt they will! Because the man you have trusted with great leadership comes with no guarantee! Why is it, do you think, that he's so reluctant to step outside the city walls and face the enemy with prowess?'

A murmur swept through the clusters of seated men, the aristocracy in particular, who had long been sceptical to Pericles' defensive strategy. Eucleides and Cosimo's eyes met.

'Could it be because he has struck a deal with his old friend, the so-called King Archidamus? Could it be, that this man can sleep soundly at night because he knows the Peloponnese troops won't inflict any destruction on his own property, having received bribes?' Cleon exhaled, the red flare on his face slowly cooling, then allowed his hem to drop again and sat down.

In the meantime, the object of his slander had risen. Pericles climbed the platform with the utmost dignity—Eucleides suspected a good portion of it was deliberate, so as to make a startling contrast to the unscrupulous opponent who had spoken before him—and raised a hand to silence the chorus of hushed voices. 'You bring false accusations, Cleon son of Cleaenetus. If there's any shred of doubt in your hearts, Athenians, that I have not served this city with diligence and honesty, I seek to erase that doubt. If, by some wily tactic to estrange me from your trust, the Spartans decide to leave my property untouched, I vow to donate it to the *polis* instead so that you may all benefit.'

Eucleides' eyes widened. The speech seemed to have struck a chord even in Cosimo; Eucleides could not help a smile at the sight of his cousin's parted lips and arched brows.

'If you will accept this reassurance, I believe we shall stand strong in our unity, protected by our sacred walls, and not adhere to brazen demagogues.'

Cleon's face reddened further at the insult. His political faction was not insignificant, yet his greatest adversary gave the impression of having every single Athenian's unconditional support even when many were disquieted. Like a hawk, he swept thousands of little sparrows under his wings with the best of intentions and often the best of outcomes, but nonetheless with a singular power that the city's constitution had been crafted to prevent any man from possessing.

The *ecclesia* voted. By show of hands, no one could deny the obvious: Pericles' position remained intact.

Efigenia treaded on light feet down the staircase, measuring every step carefully so that she might go unnoticed. For all she knew, there were no male visitors in the house, hence there was nothing forbidden in her little trip from the *gynaikeion* to the open courtyard. Still, she felt as if she lost points of decorum every time she ventured outside her designated rooms. However, she had no choice, because she had lost her toy horse earlier in the day, and dared not ask a slave to search the house for her, should they tell anyone she still had such a childish keepsake.

The courtyard bathed in cool sunlight, the rows of columns casting long shadows, the fountain rippling pleasantly. Efigenia halted abruptly and remained behind one of the columns, for she was not alone. On one of the benches at the other end of the open space sat a rigid Lady Milos with her rich *khitōn* spread out as if she was a queen. Before her stood her son—but Cosimo did not in the least resemble a prince, as he might have under other circumstances. Next to the older woman, his shoulders seemed to shrink, his eyes dropped.

Efigenia stared, realising she had never seen the two of them alone together until now. *This time, he's the mouse. Not me, at least not as long as I go unnoticed. How awful...* It was a foreign thought, almost treacherous.

'No child yet?' Lady Milo's voice was sharp as splinters.

'No, mother. Perhaps I made a bad bargain for a wife.'

'The fault hardly lies in that sweet girl. It was she who made the bad bargain, or her father did. But it's not yet been fifty days—a shred of time compared to what you have ahead of you.'

Efigenia's breath stuck in her throat. *I haven't fulfilled my purpose. He's right. And yet she defends me, though there could be no other explanation than my failure.*

Cosimo did not answer. His hands trembled slightly.

Lady Milos continued, merciless. 'After everything you have cost me, you can't even give me legitimate grandchildren?'

Efigenia snapped out of her frozen condition and turned from the scene, heart thudding against her lungs.

Eucleides' eyes met hers.

'Oh—' she gasped.

'Shh. I won't tell on you.' His voice was warm with confidence.

'I wasn't eavesdropping.'

'I'm sorry, I never meant to accuse you. But of course, you know there's little love between my cousin and my aunt?'

Efigenia shook her head slowly. 'He never tells me anything of that sort. I ought to retire.'

'I don't bite.' Eucleides smiled. 'Promise. Aren't you curious to know? It's not a pleasant story, but if you don't know it, I think you should. If it might bring you closer to him...'

Efigenia threw a glance over her shoulder. Cosimo and Lady Milos were no longer in the courtyard; a few dull-eyed slaves had taken their place, sweeping the floor, but she doubted they were cheeky enough to listen to the conversation. She nodded: anything to bring her closer to her husband.

Eucleides continued. 'Cosimo wasn't always his mother's only child. There were two older ones, both sons, sired by her husband.' He arched an eyebrow.

Efigenia's eyes widened briefly. *Sired by her husband. Then...*

'Everything was not—' A flare of aversion crossed her cousin-in-law's face. 'Not quite right when Cosimo was conceived. I don't think anyone ever tried to catch the man who did it. When the sickness took her husband and the two other children but spared the one son whom she could not stand to look at...well, the affection hardly grew over the years.'

'How...how dreadful for him.'

'Yes, yes, dreadful. But I'm sure he will tell you much more than I can, once you grow closer.'

Efigenia nodded again. *If that's his wish, I shall listen.*

Eucleides appeared to wait for a reply. When none came, he merely clasped his hands behind his back. 'Well. I must go, and take your husband with me, I'm afraid. If you like, you really should try the raisin bread one of the slaves baked this morning.'

Efigenia watched him depart with a strange, comforting sensation sparking in her chest. It resembled what she had felt when her older sister had occasionally set aside a moment to speak gently to her—only stronger, because Eucleides was not of her blood, thus he had no obligation to so much as notice her, yet he had confided in her with natural ease and given her the valuable gift of his full attention. She caught herself wishing he had been a girl, and closer to herself in age, so that she would have dared return his confidence, but she knew that would have been hoping for too much. Here was another thing she could add to the list of little fortunes she so often repeated to herself in moments of melancholy: a potential friend, a mother-in-law who was her ally one way or another, an uncle-in-law who hardly seemed to know of her existence, a beautiful house with beautiful riches—and a husband with the most sublime nature in all of Athens.

CHAPTER EIGHT

WITH THE MONTH of *Elaphebolion* came not only the first whisks of budding spring but also the Dionysia, that ecstatic spectacle spanning several days, honouring the god of the vines.

Eucleides' chest fluttered with anticipation, blissfully aware that this was the festival most specked with wonders, and that these were the days in which the playwrights would present Athens with the most preeminent of their new creations. The audience would weep at the tragedies, whistle at the satyr plays, grin at the comedies, and flit around in drunken rapture part of the time. *And are not those things the most exhilarating blend there is, so long as one is reasonable in nature?*

The festival began as it always did, on the 10th day of the month, with the torchlight procession from the city gates to the theatre of Dionysus carrying a large wooden statue of the god, as well as phalluses. Eucleides wrung his hands in embarrassment at the sight of the massive replicas of male genitalia which the citizens and *metoikoi* paraded on poles through the streets. He and Cosimo walked shoulder to shoulder, crammed and surrounded by *khitōns* of varying quality, leather aprons, thick beards, countless of limbs.

'I wish we might find a more cultivated symbol,' Cosimo hissed, his face dramatically illuminated by the warm torchlight.

'Any suggestions?'

'One solution would be to disperse with the entire madness.'

Eucleides' eyes widened in horror. 'You don't mean that! Anyhow, vulgar as it may be, we cannot change legend.'

Indeed, the fertility symbols originated from a myth telling of how Dionysus brought a plague on the Theban men who foolishly discarded his worship, a plague affecting their private parts. The issue was only resolved once they had embraced the cult dedicated to the god.

Two other elements in the procession were particularity salient: square-faced bulls with horns sticking up like white thorns, their necks bulky as tree trunks, and the swaggering *chorēgoí* who sponsored the playwrights. The bulls were there to sacrifice their blood, the men their wealth.

The Athenians had now reached their destination, the theatre cut into the southern slope of the Acropolis. There, those who could fit sat down on the rows of bleachers, one patchy body of coarse wool and refined linen, eager to hear the dithyrambic competitions.

First, though, the ten *strategoi* poured libations to appease the deities. Pericles' face bore the same dignified calm as always, the symbolic helmet pushed high on his head.

Eucleides surveyed the proud men. *One day...one day I will have some greater part in this. A strategos? No, I could never be that. But perhaps a chorēgos, using my money for something truly wonderful.*

Cosimo's eyes warmed as the poets, choruses, and flute players united their efforts. His cousin rarely admitted it, but Eucleides knew he enjoyed the musical aspects to the festival and to life in general, if not the plays. *Who wouldn't? It's like water rippling over a riverbed of silver.* Eucleides himself still preferred the spoken stories to the sung, but could not deny the beauty of either one.

The choruses each belonged to one of the ten tribes constituting the population of Athens. Eucleides hardly paid any attention to the winner, though; the playwrights' competition was of far greater magnitude, especially in his eyes.

The bulls were sacrificed as was custom, their life bleeding out on the ground, rich red spurting from where their throats had been slit. Some gave up hoarse, morbid howls as their knees buckled, while others met their death in silence.

Eucleides threw a glance at his companion.

Cosimo's complexion had turned the colour of sage, eyes glued to the slaughter without blinking. 'It's nothing,' he murmured, noticing the glance. '*Every* gory ceremony... Can they never conduct such things behind closed doors? Last year, I almost got a stain on my sandal.'

'I doubt the bull meant any offence.'

'Poor creature. A necessity, but still.'

Eucleides nodded, pity stinging his heart, watching the slaughter taking place under hymns and praise. One of the bulls—an animal the colour of milk and therefore considered an especially worthy gift—pulled at the ropes holding it with all its vigour until one of the men in charge leaped forward with the knife and sullied purest white with spatters of red. Sacrifices were meant to be executed with the animal's consent, but it appeared the priests failed to obtain it more often than not.

That evening a feast was held, featuring parts of both bulls, pigs, and sheep roasted on spits. The poorer citizens, craftsmen and labourers earning a *drachma* or less a day, rejoiced in particular since festivities like these were the only time when they could fill their bellies with good meat. With grease smudged on their lips and juices dripping from their fingers onto their clothes, they looked like something between wild animals and elated children, causing a few men of higher social strata to arch their eyebrows. However, one could hardly blame them, and all regard for table manners was soon forgotten in the drunken revelry that followed. Such intoxication was generally frowned upon, yet unavoidable on this kind of occasion.

Under night's heavy shroud, a near frenzy broke out, the masses pouring through the streets once more, lacking the relatively good behaviour they had demonstrated earlier. It was not merriment that was amiss, on the contrary, but the feast had turned even the most civilised men boisterous, shoving and shouting. The women, who were otherwise permitted to attend religious ceremonies, were banned, since no respectable wife or daughter could possibly be seen participating in something like this without having her reputation shattered.

Eucleides held a firm grip of Cosimo's *himation* as they shouldered their way through the wall of people. 'Do you know where we are? Where, in the name of Aphrodite—'

'Don't use the gods' names in vain,' Cosimo said, his words nearly drowning in the raucous. 'It seems to me the whole of Athens needs to visit a bathhouse, or keep to their houses!'

'I think we're in *Kerameikos*. We're not even in the right part of Athens, then, much too far north.'

Eventually, the crowd scattered as each man returned to his *oikos* or some other place where he might spend the night.

Dawn broke, marking the beginning of the three days dedicated to tragedy, forcing the citizens to shake off their headaches from the previous night and muster enthusiasm again.

The first of the tragedians to present his four plays—three tragedies followed by one satyr play—and thereby lord over the day, was Euripides.

Eucleides knew the man by sight: a full beard clad the rounded, solemn face, his forehead high since his hairline had crept back a little with each of his fifty years. The playwright had a habit of constantly tapping at his slightly pointed nose in his many moments of irritability, but his skill was undeniable. Once, Eucleides had tried to persuade him to attend a *symposion*, upon which Euripides had replied: *'Young man, I know nothing of you except your name, and only because you just told me. I suggest you ask a man who writes comedies, since he wouldn't mind playing the fool in a stranger's house.'*

Before Eucleides had had the chance to clarify that he most certainly did not wish Euripides to come to give the other guests a good laugh, however suspiciously random the invitation might appear, the tragedian had fled his sight.

Now, he sat adamant in the theatre, eyes shining and hands tapping in eagerness to display his first contribution this year, *Medea*.

The actors wore masks painted in stark colours, the bold expressions and lines communicating the different characters even to the spectators seated far back. They had strapped platform sandals to their feet so as to appear outlandishly tall; they wore wigs of animal hair. The cast usually consisted of three men to play every roll required, as well as a large chorus to reflect and react on the events taking place by way of singing and dancing. However, the simplicity of Euripides' first play now became apparent, because only two actors entered the stage.

The Athenians bristled like leaves in the wind, a wave of whispers fizzing through the rows of bleachers. They all knew the story of Medea, princess of barbarous Colchis, who had taken Jason for her husband and aided him in his quest for the Golden Fleece had killed Jason's second wife as well as her own children in a jealous rage. Whether she was a wronged lover claiming rightful revenge or a cold-blooded woman ridden with madness—well, that was a matter of debate, though many attested to the latter. Either way, Eucleides found the story both grisly and compelling. It was one of those tales that made horror strangely irresistible even to one such as himself, who was drawn to the bright and cheery. *Pair it with a mind like Euripides' and geniality is the only possible outcome.* He craned his neck for a better view of as the play opened and one of the supposedly female characters addressed the audience.

'How I wish the Argos' sails had never swept through the dark rocks into the land of the Colchians; I wish the pine trees had never fallen in the groves of Pelion, cut down to put oars in the hands of the heroes who went after the golden fleece for Pelias. Then my mistress Medea would not have sailed to the fortress of Iolcus' land, her heart battered by love for Jason.'

The "elderly woman", presumably a nurse, resumed her speech, fearful of the harm her mistress might inflict upon the children.

Medea—the mask painted starlight-white with scarlet lips—soon confirmed the nurse's fears: 'I am in agony; I am so brutally misused. You horrible children, of a mother who hates you, gods damn you with your father, and the whole house go to Hades.'

The other actor then changed his mask, transforming into Creon, k ing of Corinth, who informed Medea that she would be exiled, while Jason wedded the King's daughter Glauce.

The play was a lengthy procedure; for hours the actors and the chorus intertwined dialogue with lyrics, ensnaring the listeners wholly in their web.

Eucleides at once remembered the days spent on these same benches with his father. Now, Achaikos' joints were stiff not from sitting but from disease, and he could not be bothered to attend the festival. *How it would brighten his spirits to see it… Perhaps tomorrow…* Eucleides returned his attention to the *orchestra*, where Medea was now announcing her horrendous intentions.

'My friends. I have determined to do the deed at once, to kill my children and leave this land, and not to falter or give my children over to let a hand more hostile murder them. They must die and since they must, I, who brought them into the world, will kill them. But arm yourself, my heart. Why hesitate to do these tragic, yet necessary, evils?'

Because violence was never shown on stage, said necessary evils were left to the spectators' imagination. The play later concluded with Medea escaping to Athens carrying the bodies of her children, leaving Eucleides marvelling, as was often the case at the end of a tragedy. *We must have it collected for the* bibliotheca *someday soon. I should like to read it myself—* His thoughts were interrupted as Cosimo tugged at his *khitōn*.

'What?'

'We ought to stretch our legs before the next one begins,' Cosimo said. 'And get some clear spring water for my throat.'

'Something to eat, perhaps,' Eucleides beamed.

'If you like. That awful woman Medea has robbed me of my appetite.'

Did you ever *have a great appetite?* Eucleides kept the notion to himself and together they rose from their seats and ventured outside the theatre for a short while. It was midday, the sun a sliver of light against a sky of marbled greys, its rays of warmth enhanced by the crisp breeze.

Having paid one of the vendors an *obol* for a handful of walnuts and a cup of heavily diluted wine for lack of water, they strolled along the foot of the Acropolis, the wind whisking hair in their faces as if to tease.

Cosimo sipped on the beverage. 'I think Euripides should have portrayed Jason in a more flattering light. It was almost as if he wasn't the hero. *I* could write better drama if I tried.'

Eucleides frowned. 'How can he be the hero, abandoning his wife for another, after all the god-worthy trials they endured together? Didn't he love her once?'

'Your fantasies blind you, cousin. His choice was simple: a young and wealthy princess of Corinth, or a barbarian woman who murders in her hysteria?'

'Hysteria caused by his actions, surely,' Eucleides remarked.

'Oh, but you forget how she cut her brother in little pieces and threw them in the ocean to distract their father from capturing *Argos*.'

Well, maybe that *wasn't the most sympathetic choice.* A moment passed in silence save for the crunching of walnuts being cracked and devoured, and the ever-present hum of the city.

'She's impressive, though, Medea. You must concede to that, at least,' Eucleides said as they began walking back to the theatre.

'Impressive? She's all that is repulsive in women, magnified into insanity. I really don't know how you stand the whole thing.'

'Would you treat your wife the same way Jason treated his?' Eucleides bit his lip. *Surely not, never.* Fortunately, Cosimo did not have a chance to answer, since they had re-entered the theatre and the noise of thousands of voices chattering washed over them.

Two more tragedies were performed, both skilfully executed yet far from as memorable as the first. The satyr play always offered a much-needed release of tension after a day jammed with suspense and misery: the chorus dancing with goat skins thrown over their otherwise naked bodies, the entire performance burlesque and saucy.

Upon returning once more to the *oikos* by nightfall, Eucleides left Cosimo with his dear dogs and went to look for Efigenia. Under other circumstances, he would have hesitated to act so boldly as to pay another man's wife a visit at this hour, but *Medea* had left a nagging trace in his thoughts. The newest member of the household had not spoken many words to him in the two months since her arrival, but he had sensed her warming a little to him since that day in the courtyard, when he had discovered her watching Cosimo and Lady Milos. Still, she was a hard nut to crack, her shell of frightened correctness too thick to allow any true friendship to spring forth. For now, pity would have to suffice. *Poor girl, confined in her chambers while the rest of the* polis—*no, the rest of the citizens, that's quite different—watch the plays. And womanly hysteria...does such a thing really exist?* His mind was a whirlpool of similar questions as he knocked on the door to Efigenia's bedchamber as quietly as he could.

One, two, three heartbeats passed before the door creaked open and a familiar little face peered back at him, her widened eyes like flecks of sienna.

The girl's expression puzzled him; euphoria and dread deeper than Tártaros mingled and shifted.

'Oh. I thought you were—' Efigenia swept her clothes tighter around her shoulders, but her face calmed slightly.

'I'm sorry, I should have thought of that. He's still downstairs, I think, petting the dogs. I just wanted to...' *Wanted to what, honestly?*

Efigenia waited in absolute silence for him to continue.

Eucleides wrung his hands. 'Well, you see, I just wanted to ask you whether you are content here. I don't know if I've asked you that before, or if your husband has, but I thought someone should. Do you feel agitated sometimes, because of your lot in life?'

Efigenia's eyes grew even rounder and she took a step back. 'Have I given you cause to think such a thing? Have I been horribly...horribly impertinent?' she almost whispered.

Eucleides could not hold back the laugh that came bubbling, immediately regretting it when he realised she was in earnest. 'No, no. I never meant to paint you as the grudging wife, only you must feel lonely at times.'

'Not lonelier than I'm supposed to be. Cosimo *does* visit me. And everyone has been graceful.' She wrapped her arms around her torso, looking stubbornly at her bare feet. 'Perhaps...perhaps it's not proper that you are here.'

'Goodnight, then. I shall remind him that you're loving and sweet.' Eucleides smiled. *At least I think you must be, deep down, from what little I know.*

A shimmer of hope crossed her face for just a fracture of a moment at this promise. Then, she shut the door.

The second day belonged to Euphorion, son of Aeschylus, and the third belonged to Sophocles. Though Eucleides found that he still preferred the work of Euripides, the remaining mass of seventeen-thousand in the theatre cheered loudest for Euphorion.

The fourth and fifth days were devoted to comedy's exhilarating mirth. The customary five plays per day had been cut to three because of the solemnity the war required of the *polis*, yet Eucleides' cheeks ached from laughing at the end of the fifth day.

The ten judges—one from each tribe, selected by lot—were always subject to public influence, and thus proclaimed Aeschylus' son winner, steeping him in the immense glory which compensated for the scanty sum awarded. A one-eyed man named Hermippus took the comedic poets' prize, and together he and Euphorion pranced like horses having won a race, clad in luscious wreaths of ivy. Their sponsors, however, were the true feat, exuding pride gained by means of money and a lucky pick in the pool of possible playwrights and chorus members, combined with further luck being allotted the most skilled actors.

When the whole spectacle with all its celebrations and processions at last died down, the Athenians were hazy-eyed and lightheaded, their hunger for entertainment stemmed for a year to come.

CHAPTER NINE

NOT MANY DAYS passed after the Dionysia festival before Cosimo, being a *triērarchos*, had to gather his most crucial belongings—in addition to the three chests of expensive clothing he insisted on bringing with him—and travel to the port city Piraeus.

The amassing of the Athenian fleet, or at least part of it, was the result of the Peloponnese raids on the countryside, which had not gone unnoticed inside the city walls. On the contrary: every time the *ecclesia* convened, the enraged shouts telling the *strategoi* to sally out and allow the army to protect their property grew in numbers and intensity. The radical faction, called war-mongering by some, grew in numbers as the Athenians bore witness to the destruction done to their crops, a destruction equalled by that of the Persian Wars fifty years ago. At the same time, those still promoting peace claimed with a tinge of desperation that they must negotiate before the situation deteriorated further.

Cosimo, however, seemed more concerned with the household finances at the moment. 'Do you know,' he said one day while overseeing the slaves folding his *khitōns* and stacking them in the chests, 'what being responsible for this trireme has cost me—has cost *us?*'

Eucleides shook his head. Unlike Lady Milos and her son, neither he nor his father had ever taken a great interest in such matters. *Why get a headache over a* mina *back or forth, when one has never lacked it?*

Cosimo began counting on his fingers. 'There's the reparations and general maintenance, and then there's paying for the rigging. Then I supply extra wages to the *thranitai* and the officers above what Athens provides the other rowers with.'

Eucleides leaned against the doorpost, only listening with one ear, plunged deep into his own thoughts concerning *The Odyssey*. 'And how much does it all amount to?'

'Almost four thousand *drachmae.*' Cosimo flashed him a theatrical look, presumably waiting for some shocked exclamation in response. 'Cousin? Did you hear?'

Eucleides snapped out of his reflections. 'Oh, yes. But we can manage that, surely? The silver from Laurion is still plentiful and flowing like moonlight. With the gods' blessing we won't live on crumbs a single day of our lives.'

'Liturgies will be our ruin, unless my mother's hideous jewellery purchases does it first,' Cosimo hissed under his breath. Then, he returned his attention to the slaves packing his clothes. 'Not that one! I said the one with *blue* embroideries!'

A hundred ships and twenty thousand men, including a thousand *hoplite*s and four hundred archers—this was the fleet Athens dispatched from Piraeus that spring under lavish circumstances. Each trireme appeared better equipped and more impressively decorated than the last; no *triērarchos* would willingly see his vessel humbled in the shadow of others'.

In the harbour of Piraeus, a crowd large enough to compete with the audience at the Dionysia had assembled; like an enormous herd of white, grey, and brown sheep the people flocked to the pier to bid their loved ones farewell. The smell—the salty ocean and gutted fish blending with filthy clothes and skin basted in perfumed oils—made Eucleides dizzy.

'I knew it would be like this, dear,' Lady Milos said, waddling behind him. 'Look at that woman's necklace! I could just rip it off her.'

That would not surprise me. 'Is the stench disturbing you, aunt?'

'What stench?'

Eucleides did not bother to answer. His aunt's nose had long since given up.

Two slaves walked abreast in front, creating a cleft in the crowd for them to pass through. Another skipped at Lady Milos' side, fervently fanning her, and another two followed behind carrying a lidded basket.

'I think I can spot the water.' Eucleides' steps quickened. 'Efigenia would have loved to see it up close. I don't think she has ever been to the ocean.'

'Of course not, dear. How could she? But don't waste your precious head on our girl. She's eager to fulfil her duties, I know, and the journey would only have put the child at risk as well as her reputation. Look at that sapphire!'

A few steps later they broke through the last rows of people, emerging at the very front of the crowd, and nearly stumbled over the edge of the pier and into the glassy teal depth.

The one hundred long, thin triremes stretched across the ocean, fading into specks of brown in the distant, the skilfully combined fir and pine catching glints of sun. The rowers were already seated on their designated spots, the oars poking out like so many legs ready to speed the ships across the Aegean.

Eucleides squinted. *Have the rest of the crews already boarded, too? Are we too late to take farewell?*

As if called upon by the silent question, the young *triērarchos* from their *oikos* popped up by the rail of one of the closest triremes, hands resting delicately on the wood, hair untouched by wind or salt. 'I expected you some time ago,' Cosimo called.

Eucleides located him immediately and stuck up a hand for greeting, smiling broadly. 'There was a bit of an obstacle on the road, a carriage overturned. Are you ready? For your great adventure, I mean.'

'As ready as I hoped to be.'

Was that fear? Maybe. 'We bring gifts from your wife,' he gestured at the basket. 'She sends wine and sesame cookies, and a shroud, for the northern winds.'

Cosimo knitted his brows. 'She's not *with* you, is she?'

At this, his mother's voice cut through the buzz around them, like dry leaves rattling. 'Naturally not. She thinks she is with child, although I doubt if this will prove true. It would certainly be a surprise.'

'Why so, mother?'

'I never thought of you as virile.'

Eucleides tugged at his lip. 'Well, I'm sure we will know with certainty when you return. Please *do* return, won't you?'

Cosimo's face cracked in that rare, glowing smile, his *khitōn* fluttering in the wind. 'I will, cousin, that I swear. Don't be a fool without me, don't drown yourself in daydreams.'

Eucleides swallowed. *If only I were the one in danger of drowning.*

The trumpet's ear-splitting note sounded, commanding silence. Priests then held a collective prayer for the success and safe return of the men, pleading for the gods to be merciful. Libations were poured, hymns were sung.

Finally, there was another trumpet blow marking the fleet's departure. One by one, the ships set course for the sharp horizon, oars moving ceaselessly since the winds were not yet favourable enough to set sail.

'We should sacrifice to Poseidon when we return home,' Eucleides mumbled.

Lady Milos lodged her thick hands on her hips. 'For the good of the *hoplites* and archers, then, dear. They will be the most valuable.'

Whether this was true or not, Eucleides had no clue, but it hardly mattered. The gods were fickle, their voices rumoured to be thunder and the scent of ambrosia crushed against their skin. They watched the follies of mortals from their thrones, amused, and not even oracles could always predict whose side they would take in a war.

Tears welled in Efigenia's eyes when her monthly bleeding came once more. *No child. Empty womb. Silly girl, to think I had managed this time.* With Cosimo somewhere far off on a trireme which felt almost imagined, bobbing up and down on the waves, there was no knowing when she would have the chance again. Even so, she dreaded his return, because she would have the unpleasant task of demolishing his expectations. *What will he say? Maybe nothing. He shouldn't have to.*

Needles of anxiety plunged through her body. She had tried every herb, every superstitious remedy she knew, the ones she had found out about from overheard whispers during her own childhood. All it had amounted to was false hope, smothered.

And to think of all the infants exposed at crossroads or in the woods. Efigenia shuddered. She would gladly have taken any of them, even a baby girl, for her own. Just as her new *oikos* needed an heir, many other families were overcrowded with offspring, which they left for nature to deal with, and she marvelled at how much kinder the world would be if blessings of fruitfulness were distributed more equally.

Nevertheless, Efigenia was still budding with girlhood. There was time, years even, before her fears would be well-founded.

Time did pass, although it was days rather than years, while four of the family's five members resumed their routinely lives. Athens remained crowded, farmers and city-dwellers like ants crawling over one another, men and women sleeping in sanctuaries and gutters alike. Efigenia would stand on her toes to cast a glance out the high windows and be stunned by the flood of people filling the streets below at any given moment. *It is a good thing I don't go out there. The filth...*

Once word reached the city that the Peloponnese troops no longer plagued Attica, a few daring souls scuttled back to their farms, only to find the crops and houses burnt to the ground. Some stayed to rebuild what they had lost, while most returned with hard lines set around their mouths and eyes, knowing it was futile.

CHAPTER TEN

APOLONIO MOVED LIKE a bronze statue come to life on the dusty plain, bathing in light from the setting sun. There was no sound, the images came in flashes. No enemy approached, yet a spear was thrust forward, plunged into his guts. As the iron, gleaming cold blue like a clam shell, moved slowly up towards his chin, it parted the skin with frightening ease. The thin red line spread, revealing glossy flesh and protruding intestines. Apolonio's eyes froze, void of all life.

Alethea emerged from the dream with her heart beating as if it might break her ribcage from the inside. The tent was stagnant with heat lingering from the day. Two slumbering figures lay beside her, just as they had done when she fell asleep—the overseer of the camp had decided it was more suitable she shared living quarters with her husband and brother rather than stay in her own little tent. She swallowed hard and scrambled to her knees, crawling across the narrow strip of dirt between her own bedroll and that of her brother. His breaths were steady, his face peacefully caught in some dream doubtlessly more pleasant than hers had been. Alethea stretched out a hand and felt his torso, which was full of scratches and scars, but no spear had torn it apart. *Thank Artemis.* She did not know why it was this goddess in particular she thanked—it felt natural, though, that the deity who Delina had given her life to would perhaps watch over their brother as well.

The beating of her heart slowed gradually, but Alethea could not shake the nasty foreboding. *Maybe tomorrow is the day something happens. Maybe tomorrow is when I need to be there, not shut up in this tent waiting and waiting and waiting.* The itching boredom accumulated over the countless past days only added to the impulse. Once daylight cracked through the clouds and the soldiers set out to raid the countryside once more, they would not be alone.

A *heílote* was an easy target for bribes, and if bribes did not work, they were always receptive to threats. Oftentimes, neither was required, for they obeyed without question. Two centuries of enslavement tended to have that effect. An elderly man with a patchy beard brought Alethea the items she had requested: greaves for her legs, a cuirass, a helmet, and the characteristic scarlet cape and tunic. She ran her fingers over the cape, admiring the colour to the fullest, but knew she would have to remove it before battle, as did all the soldiers. Red was the most unfeminine colour, yet she felt strangely alluring fastening it at her shoulders. The tunic was a man's garment, and Alethea noted irritably that it ended just above her knee and not the middle of her thigh, as it would have done on its original owner. The clothes and the equipment had all belonged to a dead soldier, she was sure of it.

The *heílote* man had not only brought her spear, but a a *xiphos*, and the blade bounced reassuringly against her leg as she walked. *Almost like an old friend.* She stuck her left arm through the armhole on the back of the *hoplon* shield and nearly dropped it before she grasped how heavy it was.

Alethea had no illusions of passing for an ordinary *hoplite* if subjected to inspection. However, if she could blend into the phalanx, made to look like just another face masked by a helmet and another set of limbs hid behind a massive *hoplon*... With a dash of luck and the men's minds focused on the raid, her scheme just might work.

Without a sound, Alethea slipped in between the rows of stern-eyed soldiers. They had not yet perfected the formation, and since not even the Spartans bothered to maintain the rigid square of the phalanx when raids were expected rather than battle, they paid little heed to the fact that one line contained one member too many. Alethea was in luck once more, because no thorough inspection was carried out and it appeared the army had almost begun to relax from lack of opposition.

No Athenians came to battle them this time, either. No one had expected them to, but a shred of hope always fluttered, that at this point there would be real resistance. This time, troops of soldiers would emerge from within the impenetrable walls, having mustered the courage to defend their farmland. It was becoming almost tiresome to perform the same mass destruction every time they set out; a little opposition always made the procedure more interesting. Farms had been burned to piles of ash on the ground, cattle slaughtered and feasted on, the few inhabitants who chose to stay slain in their homes. Thus, it could continue—and all the while, the Spartan *hoplite*s had no chance on earth to combat the true threat: the navy of triremes lording over the Aegean Sea.

As Alethea stood squeezed between two men, hardly daring to breathe for fear they might discover the more feminine arms of their companion, she wondered once more if this would not prove a fruitless war. *Athenians will cower behind those walls like deer frightened of the hunt. Their ships will demolish the Peloponnese, and soon enough we will be the ones who are doomed, not they.* Disgust surged up her spine. *How is it that such a city built such an empire? Power should not be rewarded for sly tactics but for honest confrontation.*

The signal sounded and the troops began to march. The soles of their sandals beat against the cracked earth like a single drum, as always following the rhythm of the hymns the men sang. Alethea knew the words by heart but only mouthed them, not trusting her own voice to blend in well enough. She could not spot Apolonio, nor Crysanthos, but it did not matter. She knew she was not alone.

Alethea heard the distant clopping of horses' hooves before she saw the cloud of dust, much less the animals and their masters. When they came close though, she spotted bright tunics against dark fur glistening in the sunlight.

It was as if someone had struck a chord of pique now vibrating through the phalanx the soldiers rapidly formed; they preferred to fight *hoplites* such as themselves, rather than cavalry, whose horses their speed could not match. Moreover, Sparta had no *hippeus* of its own—even the Kings' bodyguard called *hippeis* were foot soldiers contrary to their name.

Still, the Spartans did not falter in their steps, confident that their *pentēkostyes* of well over a hundred men could easily manage the perhaps twenty mounted Athenian soldiers. After all, a spear might topple a man from his horse and kill as easily as it would a *hoplite*, and if they struck down a horse, the man upon it would be crushed or left to his own devices, which were rarely good. It was rumoured that other sections of the army had faced a few skirmishes such as this before, and a majority had turned out to their advantage.

Alethea flashed a sideways glance at the man on her left. The helmet shielded his profile from her eyes, but his stature was tall and his shoulders rippled with muscles, his skin a patchwork of scars from previous military encounters. Alethea was accustomed to the sight, and it strengthened the sense of security lodged inside her ever since she was a small child. Raised and nurtured on tales of her kinsmen's victories, she felt no fear standing amongst them.

The collision was merciless. Horses shrieked as they met with the spear tips sticking out from the phalanx. Some, however, broke through the defensive lines and began shattering the formation like small tornados. The tumult which followed was different from the previous raids: then, there had been no enemy to return the slaughter.

Alethea gasped for air as her half-open mouth filled with the blood spurting from the man in front of her, who had been impaled by an Athenian spear. The sickening iron taste made her stomach turn in revulsion. She had never been fond of the black soup the men in the barracks fed on, but at least the pig's blood the soup was made of was not raw from the animal's veins.

Alethea's gaze flickered around the dusty mass of red and white tunics, blades, and whipping horses' tails, but could still not discern her brother. Her arm ached from carrying the shield, but she forced herself to raise it to fend off a sword that came swooshing towards her. The force of the blow sent vibrations up her arm to her shoulder. She caught sight of her attacker: a short but sturdy man who seemed to have abandoned his horse to fight on his own two feet. His sword was the only weapon he had, and Alethea felt a surge of triumph. She might not have any soldier's training or experience in battle, true, but she was no stranger to handling a weapon when hunting or walking alone in the evenings, and her equipment was superior by one shield and one spear.

One, two, three times she slashed with the *xiphos*. Twice, the man saved himself, then the leaf-shaped blade severed the artery just below his chin. Two more men succumbed to her hand, one whose horse she first had to launch her spear as a javelin at. Just as she had sometimes told Apolonio, she had never truly mastered this particular weapon, and the animal's cry when she missed the heart and instead tore its belly sent shivers all the way to her fingertips. Around her, men's blood spattered the ground. Of the phalanx remained perhaps a hundred men, though many had sustained wounds and scratches. The Athenian *hippeus*, on the other hand, was near extinction.

Alethea felt as disarrayed on the inside as the battlefield looked. She could smell victory, but if Apolonio's body was one of the massacred piles of flesh on the Attic plain, this would be a loss regardless. *Even Crysanthos would be a loss of sorts*. The wind whipped her hair in her eyes as if Zephyros himself was furious with her. Gusts of dust sprayed up in her face, sending her body into a highly inconvenient fit of coughing. In the corner of her eye, she spotted a silhouette raising a blade and turned her head in a reflex. Numbness spread through her cheek. The sword had missed its target but struck nonetheless.

When she woke, Alethea merely drifted from one nasty dream to another. The entire left side of her face was pulsating with a dull heat, and the part just below her one eye had swollen up enough to blind her almost completely. When she reached up a hand to examine the area, her fingers met coarse stitches and sticky pus, sending a wave of excruciating pain through her cheek. *Ouch. That's going to scar. Mother won't be pleased.*

She turned her head and raised her limited gaze from the bedroll to her brother's face a hand's width from her own. Somehow, the scent of cloves and leather remained, despite the spring they had spent on campaign.

'You're awake,' Apolonio remarked, voice dripping of relief.

'I know that.' Alethea attempted a shaky smile. The pain it took was a thousand times worth the slither of comfort she knew it gave him.

'I could pour reprimands and rage on you. I probably will, once your face no longer looks like a flayed and butchered animal.'

'I'm sure you will. But I killed three men. I didn't make a fool of myself.'

'No.'

Apolonio fetched a bowl of water and soaked a linen rag in it. He then pressed the cool cloth against her cheek with the utmost care.

'What—what will happen now?' Alethea's pulse was like the fast falling of a spring rain as she waited to hear her doom. *I directly opposed the éphoroi's instructions. I did the unspeakable. I never would have, had it not been for that damned dream.*

'I don't know. I haven't spoken to the commanders yet. The army cannot be delayed by a wounded woman.'

'I wouldn't want to delay it, by Zeus. I only wish—'

'I know. Me too.' Apolonio placed a kiss on the tip of her nose. 'Rest.'

Alethea nodded. Though the rest of her body was merely a little sore from the battlefield, there was no point in objecting to this most simple of requests. If nothing else, she could always take the opportunity to consider her course of action. *I will never beg forgiveness on my knees. Never. The only thing to do now is take the blow. They know it as well as I do. They expect it. And yet...* Sparta punished disobedience but admired courage. Furthermore, sending her back to the *polis* meant the army would have to spare men to escort her, and even if those men were *heílotes*, those in charge might be hesitant. These were barely reasons enough to hope, but Alethea desperately gripped after anything to soothe the anxious fluttering in her chest.

The shred of hope was trampled to dust the following day. The *éphoroi* and the king were occupied with matters of greater importance, hence it fell on one of the lesser commanders to determine what would be done with the unruly young woman who trotted at the army's heels.

The palpable grimness of his mouth and the brackets of creases around his eyes told Alethea all she needed to know. However, he spoke. 'It was foolish to let you accompany soldiers on campaign.'

Alethea met his gaze as well as she could, the swollen part of her face throbbing hotly. 'I have been a good subject. What I did was a single instance.'

'A single instance is enough.'

'I killed several men.' Alethea thought she saw a twinkle of approval in the commander's heavy-lidded eyes for just a heartbeat. 'So I heard. You're a strong, healthy young woman, reared well despite this disobedience. You could contribute many thriving children to the polis.'

'I suppose so. I plan to. As soon as we return.' The throbbing escalated and she could hear the blood pulsating in her ears. *We, not I. Please don't send me back early, please don't. Not without—*

'Yes. I believe it would be best if you returned to Sparta presently, indeed. Arrangements will be made. You can stop along the coast should your wound make traveling uncomfortable.' His last word oozed of acid. Then, he was gone, leaving Alethea to ride out the chills of his verdict.

The humiliation of the defeated state in which Alethea left camp was meagre in comparison to the despair of taking farewell of her brother.

'It's only a month,' she whispered as much to herself as to him, arms wrapped so tight around his neck that it would hurt. His nose pressed against her collarbone, warm breaths brushing sweetly against her skin.

'I know that. You'll recover nicely, and I shall see you before you know it.'

'And you'll be healthy and in one piece, also?'

Apolonio withdrew slightly, nose crinkled. 'Healthy enough to beat a *heílote* or two if they prove lazy with the harvest.'

A joyless laugh escaped Alethea. 'Goodbye. For now.'

The travel was both painfully slow and painful in itself. Alethea had, after a good deal of persuasion, agreed to ride one of the cargo mules rather than walk on her own two legs. The obsidian-eyed, tough-limbed animal ambled idly, Alethea swaying a little with each bobbing step, her body stiff from sitting from dawn till dusk. She had spent many hours on horseback during her youth, since it constituted part of the exercise regime girls underwent, but had always preferred other activities and would rather watch the reckless chariot races than ride herself.

Two *heílotes*, men approaching forty, flanked the mule, their feet full of little cuts from sharp stones in their simple sandals. It was a risky endeavour to entrust them to return a wounded young woman to Sparta; the temptation to rid themselves of her and flee their oppressors with the mule and the provision was obvious. Still, the commander who made the arrangements had not been too worried. The *heílotes* knew what happened to those who revolted, they had heard the whispered stories of relatives found slaughtered or simply disappearing. Like iron beaten into shape over ember, they had been moulded by fear.

The day after the small entourage had passed the Isthmus of Corinth—looking absurdly empty now, every trace of the thirty thousand men who had camped there wiped out—and crossed to the Peloponnese, Alethea's health deteriorated rapidly. The cut oozed pus, the stitches buried deep between swollen flesh shifting in purple and amber. Her thoughts muddled with fever, her body slouched like a sack of grain under sickly exhaustion, causing her to slip back and forth on the mule. *If I fall off and this wretched animal tramples me to death, I'll be better off.* The heat only made the situation worse; the blazing sun would have given even the most vigorous person a splitting headache.

Alethea often caught the *heílotes* exchanging glances over her head, eyebrows elevated, but none of them spoke on that first day of decline. On the second day, however, there was no alternative than to stop in one of the coastal towns, as the commander had suggested.

Houses seemed to climb on one another: lumps of clay and sun-baked bricks carelessly thrown in a pile. The port consisted of steep cliffs flecked white with birds' faeces, ending in a thin strip of shore where Aegean waves licked the sand so far up that only the smallest of vessels could be pulled up on dry land.

The inhabitants were obscure dots in Alethea's compromised view. Like badly painted figures on a vase, they flitted around reeking of the ocean's salt and the goats they lived off, maintaining a distance between themselves and the happenings in Attica. *Maybe they sent soldiers...maybe not...maybe a tiny pit like this isn't on our list of allies...* Alethea could think no further before drifting back into the half-conscious state that had become her reality.

'You need to pay,' was the answer the *heílotes* received when they inquired for somewhere to spend a night or two. In Sparta, coins were not custom, for it was thought to make the people try to accumulate wealth rather than further the egalitarian *polis* and the army. When transactions were unavoidable, spits of iron were used for currency, and no one had provided the little group with coins of the sort used in the rest of Hellas. Thus, the potential hosts refused one by one.

The sacred tie of mutual hospitality was for princes and the like, not for worn slaves. Even the common tradition of generosity towards travellers appeared forgotten, until Alethea partly on purpose slid off the mule and landed in a sorry heap in one of the winding streets.

With her face and shoulders slathered in mud, two elderly women and a man supported her to one of the more respectable houses while the *heílotes* trailed behind. *I bet they're overjoyed. I bet they have longed all their lives to see a Spartan this humiliated.*

The house belonged in practice to one of the elderly women, a widow, who after a scrutinizing look at Alethea's muddied figure gave her a bedroll in one of the otherwise empty rooms on the second floor. Despite the room being plain even by comparison to her home in Sparta, Alethea felt as if she had been granted the greatest luxury on earth, resting her head on the bundled-up blanket serving as pillow. *If mother could see me now, she would slap me for being so stubborn. I would, too. But it was worth a try, even if all I got was some time with Apolonio and a battle mark on my face.*

What followed was three days of attempted recuperation. Vivid dreams mingled with hazy woken hours, the bitter soup her hostess fed her competing with her other ailments. Whether asleep or awake, one question frequently popped up: what was happening at Acharnae? This encompassed a hundred other questions. Was Apolonio well? Had the Athenians come out to fight yet? The townsfolk knew nothing, of course, and Alethea doubted they would have thought to inform her even if they had.

Her only solace was that the pus slowly left the wound and the burning fevers cooled a little. In another two days' time or so, the old woman said in a nasal voice, it would be possible to resume their journey home.

CHAPTER ELEVEN

A LETHEA WOKE TO tumult. She felt the young man's hot breath before she could discern his face with her single clear-sighted eye. High, perfectly sculpted cheekbones protruding under milky skin, a strong nose, thin lips. Wisps of dark chestnut hair hung across his deep-set eyes, having escaped from underneath the helmet in the heat of the moment.

Slim fingers yanked her hair, not hard but enough to turn her head so that he could look at her face. Had she not been sunk deep in the haze of fever, cheek pounding with pain, Alethea knew she could have warded off the man without difficulty. However, he was not alone, but accompanied by three sturdier figures, all of whom waited in the background while what appeared to be their leader inspected her.

'Take her to the ship. She'll do.'

One of the other men took a step forward and flung her across his shoulder without any considerable effort. Alethea gasped with stunned humiliation. This was not like the symbolic abduction on her wedding night; this was not on her terms, and it stung worse than the fear of what might happen to her.

The town was burning. Bright flames licked the clay and woodwork, jumping from one house to another with incomprehensible speed, turning everything in its way black. The tightly compressed houses only facilitated the destruction.

Alethea caught glimpses of limp bodies in the streets, people scuttling away from the fire and the attackers, some mowed down as they fled. Her chin bounced against the man's back, his arm clenching her legs to keep her from kicking. Once they reached the beach where the trireme—an immensely ugly ship in Alethea's eyes, with tears in its sails and damage presumably obtained on previous raids—her throat hurt from screaming.

'Make it stop,' the leader said. 'My poor ears.'

Fortunately, the blow that followed was not on the wounded side of her head, but it was no less effective in robbing her of all consciousness.

Waves beat against the trireme's side, casting the ship back and forth despite the fine craftmanship with which the pine and fir had been forged to create a steady vessel. Dashes of foam sprung up from the ocean and over the rail, the salt drying on Alethea's lips where she lay on deck. Her wrists had been skilfully tied together with ragged rope and locked behind her back, her feet held still in the same manner. *If this continues much longer, I'll have to dig these ropes out of my flesh. And when I have, I will cut up his body from the groin to those grossly pretty cheekbones.*

Alethea craned her neck, trying to catch a glimpse of her captor, who was pacing from one side of the deck to the other. For several hours now, she had studied the young man in his seemingly endless pacing—it was as if he was under the illusion that he could make the trireme reach its destination faster by moving his own legs—and concluded that he was the self-possessed type. The type that, had he been the dubious hero in a tragic play, the gods would have damned for hubris. To her great irritation, Alethea had also made the discovery that the man's appearance had not been the least dishevelled by neither the raid on the coastal town nor the time at sea; it was the same immaculate clothing, the same glossy chestnut hair, the same icy calm eyes that now looked at her from the other side of the mast. Steeped in shade and with the sail billowing behind him, he resembled a silhouette drawn on a piece of papyrus.

Once more, the trireme rode high on the sea before plummeting down again, and Alethea's stomach turned. She swallowed resolutely two, three times, determined not to disgrace herself by vomiting. No one would clean her hair and face if she did.

The faint creaking of the man's footsteps against the deck was deafening in Alethea's ears. Then, there was the contours of his fleshy shoulders and the gleam in his small, oddly round eyes. The dark enveloped him like a protective cloak, and she knew he would not have dared approach her in broad daylight where the *triērarchos* could see. At this hour, though, her captivator was likely sound asleep, perhaps dreaming of the comforts of home.

Alethea surrendered to her instincts as the man enclosed the short distance between them: to wriggle with all her strength in a futile attempt to loosen the rope stringing her wrists together and scramble to the other end of the trireme or even dive over board into the pitch-black water. This time, Crysanthos could not come to her rescue, but this time she was lucky in that her limbs did not freeze involuntarily.

Alethea recognised the man now they were no less than an arm's length apart: one of the *thranitai*, the top rowers, a short man who looked like a flustered mass of sweat and callouses when put to work.

Within seconds, one of the rower's strong hands pressed against her lips to prevent a scream, the piece of cloth shoved between her teeth having been removed earlier that day, while the other hand grappled at her rags for clothes. A whiff of sour breath stung her senses, witnessing of the cheap fish and cheaper wine the lower ranking members of the crew dined on.

Like a tied-down animal being slaughtered, she writhed back and forth, panic bubbling in her throat along with bile as sour as the man's breath. On pure reflex, she slammed her jaw shut around the man's thick arm, drawing blood as her teeth sank through his skin.

The man cried out in raw pain, pulling his arm to him, thereby making the wound worse, just like when one pulls away from a biting dog. 'You...beast! Dorian harlot!' His eyes darted over her body in the dark.

Alethea realised with a chill that he was contemplating where he might inflict the most harm without the *triērarchos* noticing someone had touched his war prize. She ran her tongue over her teeth, tasting the man's blood. Then, before another thought could cross her mind, a crushing pain diminished everything else, making her vision sway. Alethea could not see the fingers on her left hand in the night, but she did not need to. She had heard the crackle of bones when the rower squashed them under his boot like a beetle. She pressed her lips and swallowed several screams. The pain soared, sending waves from her bloody lump for a hand to her head, and blackened everything out.

When Alethea regained consciousness, bright daylight stung her eyes, the ship moving under her and seagulls squealing above her. There was no way to be certain, but judging by the state of her peplos, Alethea guessed the man from last night had retreated after trampling her fingers, probably to tend to his own wound. She could not spot him by the oars, but the angle at which she lay did not allow a full view of the ship.

None of it was the least unexpected, on the contrary, it was a small wonder it had not happened before, and Alethea did not doubt it would happen numerous times again before she stepped onto Athenian soil. There is only so much will to live in a person, and though she had always prided herself on having a large amount, it felt as if it was draining away hour by hour. The ropes carving into her wrists, her battered face, her crushed and throbbing hand, the stiffness and the constant hunger—all these physical circumstances were eating into her psyche, threatening to leave naught but a shell if not hindered. She recalled the *heílotes* forced to work like animals and humiliated in every imaginable way, occasionally slaughtered to prevent uprisings. There was a certain hollowness to their eyes, caution in their every step.

'Do you need water again?' The *triērarchos'* reserved voice mingled with the seagulls' cries and the rower's groans.

'No. A little.'

The young man gave a small wave and what appeared to be a servant squatted down to help Alethea drink from a cup.

'You look even worse than you did yesterday. It's rather gross.'

'What did you expect? One of your men saw fit to crush my hand.' Alethea did her best to shoot him a glare with her clear-sighted eye.

The *triērarchos* did not reply, but Alethea knew he was not violent in nature. If he derived some small pleasure from diminishing those around him, it was by torment of the mind rather than the body. There was no need to fear his grave silence, in fact, it suited her, because she had no desire to converse with any crewmember on the hell-bound trireme.

The *triērarchos* gave her one last, long glance, then turned on his heel and resumed his everlasting pacing on deck.

Through scraps of conversation overheard from the rowers and the rest of the crew, and from what she could see, Alethea figured that the tears in the ship's sails had been hastily patched together and the woodwork temporarily mended. Now, they had set course for Piraeus, so that said damages could be properly tended to, the wounded crew members healed and the dead exchanged.

It was obvious to anyone looking that not a single man on the ship except perhaps the *kybernētēs*, the commander of the vessel, was sorry to set sails for a familiar coast. Though they were all experienced men of the sea so to speak, many had doubtlessly acquired their positions solely out of poverty and obligation. Even if they were not allowed to stay for long and would not be dispatched home to their families, Piraeus must be a safe haven compared to the furious Peloponnese and the seemingly furious waves.

Apolonio's skin was coated in bright specks: drops of water glinting in the rays of sun like a thousand pearls. His limbs looked lean and confident yet lacked the full physique of the adult, and his face was still composed like that of a child with smooth cheeks and oversized eyes. A rippling laugh escaped him as he skipped from one slippery stone to the other by the bank of the Eurotas river, having been granted a rare moment of rest from the agōgá's rigid regime. When he turned, though, his back was one crosshatching of lashes, skin still hanging in bloody dollops—the result of the Artemis Orthia rite.

'Come! Come!' Apolonio called to her. 'I want to tell you a secret.' He ceased skipping stones and stood still as a statue, eyes suddenly pools of grey sobriety. 'You can't save me.'

A woman appeared behind him, floating upright through the water—but the creature was no woman by the ordinary, mortal definition. With her coal-black hair plaited and adorned with silver garlands, a bow slung across one shoulder and a quiver over the other, her skin giving off a faint glow like the moon itself, the deity approached swiftly. Her robe was cut just above her knees, revealing muscular calves wrapped with leather strings.

'A shame. The things you mortals do at my shrine. You should sacrifice game, not perfectly crafted youths. I am not without compassion.' Her voice flowed like the tide. 'But that won't be the final sacrifice.'

The lines blurred; Apolonio's hair turned intensely golden, his face fairer, his gaze almost mocking. Crysanthos smiled. 'You're terribly redundant. We don't need you. You—'

Alethea gasped in pain and her eyes fluttered open. Someone was touching her trampled fingers, and as she craned her neck, she saw a man squatting by her side while tying her hand to a piece of wood with linen rags. It took her a moment to realise this was not some strange way of further injuring her, but the simplest method of healing. She did not bother to ask the man, because seeing the *triērarchos* cast a glance on her served as confirmation enough. *Of course. They would not want a crippled slave. The scar on my face will already have lowered the price anyone might be willing to pay.* She winced as the man jerked at the linen rags, making a final knot before returning to the rhythmic chanting of the other rowers.

'We arrive shortly.' The *triērarchos* brushed a single strand of hair from his eyes and lifted his chin a little more.

Silence reigned. *If he expects an exchange of pleasantries, he can go to Tártaros.* Curiosity finally overpowered stubbornness though, and Alethea drew a deep breath. 'What is Piraeus like?'

'Useful, I suppose. Nothing like your own stagnant *poleis*, yet inferior to Athens.'

The brief conversation was by far the most elaborate discussion that had transpired between them, and Alethea knew she would consider herself blessed if there never was another.

CHAPTER TWELVE

GLIDING INTO THE port of Piraeus, the trireme resembled a wounded animal returning to its cave. The rowers seated at the bottom row had begun to complain their sandals were always soaking wet since the temporary pegs and rags used to mend the holes in the ship were starting to leak, and the harsh wind, which had returned the day before, had torn the hastily patched-up sails anew.

Alethea recalled what little she knew of the city: fortified quite recently, it was the home of the Athenian navy, funded by the silver from the Laurion mines. Connected to Athens by the imposing Long Walls, it was a bustling pivot of trade and commerce. The stench of fish and tar characteristic of harbours slammed Alethea in the face, filling her nostrils just as the chorus of noise filled her ears. She took short, shallow breaths to avoid it best she could, but to no use, as the trireme was hauled onto the beach—it was not strong enough to stay in the water by the pier— and the crew entered this bubble of fervent activity.

Alethea did not have to wait long to learn the fate her captivator had decided on for her. Truth to be told, it was a fate many would have considered fortunate, or at least more so than the alternatives, but Alethea cursed silently in the name of every deity she dared use for the purpose. *I would rather work myself to skin and bones in the mines, or be flaunted at some brothel, than wash that man's clothes and comb his wife's hair.* She deliberately postponed even thinking about the other, more unpleasant things she would be liable to. It was unclear as to why the honey-voiced, delicately sculpted *triērarchos* planned to drag her with him to his *oikos* in Athens at the first opportunity. A person of his standing was hardly in dire need of more slaves, and even if he were, it was frowned upon to use Hellenes rather than purchase a barbarian from Persia or Egypt.

If he had been any other wealthy man, Alethea would have held no doubt that he had abducted her because of some twisted sexual preference for mildly mutilated and decidedly hostile young women. However, he had never shown the least personal interest in her during all the time she had spent lying like a wriggling worm on his ship, hence Alethea could only think of one reason: he intended her for someone else. *I won't be a pretty gift. He chose poorly, whomever I'm being gifted to. Daft pig.*

While her abductor made arrangements for his ship and his travel back to Athens, he put Alethea in one of the storage rooms for hire by the docks. Three days passed, during which she staggered on wobbly legs from one side of the tiny room to the other, her limbs too stiff and her muscles too atrophied to do much else. Slowly, she re-learned what it was to stand upright and to move without ropes cutting into her skin. Dancing or racing with heels flashing and lungs burning was naught but a memory floating into obscurity, but with the help of a small miracle they might not always be.

On the fourth day, Alethea was put in a plain cart, and so the trip to their final destination resumed. The Long Walls connecting Piraeus with Athens was spaced perhaps a *stadion* apart, and between them ran the road on which food transports, military troops, and anxious travellers might go.

The journey was shorter than Alethea had expected. What she estimated was little more than an hour passed, the cart bumping continuously. If Piraeus had been a pivot of trade and commerce, a bustling hub of life, then Athens was at first sight the pinnacle of grandeur. Sitting on the slope of Mount Lycabettus and surrounded by three rivers—all smaller than the Eurotas—it appeared crammed with splendour. Alethea soon guessed, though, that almost every one of the sun-flecked buildings which made her eyes widen against her will as they passed, were not private houses but public investments: baths, theatres, temples, administrative quarters. Their magnitude cast a certain shade over the narrow streets and already squalid huts where common people resided. Alethea peered out from the slit again. *If you just knew to keep your whole* polis *simple in the Laconian way, you would avoid these contrasts. Overall simplicity is always superior to one part extravagance and one part ramshackle.* Of course, looking beyond her bitterness towards the city, she knew full well why it looked thus: Hellenes preferred to adorn those buildings dedicated to the gods or to the *polis* itself, not boast personal wealth. Paradoxically, they were not shy to display jewellery.

The small entourage continued its course through the city. One of the temples was perched high on a steep rock, its colonnades larger than what was customary, its intricate friezes painted in vivid reds and blues. Alethea had heard of Athens' ridiculously expensive building project and freshest pride, the Parthenon, from travellers coming to

Sparta during the past decade, and as she beheld it from the cart, it was indeed a pride and would probably remain one for hundreds if not thousands of years.

The welcoming party in the vestibule—save for the numerous slaves—consisted of an odd trio. The first to capture Alethea's attention was a fair-skinned woman with a bracelet the shape of a spiralled snake embedded between the fat on her upper arm and with dignified little crinkles around her eyes. She took a few steps forward, waddling like a goose, and greeted the *triērarchos* with a single nod.

'Mother.' The word came reluctantly from his lips.

Alethea suppressed a tiny smile. *I thought my mother could be a nuisance.* She turned her curious glance to the man standing next to the woman, leaning heavily on a beautiful cypress cane, the expression on his ruddy face kind but distant, almost sleepy.

'We ought to...ought to carry out the necessary...' he grunted.

'The necessary rites.' Cosimo nodded, referring to the initiation ceremony welcoming a new slave into the *oikos*, presided over by the mistress of the household. There was no point in delaying, for the sun had dipped below the horizon and the fleeting colours of dusk were already fading.

The goose-like woman, however, gave no sign of being about to perform the rites, but instead shuffled forth a much younger lady—a girl of perhaps fifteen, Alethea realised—who had previously stood silent and still enough to blend in with the wall. Fine-spun hair framed her face, held in place by a superfluous number of ivory pins and combs engraved with gold. Alethea could only marvel at the bright colour. The girl's face was not in any way unpleasant but the kind Alethea would forget in a blink of an eye, and appeared to have been white-washed along with the plaster on the walls, void of colour and expression. In a peculiar way she reminded Alethea of Delina: terribly young and terribly old at the same time, though she doubted this girl possessed any of the startling character her sister did. Indeed, the more one looked at the her, the hollower she appeared, as if someone had sucked out her insides, leaving a gaunt shell both in body and in spirit.

'Efigenia can conduct the ceremony. She is, after all, the wife in this house,' the older woman said drily, then turned to her son without meeting his eyes. 'Take your war prize inside, Cosimo.'

Cosimo. So that's it. Cosmos—the order of the universe. Even your name reeks of hubris.

The Athenian house was beyond Alethea's wildest imaginations, beyond anything she had seen in Sparta. The countless rooms were arranged around an open courtyard lined with colonnades. The polished stone floors occasionally covered in animal skins, the woven tapestries, and the ample woodwork all gave the impression of a small palace. When the little party reached the hearth, Cosimo gave Alethea a hard poke and she eventually sat down for the ceremony. The girl with the ivory adornments proceeded to shower her with dried fruit and nuts, and presented her with the name she would go by from now on: Doris.

Alethea shuddered with disgust and brushed a walnut from her shoulder. *Doris. Dorian woman. How imaginative of you.*

Alethea promptly refused the barley bread and cheese that the old woman pressed against her lips with equal determination. Finally, the woman gave a low scoff and put the food down, upon which Alethea broke a piece of the *artos*, ravenous.

The female slaves' quarters were no grand metropolis, yet the sparsely lit dormitory was by far preferable to every space she had occupied since being taken from the coastal town. Sheets of wool substituting beds lined the walls, along with a couple of chests used to store linen. In one corner was crammed twenty or thirty *amphorae* spilling over with grains and dried legumes, and in another a stack of lumpy sacks, all of which would ideally have fitted in the storage rooms. *But we're little more than goods ourselves*, Alethea reminded herself, a bitter taste in her mouth as she ran her eyes over the girls and women crowding on the sheets trying to get some precious sleep before being forced to rise at dawn. The youngest—a doll-sized girl huddled up against the wall, resting her chin on her knobby knees, a cascade of hair shielding her face—could not be older than eleven or twelve, while a few other members of the group were withered with age. The majority, however, were in their prime years, fit for arduous labour as well as managing their mistresses' beauty routines.

There must be...fifteen of them, and I bet the men are just as many if not more. But then Athenians put more emphasis on private slaves than public ones. Not like we do. Though she had lamented her fate for what seemed like forever, it still felt foreign to think of the slaves as her new peers rather than a remote mass.

The old woman slipped the remnant of the bread in her own pocket and held out her hand, then spoke in a wheezing voice painful to hear. 'Let me see your hand. The undamaged one.'

Alethea obliged, too exhausted to resist.

'Hm. A little calloused already. Then perhaps you won't mind the laundry.'

'I do mind. I wasn't born for *laundry*.'

'Hm. Did the Master bring you from the Doric people's lands as they say? Hm, I think so.'

Alethea withdrew her hand and flashed the woman the most intense glare she could muster. 'The so-called Master is a snake.'

'Hm, yes. Not like the other ones—the father's wits long gone and the son a reasonable one. A little too eager to please, even. Head full of ideals and scrolls. Hm,' she wheezed, squatted up from the floor and shambled away.

Alethea sighed, lying down on the sheet, still surveying the others. None of them appeared to be with child: a rare but good sign. Although she doubted the *triērarchos*, Cosimo, possessed even a dash of respect for women in general, not to speak of women legally belonging to him, she could not imagine him rumpling the sheets with just anyone. No, that frosty gaze would select carefully, not even for a heartbeat stooping to ordinary men's primitive standards.

And if the father is half-witted, whatever that means, it leaves only the son, whoever that is. With some luck, he's as impotent as Priapus after Hera's curse.

'Where's my cousin this evening?' Cosimo stood with his back towards his wife, one hand stretched out so that the fountain's water could trickle over his fingers like liquid moonlight.

Efigenia took a step forward, chest fluttering violently at the genuine interest in his voice; the question might not concern her, but it was at least directed at her. 'He's dining with Paralus and Xanthippus and perhaps...perhaps twenty others. It was truly marvellous when the invitation arrived... If only you had been there—' She stopped before her voice reached a much-too-excited pitch.

'Yes, if only I had been there for such an honour. How good of you to remind me.'

'I didn't mean...'

'Never mind. And when does he return from his escapades with Pericles' sons?'

'He didn't say. Was...was your journey comfortable? Was your mission terribly dangerous?'

Cosimo withdrew his hand from the fountain and wiped it on his *khitōn*, then turned to face her, tendrils of hair dancing on the breeze just above the sharp contour of his collarbone. 'I wonder if Penelope had to ask Odysseus the same when he returned after his perilous adventures.'

'I don't know,' Efigenia said truthfully.

'I'll visit you tonight. I'm expected to return to my duties as soon as the reparations are done, and by Zeus, it's high time you fulfilled yours.'

On that note, he glided past Efigenia and into the house in a flurry, leaving her standing in a pool of moonlight, digging her nails into her palms. It was the same tangle of dread and delight one might feel when faced with a beautiful beast. Regardless, she knew her husband to be right: more than a third of a year had passed since their marriage and still they had only performed their marital duty a handful of times, with the only indication of pregnancy proving false. She had not said anything about it, but he had known by a quick glance at the flatness of her stomach and the defeat in her eyes the moment they met again.

Of course, they were both considered to be in the blossom of their fertile years and that blossom would not die yet, but legitimate children were always eagerly sought-after by those who had none. Furthermore, Efigenia had heard more than one daunting tale of wives whose childless months turned to years and before they realised it, they were rumoured to be barren. They then suffered a quick divorce and were whisked back home to their father's *oikos* with measly hopes of ever remarrying.

Efigenia's determination proved to be a great aid in the macabre task she had adopted during the past few months: that of suppressing every whimper or flinch threatening to escape her. There were always two forces pounding in her head, almost pulsating through her veins, namely the determination and the sweet ability to pretend that she was at the centre of his senses for just a brief moment. She knew that not even this was true, but the pretence was all she had. By clinging to these two forces, she managed to endure with a docility disguised in her own mind as excellence.

CHAPTER THIRTEEN

THE FIRST THING Eucleides noticed as he stepped inside the house, hidden in the dark of night and as intellectually stimulated as if he had dined with the Nine Muses, was his cousin's immaculately clean sandals. A surge of relief ran through his limbs. The messenger announcing Cosimo's impending homecoming had arrived two days ago, but nothing was certain in times like these, and Eucleides had not quite believed it until laying eyes on those sandals. More times than he could admit without sacrificing a plentiful part of his dignity, he had imagined Cosimo floating face-down in the vast Aegean Sea, plumes of blood curling to the surface from his battered body. Though no significant naval battles had yet occurred, the raids on the coastal cities were not met without opposition and often resulted in the loss of a few Athenian crew members.

But he's home now, the two of us right where we belong. Fifteen years together would be a shame to waste. Eucleides removed his own sandals and advanced on light feet into the sleeping house where even the last of the slaves had taken to their beds after a strenuous day. For a moment, he considered waking his cousin, then recalled one or two unpleasant incidents involving a sleepy-eyed

Cosimo, and decided against it. *Tomorrow. Tomorrow we'll spend the day in the* gymnasium *and the* agorá, *discussing all sorts of wonderfully pointless things.*

Eucleides was not disappointed. A sharp-teethed smile reaching his cousin's hazel eyes, melting the frost set in Cosimo's features, met him as he woke at dawn the following day.

'I heard you wined and dined with the two cuckolds yesterday.' Cosimo crossed the bedchamber with an uncharacteristically sanguine stride.

Eucleides yawned before he was able to reply; the late hour, the cups of wine, and the strain of maintaining his most charming manner had taken their toll. 'Oh, yes.' He smiled back, running a hand through his dishevelled locks to remove the worst tangles. 'I wish I could have been here to welcome you home from your endeavours. The messenger never said whether you would arrive at midday or at dusk.'

'No matter. It would gall me if you neglected our political contacts in my absence.'

'I have eight years until I can hold office.' Eucleides yawned again. *And which office do I opt for?*

'And I have four, yet we ought to be well prepared when those years have passed. You haven't eaten?'

'By Theseus, I'm barely awake!' Eucleides laughed. 'And you?'

Cosimo cocked his head slightly. 'Eat now then, cousin. Don't grow lazy. I brought you something from the Peloponnese.'

Something from the Peloponnese? How oddly diffuse! 'May I ask what?'

Cosimo smiled again, though this time the radiant glow had shifted to cunning gratification. 'I suppose you may. A trinket, really, a slave girl—Spartan, it seems, horribly fierce. Despite that brutal cut on her face, I think you will find her fascinating. I never cared for the type myself, but you were always inclined to observe the barbarian.'

Eucleides stared at the other man. Indeed, he found people of other customs delightful to surround himself with, although he rarely adopted any of said customs but remained the observer, Athenian to the very bone. *But a slave girl? That would be like looking at an animal in a cage.*

'I—Thank you,' he said, floundering.

'Yes.' Cosimo started for the door. 'I wouldn't take her to my bed, though, if I were you, cousin. She's only harmless when kept at bay.'

Eucleides remained on the spot a good while, contemplating whether he would ask to see the Spartan, or perhaps attempt to make Cosimo understand the morbidity of the situation without inflicting a splinter in the precious little time they had together before the trireme's crew demanded their *triērarchos'* return. *No... It would only lead to unpleasantness. If I simply don't seek her out, I shan't trouble her, and he need never know that I didn't.*

Eucleides changed his *khitōn*—which was spotty with wine and crumpled from having been slept in—for another, the thin white linen a gracious companion in the broiling summer heat. It was still early in the morning, but by the time Helios' sun chariot reached its peak on the sky, the air would practically be simmering.

To Eucleides' relief, the day, as well as those following it, passed without further mention of the slave. The *ecclesia* was not summoned, hence they spend the hours practicing *arete* in the *gymnasium*, toes sunk deep in the hot sand, skin glistening from oil like polished wood, the scent of olives hanging thick in the air. Eventually, the lines blurred and the colours shifted, bringing on that soft shimmer unique to summer evenings; the wind's rustle mingled with crickets and conversing Athenians to create a full chorus.

In those moments, nothing seemed more forlorn, more bizarre, to Eucleides than the idea of a blood-soaked battlefield or the Parthenon put ablaze by Peloponnesian troops.

CHAPTER FOURTEEN

ALETHEA'S ARMS THREATENED to buckle under the weight of the *amphora*, water slopping against the edge and landing on her sandals every other second. *If it continues like this, I won't have any water left to show for my efforts.* The strain on her muscles reminded her of that fateful day when she had hooked her arm through the strap on the *hoplon* shield, how the weight of it had made her feel both weak and immensely strong at the same time. Now, she resembled a curtailed sparrow rather than a blackbird flying securely and proudly among its peers. Her crushed fingers—still splinted to the small piece of wood and hurting at the slightest touch—did not make matters easier.

It was only the day after her arrival in Athens, but she had not been surprised when she without further ado had been put to work with five other slaves to tend to the laundry. The labour was duller than the Asphodel Meadows, Alethea was certain of it, hence she had volunteered when the younger of her mistresses requested water to be brought to the *gynaikeion*.

A flash of chestnut in the corner of her eye made Alethea's head turn, her body to instantly lean over the banister. *That bastard shan't see me trip and toil with something as simple as carrying water.* As she put the *amphora* down, though, and raised herself on her toes for a better view of the floor below, she did not see Cosimo's slender wrists and resentful mouth, but an entirely different figure. Alethea could not quite pinpoint what separated the two men so absolutely, so vastly—they both wore the same simple but elegant and clearly expensive clothing, both wore their hair in glossy, thick waves reaching to their chins, both were young and walked with enterprise in their step—but there was a fundamental difference. She just could not find the words for it yet.

The *amphora* slipped. A fragment of a heartbeat passed as it fell from one floor to another, then smashed against the stone tiles in a cascade of water and potsherds.

Alethea's breath knotted and stuck in her throat. Although the slip had been largely accidental, she knew part of her had allowed it to happen, craving revenge on anyone even remotely associated with the fact that she was a chattel slave and not a free woman. A hand's-width to the left, and the *amphora* would have cracked the skull underneath. *I mustn't be a fool. The only thing to come from that would be a man punished too harshly, brains and blood all over that spotless floor, and a few outraged relatives seeking to kill me in return.*

Dark eyes struck with terror squinted up at her from the floor below, but they quickly softened and Alethea could have sworn she saw a curious glitter even at that distance. The young man squatted down and began collecting the potsherds in his palms, face still turned upwards, while Alethea remained frozen in her step. A low curse; a fat bead of scarlet red erupted on the man's finger.

He'll need some help with that mess. Alethea snapped out of her trance and descended down the first step of the staircase before quickly retreating, turning on her heel and rushing back towards the *gynaikeion*. She recalled what the old slave woman, Agathe, had said about the son in the *oikos*—because that must indeed be the identity of the young man with the bleeding hand: *A reasonable one. A little too eager to please, even. Head full of ideals and scrolls.*

The description was appealing enough, but the mere thought of a master made Alethea shudder. To have a reasonable master, even a good master, was a repellent situation, and any master would only gain some much-needed humility from having to clean up potsherds himself. She calmed her pace and pinned an expression of sombre stone to her face as she entered Efigenia's realm of womanly solitude. *Perhaps he doesn't have an inclination towards memorising faces. Perhaps he won't be able to tell which slave girl out of fifteen who almost smashed his head with an* amphora.

Efigenia, or Mean Mousey—Alethea had secretly assigned her new mistress the nickname hours after she first saw her—sat on a *klismos*, ankles as white as the ivory in her hair sticking out from the folds in her *khitōn*, her comically small feet resting in Agathe's sinewy hands. The old woman was flat on her knees, back hunched, flick fingers strapping a pair of sandals onto the girl sitting before her.

Alethea crinkled her nose. The sandals were unlike any kind of footwear she had ever seen before: the sole was attached to a thick platform of wooden cork, which would make whoever wore them appear taller by half a head. *Ridiculous. Hindering one's movements, no doubt.*

Agathe fastened the final strap, wiped her palms on her thighs and wiggled back on her heels as if to stand up.

However, Efigenia gestured for her to stay where she was. 'You may remove them again in a while. I'll just walk a little and see if I want to keep them.'

On that note, she rose from the *klismos* and took a few wobbly steps in the platform sandals, much like a new-born foal, across the room and back twice.

The process of deciding whether the new shoes would be a permanent addition to Efigenia's wardrobe was lengthy and tedious: pondering, walking, adjusting *khitōns* to fit her taller stature. In the end, it was all abruptly decided by Cosimo, who at the carefully put question of whether the shoes were to be kept replied curtly: 'Are you trying to imitate an actor in a comedy?'

Alethea remained by the doorpost throughout the dreary business, not daring to leave without explicit permission, yet hoping she would not be questioned about the fact that she had not brought the requested water. To her relief, it seemed Efigenia had forgotten said request, being immersed in the matter of the sandals, and she did not address the Spartan slave by the door with a single word. Alethea slipped back to the laundry, where the other women were still scrubbing cloth, the blisters on their fingers and the apathy in their eyes just as she had left them.

The cut on Eucleides' hand bled profusely through the improvised bandage made from an old sheet, a streak of deep red staring back at him. He gnawed on his lip, using his right hand to tear a new shred of cloth with a *ritch*. The injury looked far worse than he knew it to be, and he would rather not have his aunt or Cosimo dive head-first into a pit of worried accusations. His father rarely noticed petty details in one's appearance and Efigenia would sooner chew grass than question his private undertakings, but the two other members of his family were a different matter. *That poor girl would not live to see the sun set.*

Eucleides held no doubt concerning the identity of the slave: the most recent addition, the one intended by Cosimo not only as free labour but as a bemusing creature. Although Eucleides constantly struggled to associate the right faces with the right names of the ample number of slaves in the *oikos*, that particular face was not easily forgotten with its strong jaw and the protruding scar spanning mouth to eyebrow. The grey, unrelenting cat's eyes peering down at him from the top of the staircase had not once blinked, their gaze indiscernible though hardly amiable, and then the young woman had been gone in a flash of rag-like clothing.

Of course, the deadly projectile falling from above, and later the shattered pottery and cascade of cold water released, had initially frightened him to the core, but the more he contemplated the incident, the more those eyes gained prominence in his recollection of it. Once the first chills of a near-death experience ebbed out, there had only been the impulse to inquire for her name.

Cosimo knows me too well. But I wouldn't want to know her like that, not like an animal in a cage, but as an equal and a mystery. Eucleides repeated this sentiment to himself. It did not occur to him that his intentions hardly mattered, for they existed solely in his head, and inequity was still the reality.

During the days following the strange, brief encounter, Eucleides tried to seek out the Spartan slave, soaking up the way she gave a one-shouldered shrug or crinkled her nose while never omitting a single word other than a reluctant '*Yes, Lady*' spoken in Doric dialect. However, the occasions when he found himself in the same room as her were few and torturously remote. Not once did he catch a second glimpse of her eyes, because although they were never pinned to the ground like so many of the other slaves', they never met his.

Why should they? She must loathe the lot of us. His stomach turned at the realisation; he had never before lived under the same roof as someone who rightfully—or even erroneously—made him feel like the villain in a tragedy. Of course, there were those who differed with his and Cosimo's agenda in the *ecclesia*, but the difference was purely bureaucratic as far as he knew, and this new sensation clashed violently with his habit of gratifying others for his own comfort as well as theirs.

If she proves a hopeless case then so be it, but where's the harm in trying?

Itching with curiosity, he summoned the Spartan slave girl to the *bibliotheca*. The room practically sizzled in the heat. Eucleides' palms were sticky with sweat and the scrolls he had been studying since shortly after breakfast bore marks from his fingertips. What felt like a small eternity—a concept he rather liked—passed before two rapid, deliberate knocks sounded against the doorpost.

Eucleides' started at the sound, accidentally biting down into his tongue. 'Please, come in.'

Though he had anticipated finally meeting those eyes, it proved more difficult than he had imagined, because their message was suddenly as clear as spring water: *We're not friends, you and I. We're not meant to sympathize.*

The young woman treaded cautiously into the room as if some wild beast lured in the corner. She halted several steps away from him, but it was close enough to reveal the poorly treated hand hanging limp at her hip, and Eucleides could not help but cast a glance at his own injury, insignificant in comparison.

He gestured to a bowl filled with a blackish, thick liquid smelling sickly similar to slaughtered cattle, stirred with a hint of vinegar. A few drops smeared against the table, revealing an undertone of red.

'I asked the cooks to prepare this for you, if you're hungry. I imagine you must be. I heard the people in your *polis* are fond of this, well, this soup. Would you like something to drink?'

The cat-eyed girl stared at him, then shook her head. 'I never liked *melas zomos.*

Can anyone *truly care for such a nasty thing?* Eucleides swallowed at the fumes and pushed the bowl farther back on the table, lumps of unidentifiable meat swimming up to the surface as he did so. 'Figs, then? Or—' He reached for another, more appealing dish with eager fingers. '—bread with honey? It was baked this morning, I believe.'

The slave said nothing; a garland of hair had escaped her hairnet and dangled by her unblemished cheek.

Eucleides resisted the urge to tuck it behind her ear and instead slathered two pieces of bread in honey, one of which the woman accepted, chewing slowly.

'My name,' she said, sucking her sticky fingers between the words, 'is not Doris.'

'It's not a flattering name. I'm sorry they decided to call you that.'

'I said it's not my name.'

'Will you tell me what is, then?'

A sharp breath of hesitation. 'Alethea.'

Eucleides struggled to hide the curiosity in his voice. 'What happened to your face—if I may ask? And your hand?'

No answer. Only a face carved from stone. Finally, Alethea's gaze shifted to the bundle of scrolls accumulated on the desk, and she reached out a finger to poke at the one presently unrolled. 'The Iliad?'

'Oh, yes,' Eucleides beamed, heart racing. 'Do you have a favourite part?'

'Patroclus scaling the walls. And the struggle for his body.'

'Really? Violent events, odd contrasts to such a melodious verse... Hades claimed many souls in those parts, not to speak of Achilles' final slaughter of the Trojans.'

'I call it enticing—and are not all parts like that?'

Eucleides thought for a moment. 'Well, not the *Catalogue of Ships*.'

Alethea crossed her arms as if shielding herself. 'I never read the *Catalogue of Ships*,' she said flatly.

'I hope...I hope we need not be agitated by one another merely because of the current circumstances. If we think about it, isn't this a war between Athens and Corinth, with Sparta pushed into the conflict out of loyalty to her allies? I'm sure our differences are narrower than they might appear at first sight.' Eucleides fired off the smile he so often used in the *ecclesia*. 'One can never have too many friends.'

Alethea reached for another piece of bread before answering. 'Are you always this nauseatingly *charitable* towards those you consider property? I'm no *heílote*.'

Eucleides' prickled with frustration entwined with guilt. Indeed, he had never been this charitable with any other slave. It was not in his nature to beat and bark at them, yet that did not mean he had tried to cultivate personal relationships with the oblique mass that was the thirty-four souls toiling to maintain the illustrious life he led. *How can I make her see she's no slave to me, when I don't even know why that is? Because she's Hellene? Because I wish we had met under more pleasant circumstances?* Unfortunately, wishing could not reverse his cousin's actions, nor could it change the view she held of him.

'And this?' Alethea said, cutting through the silence with obvious difficulty, like a dull knife cutting through leather. She gestured at another scroll.

'*Nostoi*. I haven't studied it yet—it is so gruesome. Though fair, I suppose.' The papyrus telling of Agamemnon's meeting with the splitting axe seemed to observe them both from its place on the desk.

'Yes. Fair. I think so, too.' The tiniest inkling of a smile pulled at her lips, gone in a heartbeat. 'Is it some twisted Athenian custom to sit inside reading all day?'

'We do other things also. We cultivate our minds and bodies in every art.'

'Hm.'

Eucleides' patience was seeping away little by little. However dearly he wanted to extract a friendly word from the woman standing before him, it felt easier to solve the Sphinx's riddle. 'If you want something—bread, better sandals—only ask for it. Forgive my cousin, for he can sometimes be...foolish, and know that I would rather learn your thoughts and ideas than see you suffer in silence.'

Alethea jerked her chin forward. 'I want my freedom.'

'You're still legally Cosimo's, not mine. And how would you manage, how would you survive, if you travelled alone back to Sparta? Even if the rest of the *oikos* agreed and even if you escaped the city without being stoned...you would be unsheltered and—'

'*Exòloio*,' she said in little more than a whisper, turning on her heel and marching toward the door. Then, under her breath before departing: '*Gràson*.'

Eucleides, stunned, considered the insults while wiping his sweaty palms on his *khitōn* for the hundredth time that afternoon. *"Drop dead". She really means it. But "one who stinks like a goat"? A little unfair.*

CHAPTER FIFTEEN

THE *ECCLESIA* CONVENED as usual a few days after Cosimo's homecoming and Eucleides' futile attempts to appease the Spartan slave girl. As they made their way to the Pnynx Hill, however, Eucleides' thoughts were not on the political and marshal matters they would be expected to vote upon.

'What ails you? You look like an owl beaten out of its wisdom, eyes all dazed,' Cosimo said as they passed the Acropolis. He made a dismissive gesture at a beggar approaching, the flute-like bones in his underarm showing through the skin.

'Well, the young woman you brought—'

'Your present? You like her? I knew you would be entertained.'

'Must you call her that? She wishes to be set free. I told her even if you and the rest of the *oikos* agreed, she would be alone without money or shelter, many days' of dangerous travel away from home.'

Cosimo's gaze was piercing. 'Of course she won't be freed. You almost make it sound as if you would consider it, were it not for those obstacles! I'll tell you the true obstacle: she's a savage and a trophy, and she will serve just as her kinsmen will serve when this cursed war is won. Perhaps we could even get a ransom, albeit Spartans are not famous for their wealth and generosity, are they?'

Eucleides clenched one fist, hidden between the rich folds of his *khitōn*, and cooled his voice before speaking. 'I think it should be my decision.' *But I know it's not. Not if you convince my father, at least, and you do that so easily.*

'Think of other things, then, cousin dear. I assume you will vote against pitch battle.'

'Yes, if it is brought to a vote. But I doubt Pericles would allow it to be, when the radical faction is so strong and the anger brewing so hotly. Maybe things will settle a little now, with the raids over and all. It seems my father won't have to pull any strings, as long as the army keeps inside the walls,' Eucleides was grateful for something to finally brush Alethea off his mind, if only for a day.

'No strings can save me from the fleet, that is certain. The raids will continue. If not this autumn then next spring.'

Of course... How did I not see that? They can continue in near eternity to destroy our land, just as we can continue in near eternity to get supplies through Piraeus. 'It's only a question of which lasts longer, Delian coins or Peloponnese fortitude. Unless the radicals get their pitch battle.'

'Precisely.'

Upon arriving at the Pnynx Hill, they received brighter news than they had been expecting.

'We may now count Thrace as our ally. King Cytakus has promised to send both cavalry and light infantry, aiding us at Potidea,' Pericles declared.

A surge of approval swept through the crowd. The besiegement of Potidea was rapidly draining the Athenian treasuries, gobbling up tribute from allied *poleis* intended to pay for ships and supplies.

Pericles motioned and the noise died down at once. 'Furthermore, as the Kingdom of Thrace presses close against that of Macedon, King Cytakus shall attempt to reconcile the latter with Athens. If the attempt is fruitful, we will be not one but two strong allies richer.'

Eucleides' eyes went at once to Cosimo's, exchanging a few unspoken words. *Perhaps it won't be an endless war, with the help of those two. What do you think? Yes?*

When the right to speak passed from the *strategoi* to the rest of the assembled men, no heads turned in surprise upon hearing Cleon's voice.

'With this new addition to our forces, the time *must* have come to strike! The fleet is not enough! The enemy cannot be defeated by petty attacks on coastal towns. *Triērarchoi* and their crews cannot substitute a *real* army.'

Red spots burned on Cosimo's cheeks like a sudden rash. However, he remained seated, knowing the damage it could do to one's renown to speak in affect.

Eucleides, on the other hand, heard his own voice before he quite realised what he was saying. 'With all respect, Cleon son of Cleaenetus, I think you are wrong to urge for a *hoplite* encounter with the Peloponnese. Have you seen their army, their soldiers? I haven't, but I have heard of the way Sparta moulds her youth to withstand anything—flogging and...' He searched his memory for the word Alethea had used. '...*melas zomos*. And from what I have heard, there is not the slightest sense in risking our lives in a battle we cannot win, rather than trust in our fleet, a fleet grander than any city in Hellas can compete with. I'm sure the honourable citizens of Athens agree with reason.' He gave the *ecclesia* a broad smile, putting as much bright attraction in it as he could, and sat down again next to Cosimo.

The men sat tight-lipped, silent. This was not what they were used to or what they craved; the notion that their *polis'* land-based army did not stand a chance was far too unpatriotic. Yet they seemed to understand the boyish figure who had spoken before them had not intended it as such, nor as a display of marshal knowledge, but rather as pure honesty, a plea of sorts.

'Well-chosen words,' Cosimo whispered in his Eucleides' ear, the red spots on his cheeks flushed out.

Eucleides only nodded, hoping the audience would take his statement to heart.

Neither the possibility of sending forces to raid the Megarid, the land surrounding the city of Megara, nor anything more daring was put forth that day. As they walked home again, Eucleides felt as if a benevolent force had lifted an immense weight from his chest, if only temporarily, levitating the pressure on his ribs. His words had bought him another sliver of time, which would have to be enough for now.

While the sweat prickled and pooled on his skin in the afternoon heat, he came to think of another issue. 'Did Efigenia speak to you yet?'

Cosimo's tweezed brows knitted. 'What about?' Then, his face drained of all emotion. 'Ah. She's not with child after all. I should have known better than to harvest such hopes.'

'Half a year is not a long time, on the contrary,' Eucleides pointed out.

'No, but I have a feeling it will be far longer than that.'

'And I have a feeling that someday you will have more sons than you can divide your property among and more daughters than you can marry off.'

Cosimo gave a short, sharp laugh, like the sound of silver blades colliding. 'May the gods fulfil your prophecy, cousin.'

May they indeed, if only to make you more graceful towards her. You have enough grace to shower around you without running dry.

CHAPTER SIXTEEN

IT WAS THE fifteenth night in the slave quarters—she had counted them by carving marks into the wall where she slept—when Alethea discovered the spare key one of the other women used to steal away an hour or two with her lover.

The door to the male slaves' dormitory was merely closed, not locked, at night, but Lady Milos made a show every evening of turning the key to the women's door with a characteristic *click*, firmly patting the smooth wood with her pillow-like palm. The message was clear: those who slept within could not be trusted, presumably because she considered women more prone to lay their dirty pawns on her jewellery. However, as it turned out, the door could be unlocked from both sides, and the slaves were not as witless as Lady Milos seemed to think. Every other night, one of them would borrow the spare key— which they must have acquired with aid from their male counterparts, whose outdoor chores gave ample opportunity to have a replica made of the original—and slither out quiet as a shadow.

Alethea bided her time. *She went yesterday, so she won't go today. And the others dare not ask too often. It's my turn, then, to escape this...this cage for a little while.* She knelt by the woman, whose hair hung in thin whips across her face, fluttering with every erratic snore. Forcing her fingers steady, Alethea reached inside the folds of the woman's blanket, searching with her breath knotted in her throat, until she felt the cool metal against her skin.

The door unlocked and opened swiftly; Alethea breathed a sigh of relief as the narrow staircase only creaked the slightest. The house was heavy with silence and sharp-cropped shadows, much like one might imagine a gigantic grave. Without the bustle of the street trickling through the windows and the daytime activity of slaves and dogs inside, it was an entirely different world.

Alethea tip-toed at first, then quickened her step, overcome with the rush of being completely free of intrusive family members wishing her to perform some chore, free of other slaves spewing remarks about her jagged face or bad manners. Time seemed infinite though she knew it was scarce. She half-ran on light feet through the house and out in the courtyard, remembering the intricate dances she had used to perform in Sparta.

If Eucleides had not spoken, she would have walked straight past him, assuming the frozen silhouette on the bench was a new addition to the sculpture of Aphrodite and Adonis by the fountain. His face was churned grey, every curve and angle chiselled forth by a master artist and eyes faceted like gemstones.

'Alethea?'

She halted, swallowing hard. *They can flog me, accuse me of almost anything. Not to speak of what the others might do when they learn I've robbed them of their one freedom.*

'You have someone to visit already?' There was a note of genuine surprise. 'I know some of the slaves do. It's romantic, really, I wouldn't spoil such a thing, but you didn't seem the type.'

Alethea stared at him. *You sanction it?* 'No. I just wanted... I'm married, anyhow, if you must know.'

'Oh. You're very devoted, then.'

'I wouldn't say that.'

'Do you want to sit? I don't like being alone at this hour. I'm not usually, see.'

Alethea hesitated a moment, then sat down on the very edge of the bench, cold stone pressing through her tunic. Slanted beams of moonlight broke through the veil of clouds above, and she was infinitely grateful for the openness of the courtyard. *If I could, I would spend* every *night here.*

'Do you suffer from nightmares?' Eucleides asked, tilting his head.

Alethea frowned. 'Everyone does.'

'Yes, yes, of course.' There was a solemnity she had never observed in him before. 'What are they about?'

'This place. Everything. My brother. Why?' Alethea folded her arms, pressing her lips together, marvelling at the unlikely conversation. Perhaps she had already exposed too much.

'I always dream the same nightmare every time. It's not really a dream in itself, just fragments dwindling away, flashes of things. It doesn't go away, except in the morning, when it does. I'm sorry. My words are a little unruly tonight; I should save them until I can compose them better.

'Save them always.'

Eucleides nodded, swallowing several times. When he spoke again, he regained his usual winsome tone. 'I'm still curious about your scar.'

'Curiosity can be dangerous.' Alethea could not help the smile tickling the corner of her mouth and cursed herself.

'But what's life without it? You'll tell me someday, I'm sure, and then I'll tell you anything you want to hear in return.'

'Anything?'

'Almost. That's the secret to pleasurable company.' Eucleides managed a faint smile.

Alethea studied him for a moment, before the absurdity of the situation dawned on her. *Here I am, chatting away precious time with the man they dare call my master. I ought to be back by now.* 'I should go. If anyone awakes, well, I don't think they would be as *lenient* as you.'

'You make everything sound like an insult, did you know that? I haven't been unkind to you, have I? I don't think I have.' His smile no longer looked as effortless.

'I wish you would be. It would be easier to hate you.'

'Then at least you don't hate me.'

'I...maybe I do!' Alethea burst. 'I don't know. I will go now.' Her feet stumbled as she marched back the way she had come, climbing the staircase and shutting the door behind her as carefully as she could, tuning the key in the lock again.

The slave women were as she had left them: curled up or sprawled out on the coarse wool, a chorus of heavy breaths and snores filling the room. Alethea returned the key to its owner, then sank down against the wall.

She had spoken truth: it *would* be easier to endure her new circumstances if she could hate each of the family members. Cosimo she loathed with all her heart and soul; his wife was only a peg lower on the scale, with her tedious flatness and vain commanding. Lady Milos was an annoyance, at least, the unyielding chief over the *oikos* who failed to see how ridiculous she looked decked in all that gold. Her brother kept to his chamber, both forgetful and irrational, it seemed, but rarely present.

And at last the greatest problem of them all. The one who smiles and beams and expects the very stars to align with the right words. Perhaps they do. Alethea squeezed her eyes shut until bright spots danced against the back of her eyelids. Sleep would not come easily now.

The following days were a complicated game of manoeuvres to avoid Eucleides' presence. To Alethea's relief, he did not seek her out again, but merely cast quick glances, always with a slight crease on his forehead, as if for the first time in his life he did not know what to say or do.

Little changed in the rest of the *oikos*. It appeared to Althea that each family member had their fixed spot in the house, and each had their fixed role to fill. *At least there's some order and tradition. Not like home, but still.*

The days were not unbearable, for her nor for the other slaves, if one only swallowed the bitter fact of working from dawn till dusk and obeying the wink of one's master's little finger. Of course, swallowing that fact was easier said than done, yet the slaves' diet was almost becoming a more pressing concern in Alethea's eyes. *How do they survive on so little without fading to shadows, and with almost no meat! No wonder the women of Attica grow quiet.*

Unfortunately, in order to stay clear of both Eucleides and Cosimo—the latter of which took no personal interest in her but nevertheless insisted on giving her pointless little tasks—often meant she had to keep to the *gynaikeion*. There, Mean Mousey, sometimes joined by a bracelet-clattering Lady Milos, passed the time in what seemed to Althea like endless drabness. Sometimes, they would exchange a few words other than commands with the other slave women—a piece of gossip or an absent-minded inquiry—but never with her. *It's me they gossip about. It must be.* On the rare occasion when one or two of Lady Milo's female friends came to visit, the curious glances only grew in number.

Eventually came the day when she could stand the atmosphere no longer and ventured outside the house, though the price she had to pay made her clench her jaw until her teeth hurt: to act cargo mule on one of Eucleides' frequent excursions to the *gymnasium*. In truth, she only had to carry a piece of bread, while he carried his satchel, but that was scant comfort.

'Have you ever been to a *gymnasium* before?' he asked as they made their way between the rows of tightly wedged houses. Humans and animals alike crowded the filthy streets and alleys, the sun like white gold burning their skin until they all carried its mark.

'No.'

'I thought Sparta was a great champion of athletics.'

'Yes. But we exercise in the open, and the men with their comrades.'

'I don't think they will allow you inside. I should have thought of that.' Eucleides bit his lip.

'Must you do that?'

'Oh. Sorry, just a bad habit, I suppose. You have a few of your own. Anyways, the gymnasium isn't entirely suitable to female eyes.'

Dear Zeus, strike me down with one of your thunderbolts. The open air wasn't worth it. 'I'm not a prude.'

'Neither am I.'

A dense silence settled then in their little sphere of two, while the raucous of the street remained. They had not spoken of what had transpired during those brief moments of courtyard moonlight, and Alethea had no intention of doing so now. *The less we talk, the better. What does it matter what his nightmares concern, or whether I can't hate him?*

The gymnasium was an impressive, oblong building, but Alethea saw little difference between it and the countless other public houses with their fancy colonnades and bright marble. What appeared to be a guard stopped them at the entrance, his gaze fixed on Alethea, his brows knitted.

Eucleides gestured to her. 'Can my...my slave enter?'

The man chortled. 'She's a woman.'

'Then perhaps she could wait for me in some enclosed space. I should have thought before bringing her, I know, but I fear she wouldn't find her way back to the house. Please.'

Having handed Eucleides the bread, Alethea followed the man past a row of doors, one of which he opened swiftly and closed behind her. She squinted in the dark room. From what she could discern, the space was narrow enough to send those prone to hysteria into a fit; the walls seemed to push inwards, leaving room only for a pallet and a few *amphorae* smelling heavily of olive oil. One of the walls, she discovered, was in fact nothing but a curtain separating her from the men in the *palaestra*. A blinding streak of white ran across it, a slit offering the sole source of light. Alethea could not help herself but peered through it, landing her eyes on the exercising Athenians.

Their skin shone like polished wood from the oil they had rubbed on themselves, patches of it coated in sand from wrestling or stumbling. Their limbs arched in the throw of a discus; their calves tensed in the long-jump. Some were graceful with muscles dancing as they moved, while others sprawled and struggled. There was much greater variety of both bodies and ability compared to the uniform perfection of the Spartans.

Just as she was about to let the curtain fall back and close the slit, Alethea caught sight of Eucleides.

Nude, just like most of the other men and boys, he ran the length of the *palaestra* and back, locks of hair flitting behind him in the wind. *I could outrun him easily, at least if I had somewhere to stretch my legs.* Indeed, Eucleides' movements were not as swift nor as natural as those of a born runner, and his face was glazed with disinterest as if he only did it out of necessity, to maintain fundamental health. The sculpted limberness of his body was decorative rather than useful.

Alethea stepped away from the curtain, much to her annoyance feeling the familiar burn of a blush on her cheeks. *Don't be an idiot.* It was true what she had said about not being a prude. Sparta had not allowed for that kind of luxury, girls and boys both brought up with only the most necessary garments and with more important ambitions than modesty. To busy her mind, she indulged in the searing envy she felt towards each and every one of those exercising freely in the gymnasium. *Why not me? Because I'm a woman. Because they think I'm incapable. Or maybe they think I'm capable and are afraid I would outshine them, yes, that must be it.*

The stretch of time that passed before Eucleides reappeared by the door could have been an hour at most, but Alethea felt as if it would have sufficed to recite an epic. His *khitōn* was carelessly fastened, his ankles still stained with sand.

'I hope you weren't too bored. Come.'

Alethea puckered her lips, shooting him a single glance. 'How could I possibly be bored? Waiting is my favourite pastime.'

'What else would you have done? It's no fault of mine you weren't permitted inside.'

Maybe you could use that doe-eyed face to make them change the rules.

'Are you coming?' He shouldered the satchel.

'Must we...must we return at once?'

'If you rather wander the streets for a while, I wouldn't mind wandering with you. Of course, it really is too hot, but the Acropolis is marvellous this time of day, like something built by gods. Do you want to see it?'

Alethea hesitated a moment, then nodded. The stiffness that had existed between them felt softened somehow, having taken with it a tiny bit of her aversion. One moment she loathed him, the next she found herself unable to blame him for her misfortune. Regardless, she knew she could attain noting by always declining what he offered.

They left the gymnasium and made the short journey back to the heart of Athens, where the Acropolis stood like a monument of public wealth and glory. The Parthenon, which Alethea had before only spotted briefly from the cart when brought from Piraeus, towered most prominent of all the temples and sanctuaries, theatres and statues accumulated on the elevated rock.

'Do you see the columns? How straight they are?' Eucleides asked, pointing.

'Too straight. Not like regular temples.'

'Precisely, that's the trick of it. Regular temples look just a little lopsided because they're straight. The eye is fooled by the light. These columns, however, are built with the slightest, slightest lean so as to make the temple appear perfectly straight. You understand?'

'Yes. How do you know this?'

'I spoke to one of the architects at a *symposion* once. He was awfully dull in other respects, but this he told me.'

Alethea craned her neck for a better view of the other buildings. In one of the slopes, a half-circle was cut into the stone and earth as if someone had taken a large spoon and scooped out a piece of soil.

'A theatre?'

Eucleides nodded, smiling. 'Oh yes. The theatre of Dionysus. It's where we hold the Dionysia in the spring each year—the most wonderful of festivals. I think you'd like it. Anyone would.'

'I bet I'd be barred from it.'

'I've seen slaves in the theatre, and women too.'

'What a sensation.'

The afternoon was fading to evening; the stark cornflower-blue sky washed to silver, the air like the brush of feathers against their skin. Walking back to the house, they said little, yet Alethea was infinitely glad she had exhausted her feet outdoors rather than her fingers scrubbing bedsheets or her ears listening to Lady Milos' ranting about household assets. The choice was rarely hers, but perhaps the young master in the *oikos* would not be opposed to brining her along again, if only she behaved reasonably. The thought made her queasy, because she felt like a naughty dog finally brought on a walk, but there was no denying the truth in it.

Turmoil smacked down upon them like a hawk on a mouse the moment they crossed the threshold.

Achaikos, Eucleides' father, tumbled down the last five steps of the staircase in a ball of arms and legs and alarmed howls. Eucleides, in a flurry, leaped forward but was too slow, stumbling on a strap on his sandal come undone. His cousin, however, who was half-way through descending the stairs in a decidedly more graceful manner, managed to latch onto the old man's wrist, the only result being Cosimo's own fall.

Alethea put a hand to her lips so as to not smile. *How unfortunate.*

No one else appeared the least amused, though. Eucleides dropped the satchel to the floor, pulled off the loose strap from his sandal, and sank to his knees by his father's sorry figure.

Achaikos' ruddy face was blotched with blood and the usually so bright stone tiles around him were sprinkled with the same colour. His lip had a deep cleft from which the blood poured like wine from an *amphora*, his legs twisted in a strange angle where he lay.

On instinct, Alethea joined Eucleides by the poor man's side, but knew not what was expected of her.

'Father? Father? Can you hear me?' Eucleides' voice bore the strain of a panicked animal's cry.

Achaikos turned his head and tried to lift his unwieldy legs to a more comfortable position, but in vain.

Cosimo had picked himself up from the floor and stood rubbing his bruised elbows. He froze and stared for several moments at the scarlet splatter on his expensive *khitōn*—not his own blood, Alethea realised grudgingly, but his uncle's. *His hair is still in place. It shouldn't even be possible.* Cosimo's attention shifted from his spoiled clothes and sore elbows to an even more unpleasant sight: his mother in the doorway.

Lady Milos' eyes were surprisingly calm. When she spoke to her son, her glance passed straight through him. 'Eucleides and I can care for my brother. Go and fetch help.'

Alethea watched as her malefactor swallowed and, having cleared his face of all expression, departed from the vestibule.

'Aunt? Will you help me sit him up properly? I think his legs may be taking damage. They were bad enough as it was,' Eucleides said.

'My dear, I would, were it not for my own knees. The slaves can lift him. Ah, good.'

Two men with sturdy shoulders—Zesiro, whose skin glistened dark like ebony, and another whose pointy little beard and knobbly limbs reminded Alethea of a goat—entered the room and squatted down to lift their master. They placed Achaikos sitting erect on a *klimos*, his misty eyes sparking recognition as he saw Eucleides before him.

Alethea wiggled back on her heels and stood. 'Should I get some wine to bring him to his senses?'

'No! No, thank you. I don't think it would have that effect. No,' Eucleides repeated.

She frowned. *Whatever is the matter with him? A little wine never hurt. Ungrateful Athenians. Strange and...*

Cosimo came sauntering from the *andron*, his stained clothes exchanged and his elbows sticky with salve. 'I've done your bidding, *Mother*.'

Lady Milos continued firmly patting her brother's shoulders and arms as if making sure his body would not dissemble. 'I see.'

'Eucleides?'

'What?'

'You should send for a physician, or we'll never know the damage. Come now, cousin, don't dawdle.'

'Of course, yes, of course.'

So they did. Alethea glided step by step along the wall until she could escape the commotion through the doorway leading to the courtyard, where she sat down on the edge of the rippling fountain. With the entire family—save for Efigenia, whom Alethea suspected still lingered by her loom, debating whether she should show herself in the bustle downstairs—there were few who might intrude on her.

Her thoughts galloped back over the months and years, flipping through a seemingly endless gallery of memories. *I think too much here, too much about the past. I grow too sentimental. But what else can one do?* Apolonio's laughter like peals as they chased through pitter-pattering summer rain, Delina's frail little legs as she learned to walk from the table to their mother's outstretched arms, the dark-haired clusters of boys and girls Alethea had spent years playing, competing, and hunting with.

Eucleides' voice made her jump and she looked up to see him leaning against the side of the doorway. 'My father is well. He shouldn't have walked down the stairs without aid.'

Alethea arched an eyebrow. 'He didn't *look* well.'

'He must be. He didn't look it, I know, but he has survived many ordeals. He won't leave us yet—he cannot—if we just care for him properly.'

'Perhaps.'

'Well. What were you thinking about? You looked quite mesmerised.'

'Nothing.'

'Daydreaming is no shame. I do it a lot myself.'

'I said it was nothing.' *Nothing you would understand, at least. Not in your world.*

Eucleides sighed and nodded as if he had really not expected anything more satisfactory from her. He turned to leave, but something in Alethea made her raise her voice.

'What did you dream of when I came upon you?'

'My father,' Eucleides confessed. 'How it used to be.'

'Is that all you'll say?'

'Will you tell me what you were daydreaming about?'

'No.'

Eucleides nodded again. 'Then that's all I'll say. What did you think of our Parthenon?'

Alethea shifted her weight where she sat. 'Too flashy.'

'If it was simple, it wouldn't bring so much beauty to the city, don't you see?'

If the people are devoted enough to the god, then the exterior of a temple is of little importance. 'Go to your father.'

To her astonishment, Eucleides left her, perhaps not realising he had taken orders from a slave, or perhaps seeing sense in the suggestion.

Alethea sank back into the tempting pit of nostalgia and was remarkably undisturbed for a good while. Then, the household resumed its usual rhythm of domestic activity, and she was put to work carrying water to fill a bath for Lady Milos.

CHAPTER SEVENTEEN

THEY WERE STANDING in the vestibule, nightfall pressing down upon them. Eucleides had a few songs of Homer's epic poems tucked under one arm. He had been on his way to his chambers when a certain Spartan had crossed his path and given him what had probably been intended as a light pinch.

'Why are you barefoot?' he asked.

'Oh.' She glanced at her feet. 'One of the slaves took my sandals. She'll regret it soon.'

'I see.' *I wouldn't want to be in that woman's shoes. Quite literally.*

She pointed at the scroll. 'You're reading that again?'

'I never tire, although I suppose it's ghastly of me to enjoy such a series of events.'

Alethea's eyes flashed with heat, and Eucleides wondered whether it was the terracotta lamps reflecting in the pitch-black of her pupils, or whether it was something deeper. 'You don't think it was the pride of Hellas? The victory, the war?'

'Only the gods know how many died. Perhaps not even they know. How can such a thing be glory?'

The heat in Alethea's eyes grew as he spoke, and it was no merciful fire. 'You're far too sentimental, did you know? Heroes are sprung from war, Achilles for one.' Her voice trailed off, and Eucleides wondered if she had lost herself in a shimmering fantasy, but then her attention returned to him. This time, her voice was softer. 'I can imagine them fighting sometimes. His golden locks under the helmet, the arrows buckling against the god-made armour. And gentle Patroclus, washing the blood of Trojan princes from his unblemished skin afterwards. Can you see it?'

He had never before thought of the scenes like she described them, yet the image she painted was so vivid that Eucleides could only nod. 'I can see it.' He hesitated. 'And...and wily Odysseus scratching his chin, knitting his plans while watching the funeral pyres.'

Alethea nodded enthusiastically. 'Yes. He's your favourite?'

'I don't know. I admire a man who can think rather than crush skulls.'

'I suppose so. Though, bear in mind, it was Odysseus' thinking that allowed the army to finally break through the stoic walls and slaughter everything inside, to burn the city. I prefer those who killed honestly on the battlefield. And—' She was interrupted by light footsteps.

Efigenia's skin was yellowish in the light from the terracotta lamps. Her lips parted slightly, revealing rosy gleam. 'I know I ought to be sleeping, but I needed some help with my toilette,' she said, eyes fixed on Euclcides' feet. 'My husband asked for you. Is the Spartan bothering you? She's quite impossible...'

'I'll see Cosimo soon—he won't perish without me. We were just speaking of Odysseus. Now that I think about it, Penelope was far more admirable. You agree, don't you?'

Efigenia's eyes darted up to his, flickering with confusion. 'Yes. I agree. A good weaver. Right...?' She turned to Alethea. 'You'll help me with my balms. You shouldn't loiter here.' She turned and tripped away, one ankle swollen and tender after the peril involving the platform sandals.

Alethea crinkled her nose, the glow in her eyes extinguished to damp grey ash. 'Balms. A subtle torture.'

'I wish you didn't have to go. If I ask, I'm sure she can find another girl to help her.'

'I can manage.'

'I don't doubt it.'

Alethea graced him with a quick glance before following her mistress, the hardened soles of her bare feet bright against the dark floor.

Eucleides remained a long while looking at the door she had shut behind her. Then, he wiped the clammy sweat off his palms and went to find Cosimo.

From Alethea's viewpoint on the flat part of the roof, the houses stretched out on all sides: squares of limestone and brick entwined with alleys and a handful of proper streets that ran like veins through the city. She could see as far as the towering walls and beyond them the heat-struck earth of the Attic countryside. In the other direction lay the ocean, she knew, but it was not visible at this angle.

Soon, slaves would prepare bedrolls on the roof for the men so that they might sleep under the stars, but for now, she drank in the solitude. Alethea began to pace, her thoughts involuntarily straying to the words she had exchanged with Eucleides. *That fanciful boy. At least he loves some of the right stories.*

The ambivalence only grew each time she saw him, much more so when she spoke to him. Pangs of hatred and resentment stirred with something she could not pinpoint, a pleasant flush tempting her to chat for hours, pulling at the corners of her mouth. It was different from anything she had felt with Apolonio or the other youths she had spent her days with by the Eurotas river, and it added to the suspicion she already held. Eucleides would tilt his head, voicing an opinion contrary to her own, and Alethea balanced the edge between giving in to temptation, or simply glare. When the light animated the curious twinkle in his eyes or the curve of his lip, the decision was even harder. It struck dread into her very marrow. What was uncertainty if not potential danger?

What would Apolonio do? She had mused over this before but without success. Now, the answer was obvious: Apolonio would do everything in his power to preserve himself and his ideals, to escape, to further Sparta's interests if at all possible. Apolonio would not dawdle away but act. *Ideals...yes. Ways of life. Frugality, conformity, patriotism.*

Frugality was not an issue. The wealthy Athenians might bathe in culture and riches, but these things were rarely offered slaves, and she did not have to accept any more of Eucleides' honey-slathered bread.

Conformity, well, that applied to those *living* in Sparta, not those placed in a context such as this, where every adherence to Athenian norm was a violation of the Spartan.

Finally, there was patriotism. *Patriotism would be to return home, to bear children and raise them to soldiers, to put forward my polis' agenda. He's a politician, right? And privileged. Susceptible. Prone to influence.*

As the sun sank and the sky shifted in bruised purples, the streets turning quiet in dawn's embrace, Alethea wove a plain scheme. Jagged and raw, it filled her with the sense of purpose she had lacked for months. Had she not seen Eucleides' simplicity, his mind an open well of sincerity and goodwill where one might retrieve as much as one needed? With one foot firmly placed in his land of fantasies, it seemed he refused to treat other people according to their less favourable qualities, even if he did spot them.

Not a true leader, for all his charisma. A target, a tool, if handled correctly. Poor one. I bet the woman who shares his bed shares his heart, too, a heart easily swayed.

Eucleides sat cross-legged on the roof with Chionides' *The Heroes* when the first drops of rain landed on the scroll, making the ink bleed. He tore his eyes from the text and scrambled to his feet, fingers fumbling to roll up the papyrus and tuck the scroll under his arm. He had always found rain a massive nuisance. It spoilt good literature and made one's clothes heavy and damp, the only profit being that the crops grew, providing said crops were not destroyed in raids.

The rain now came in a steady shower, beating down from the clusters of ominous clouds in a furious smatter. The summer heat sapped away in a heartbeat; the earth cooled to its core.

Eucleides wrapped the scroll in a fold of his *khitōn* and turned to climb back into the house.

'You're not staying?' The Doric dialect was as distinct as ever. Alethea's face was flushed and covered in droplets, her coarse tunic somehow elegant by the way it clung to her body.

'When did you—are *you* staying? You're already dripping!' Eucleides gave a strained laugh.

'I know that. I'm not stupid. Rain is lovely.'

'It's awful, really. We should go inside. I'll ask Agathe to fetch other clothes for you.'

Alethea gave no reply. She closed the space between them in three long steps, halting a hand's width from him, eyes fixed on something in the distance, only flickering to meet his for a moment. He could feel the warmth of her breath, see the individual strands of hair slicked against her temples and the water quivering on one eyelash.

He swallowed. 'Is something wrong?'

'No.' Her arms clasped stiffly around his neck. 'Stop talking.'

Eucleides complied with difficulty. *I know where this leads. If I could solve her puzzle...* The prospect was as alluring as ever. *If I could solve the puzzle entirely and peak beneath that ragged surface—*

Alethea's lips were slippery but firm as they pressed against his. Enveloping her with his arms, he deepened the kiss, feeling much to his relief how her stiffness softened under his touch.

What felt like forever and nothing at all passed before Eucleides finally withdrew to catch his breath and wipe the rain from his eyes.

Alethea unclasped her hands from him and took a quick step back, once more a statue of austerity, save for a strange little smile. 'You can go inside now, if you want.'

'Will you come with me?'

'Soon.'

Eucleides nodded, heart racing. *What was it Cosimo said? Don't take her into your bed. Maybe he was right, maybe one shouldn't play with fire. But the fire is so wonderfully luminous.* Besides, Cosimo had left once more to join the fleet the day before. He would be unable to give any curt comments on what transpired for quite some time, and when he returned for the season, it would be too late.

Alethea soared with triumph the moment after Eucleides had left her alone on the roof. The act had been easy—surprisingly pleasurable, even—as soon as he kissed her back, allowing her own awkwardness to fade. In the midst of all that chilling rain there had been a pool of warmth which she had not expected, worlds away from Crysanthos' passionless embrace.

All the better, I suppose. As long as it's not...love, not ever, then I can have warmth and pleasure in the process. It makes it easier to survive these things. She clutched her arms, shuddering. The rain, though lovely, was too cold now. Still, Alethea remained on the roof for a good while before sneaking back inside, careful not to encounter Eucleides. Their relationship had changed too abruptly for her to know what to say or do. The entire concept was so foreign, so easy and difficult at once, that she felt suffocated with questions. *What do I have to do, and what do I want? Do I want any of it? How do I speak or move or touch? What have I embarked upon?* She would have to visit his chambers soon, and a kiss would not be enough.

She knew only one thing with certainty: she would not act the slave girl with him. They were not considered equals in the eyes of the world, but she would not compromise herself any more than what was absolutely necessary. Through every lie and every deceit she had carried out in her life, she had never sacrificed the fundamentals of her identity, and she had no intentions of breaking that principle.

CHAPTER EIGHTEEN

ALETHEA BRUSHED HER fingers against the large, uneven birthmark on his shoulder, tracing the contour of his collar. The skin was soft as crushed rose petals, coloured bronze by the sun over many years.

Eucleides caught her hand in his, allowing her palm to rest at the base of his throat. A strand of hair fell down over his brow as he spoke. 'Why are you here?'

'What do you mean?' Alethea tried to tear her gaze from his eyes before she drowned in that dark abyss, but she was no more able of doing so than Tantalus was able to reach the supple fruit above his head.

'I mean why are you here?'

'Your dear cousin took me for a war prize, if you recall. I guess he aimed to add to his *glorious renown*.' She did not bother to hide the distaste creeping into her voice.

Eucleides reached out, touching her cracked lips with his thumb. 'Maybe. But not even the women of Sparta join their men on the battlefield, do they? How come you were within Cosimo's grasp?'

A throng of possible lies and explanations flashed through Alethea's mind in a matter of seconds. Several were plausible enough, but none would be necessary. 'My sister is a priestess. She said my brother would leave the land of the living, never returning from the battlefield. I thought…I thought I might prevent it. I persuaded my husband to bring me, with the blessing of his superiors.'

'How did you persuade him?'

Always searching for the roots of the drama. 'I told him that if he didn't, I would take a draught to make our future children stillborn.'

'I've never heard of such a draught.'

'Neither have I, and I would never have taken it. Crysanthos' intellect does not match the fineness of his looks. And, though I doubt he thought I'd be of much use, he didn't look with eager eyes on the prospect of losing his *philtatos*, his most beloved.'

Eucleides had released her hand, perhaps without realising it, his eyes wide in disbelief and his lips slightly parted. 'It is a tragic thing, to be caught in the net of forbidden love, or rather a love that is encouraged and praised at certain times yet scorned and forbidden at others. It has always struck me as peculiar that some never leave the stage of pederasty as they age, but peculiar still that others take issue with it. I remember when I was younger and one of the men competing for my devotion said—'

If only you could stop weaving your words into an infinite fabric. Is there no end to such speeches? Alethea did not listen any longer; Eucleides' voice had become a soft melody without distinction, and only one thought was truly present: *I cannot let this moment slip away.* She knew she was not a master of sweet-talk like him, neither did she have Crysanthos' experienced lover's touch or Efigenia's gift of submissively beaming. In truth, she had never imagined a situation such as this. Romance had never been on the table. Marriage was for begetting children and maintaining the basic structure of society, and although she knew plenty of Spartan youths who had indulged in dalliances, Alethea had not felt the urge to be one of them.

Now, everything she had planned depended on the affections of a young man whose dark eyes were no less infatuating than Paris' must have been. He was not distasteful prey, yet Alethea failed to discern what her next move should be.

'Would you like some wine?'

She snapped out of her thoughts at the inquiry. 'Yes. Wine would be nice.'

Eucleides nodded and, reluctantly, took a few steps back so that he might reach for the jug and the cups that stood neatly on one of the small tables. The wine was diluted, of course, but Alethea suppressed the tart comment about to escape her. Nevertheless, a sorry grimace passed over the young man's face for a heartbeat.

'I know you prefer it otherwise. It would appear strange, though, if I asked for something so...different to be brought to my room.'

Different. You want to say barbaric. 'No matter.' She accepted the cup he offered her and drank.

'Would you like for me to call on a slave to play for us? I could play myself, if it pleases you, but I'm afraid I'm no great talent.' Eucleides' eyes flickered from her mouth to her brow to her hands.

'Why?'

'I believe I've only seen you truly passionate when we spoke about the Trojan myths. Add some music to it—' To her surprise he faltered. 'You sometimes remind me of a blackbird who used to soar high but who has forgotten how to fly.'

'I haven't forgotten, but you have cut my wings.' *Easy. Not so sharp now.* Alethea sank down on the *kline* and gave him the most genuine smile she could summon. 'Well. I think a blackbird sounds a little dull, don't you?'

'A Stymphalian bird, then, with feathers of gleaming metal and a beak made for picking out a man's heart, equally cruel and beautiful.' Eucleides' weight caused the *kline* to creak as he sank down next to her, placing his cup on the floor to prevent permanent stains on the bone-white linen. 'You *are* cruel, don't you see, to keep so much to yourself.'

That's about to change, but little do you know. 'I love the Stymphalian birds,' she smiled. It was true. 'But I'm not sure Athens is the best place to be one.'

Eucleides arched his eyebrows and discreetly reached for her slave's hairnet so that her short locks might fall freely, then placed it on the floor by his cup. 'How so? What about this pearl for a *polis* could possibly displease any bird, any creature, if one ignores the unfortunate circumstances?'

'Did you know that in Sparta I used to race with the other youths wearing nothing but a side-slit *peplos* cut above my knees? We all did. It allows the highest velocity. And when we danced, it was almost in the nude.' Alethea savoured seeing the shock wash over her prey's face once more, and marvelled at how well her foreign customs worked to entice him.

'I can't imagine it. I can, of course, but I do wonder if the things you tell me are crafted from your own imagination.'

'Oh no. It's entirely true.'

'I believe you, then.' Eucleides' smile was sweeter than ripe figs. 'Will you stay the night?'

Blinding rays of sun crept through the shutters in the shape of thin lines, warming the stone floor and banishing night's chill. There was a certain fragrance to it: a room saturated with morning sun and yesterday's wine.

Alethea ran her fingers quickly through her dishevelled hair to undo the worst knots. With sleep still lingering in her limbs, she slowly rose and strode across the room to peer out the narrow slits in the shutters. There was no telling the time, but it must be early, she concluded, because the street below was still comparatively empty of people. She turned again, and her eyes fell on Eucleides, who lay sleeping as soundly as a cat on its favourite spot, one arm slung across his eyes. His skin no longer looked like dark bronze now the candle-lit night had been exchanged for daylight, but had returned to its lighter nuance.

Am I one of them now? One of those they slowly grind to dust? A wave of queasiness washed over her as she thought of the girls she had seen in the halls and occasionally on the street, some hardly yet turned fourteen, their eyes flickering with fear and their shoulders slumped under invisible burdens. They might have been bursting with life once, yet countless of agonies appeared to have fed on them, leaving nothing but a ragdoll that their masters might use as they pleased. *No. no, it's not the same.* Alethea forced herself to breathe deeply, in and out. *I have my own motives. I won't be crushed under their sandals. It was even...even wonderful.*

'Good morning, Stymphalian bird.' Eucleides pushed himself up on his elbows, squinting as a beam of sun struck his eyes.

The greeting lured a smile to Alethea's lips. 'Good morning. What should I call you?'

'Whatever you like. You'll have to think of something.' He rubbed his eyes, then seemed to fully take in her silhouette. It was the adoring gaze an artist might cast upon a perfectly crafted sculpture; it was the same gaze he had cast upon her so many times before, only stronger. Alethea picked up her crumpled *khitōn* from the floor, hastily draping it over her shoulders, and silently cursed the blush rising on her face.

Eucleides tilted his head. 'You must be hungry—
are you? I am. I'll send for some bread and honey,
and figs, and—'

'They will notice my absence.'

'They know where you are. They won't disturb
us.' He smiled. 'Please, come and sit with me.'

CHAPTER NINETEEN

THEY MET AGAIN the following evening, and this time, Eucleides was certain to extract as much information from the Spartan girl as he could, tingling to know the depths of her mind. It was no easy task, but throughout the night he learned more than he had dared to hope, receiving quite the education in life as Alethea had known it. She asked little in return but listened when he spoke regardless, and when morning came, the pleasant brewing in his chest had only grown stronger.

Eucleides followed the outline of Alethea's jaw with his finger, tracing the smooth skin with the lightest touch possible. She exuded warmth where she lay in his arms, her own limbs crossed in a defensive gesture which he, with a sting in his chest, presumed had become her habit. Her cheek rested on the pillow, face turned towards him, her short dark hair spread out like a fan. Her entire body rose and fell slowly but her breath sometimes quickened or ceased for a moment, and her eyelids twitched.

His finger passed over the bulging, knotted scar running from one eyebrow to her upper lip. Alethea's warmth—which, Eucleides realised, was something far softer than the sharp heat in her speech when awake—seemed to spread to him and fill him. It was not a foreign experience; the numerous slave girls and courtesans, *métoikoi* and even the occasional Athenian girl, were like pearls on a long necklace. For each pearl he added, he found another one an arm's length away, and though none of them lost their shine, each appeared brighter than the last. It was not cruelty on his part, only the constant allure of new discoveries, the endeavour to find a romance equal in greatness to that of the tragedies performed at the Dionysia. *Perhaps this will be it.*

Alethea stirred. 'I must return to the slaves' quarters.'

'The sun hasn't risen over the horizon yet. Stay a while.' Eucleides smiled as she opened her eyes. 'Won't you tell me more of Sparta?' he asked, itching with curiosity. 'Or your family?'

'What have I told you?'

'I know of your brother. You haven't mentioned anyone else.'

Alethea hesitated. 'I have a sister, also. She's a priestess of Artemis. Sometimes I don't know whether it is the gods that speak through her, or if she's just mad. No one really knows. I have a father and a mother. I never see my father anymore.'

'Do you miss them? I would miss my father terribly, and my aunt.'

She only jerked her head a little to the side, like a shrug. 'Only Apolonio.'

'I hope you'll make friends here. I know it's not custom for a slave to share a confidence with the women of the *oikos*, but I believe a great deal of lonesomeness could be remedied.'

A quick crinkle of her nose, an annoyed little twitch of her mouth.

Was that not the right thing to say? 'My cousin's wife is quiet, it's true, but so are you.'

'I doubt our reasons are the same. Lady Efigenia might be a bitch in her own right, but I daresay the life she leads is part of it.'

Eucleides stared, startled once again at the ugly words jumping from those peachy lips almost as often as they omitted no sound. He could not recall another slave who dared speak thus about their mistress. Efigenia's behaviour had never struck him as anything but utterly decorous—solemn, perhaps, but that hardly turned heads.

'Has she been harsh with you? I can't fathom it. She's like the sweet child of a nymph. I mean nothing amorous—'

'You're very naïve.'

Eucleides opened his mouth, then closed it again. For once, he was unable to produce an answer and his tongue felt like a lump of clay in his mouth. The first streaks of morning light illuminated Alethea's face, highlighting the garnet-red scar, making it look like a worm had entered under her skin and was crawling towards her scalp slowly, slowly. Eucleides snapped out of the thought.

'If she acts with malice in your company, why's that then? Is she unhappy? She lives in the most splendid, democratic *polis* in the whole of Hellas, in a wealthy *oikos*, and has both her youth and her health intact.'

A snort escaped Alethea. 'All the splendour and democracy you have is of little use behind the closed door of a *gynaikeion*.' Then, she swallowed rapidly, and Eucleides could have sworn he saw her pull a figurative sheath of charm over her face so that it looked as welcoming as it had in the candlelight the night before. 'But if you're my friend, I'm content.'

'Then you'll never be discontent.' He drew her closer, letting his hands slide over her hip and up her back.

'One more thing.'

'What?'

'Never refer to me as a slave again. Swear it.'

'I swear on everything sacred, everything dear.'

Efigenia stared at the young woman who lay curled up on her cousin-in-law's bed as if the piece of furniture belonged to her. Her bare thighs and the slight curve of her stomach was plain to see, for there was nothing to cover her body except for the twisted and rather inefficient sheet.

No morals. No manners, no— Efigenia curbed the alarm rising in her throat at the sight of such a fallen woman. She tried to remember the name she had given the slave girl some time ago when Cosimo had brought her back with him. *Doris.* At first, she had feared her husband intended the Spartan for himself, but this was apparently not the case. Nonetheless, the slave had been utterly useless, incompetent in her chores and hostile in nature.

Efigenia hesitated, then stretched out a finger and poked the woman, who fidgeted and pulled her legs closer to her chest like a conch withdrawing inside its shell, but her eyes remained closed. *Has she no laundry or weaving to tend to? She must have...*

Efigenia took a few deep breaths, raised her chin, and cleared her throat. The sound was not quite as confident as she had intended. 'Slave. You—'

Finally, Eucleides' new favourite snapped awake and quickly scanned the scene. Her eyes were the colour of iron and their gaze as hard. 'Yes?'

'You ought to be working. And you must cover yourself. I shan't have slave girls...loitering around naked in...in this house. My house.' She swallowed and squared her shoulders. *A good wife must know how to conduct her husband's* oikos.

The object of her reprimands blinked away the haze of sleep and rose from the bed, the thin sheet effortlessly wrapped around her body. To her vexation, Efigenia realised that the top of her head only reached the woman's shoulder. It could not solely be a matter of the perhaps five years separating them, for the stories of Spartan women's peculiarities had long since reached every ear in Athens.

'Yes, Lady.' Despite her words, there was a stout defiance in the way she spoke them and the way she refused to lower her eyes.

Efigenia resisted the impulse to crane her neck for a better look at the slave's face. 'You can go now.'

Once the slave had scooped her simple clothing from the floor, shamelessly dropped the sheet and dressed herself, she slipped out of the bedchamber on feet light as a dancer's.

Efigenia remained for a few moments, anxiously reaching up to make sure not a single strand of hair had escaped the ivory and gold hairpins fixing the chignon at the nape of her neck. Cosimo had mentioned once how he thought ivory had the qualities to make any woman bearable to the eye. *Vulgar, promiscuous Spartans.* Naturally, voicing any complaint to Eucleides was impossible—such a thing was unthinkable, regardless of the friendliness he had previously shown her. *Perhaps she knows her place now. Then I won't need to speak about it again.* There was, however, one other person in the *oikos* who might be willing to commiserate if she was fortunate, one other woman who had been raised to obey and command in just the right proportions, taught the weight of virtue.

Efigenia found Lady Milos fanning herself in the courtyard; she had persisted in this pastime of hers although the most blazing heat of summer was beginning to fade, and Efigenia suspected she would not cease the flapping of her wrist in the winter either. Often, she employed a slave or two for the task, but today she was alone.

'Lady?'

The older woman patted the stone bench where she was sitting, her hand more wrinkled than a dried prune.

Efigenia obliged, sitting down and clasping her hands in her lap. 'There is a delicate matter I would like your advice on.'

'If it concerns my son, you have my sympathies.'

'Oh, no, Lady. My husband has never given me cause to—' Efigenia smoothed her hair again, fastening a loose pin. 'It concerns one of the slaves.'

'Continue,' Lady Milos prompted, reaching for one of the honeyed sesame cookies piled on a plate on the bench between them.

'I don't like how the Spartan girl behaves. Your nephew is...is as if struck by Eros' arrow.'

'My nephew is a sweet boy. If the gods had been more merciful, I would have been blessed with a child like him.'

'It's not your nephew who concerns me, but the Spartan. If she takes part in carnal acts, well...I fear the consequences.' *That ought to reason with anyone. Children are expensive. Children...* She forced herself to continue. 'Eucleides' tender heart might cause him to bring up the result with all the circumstance due to a legitimate child.'

'I see.' Lady Milos stole a glance at the extravagant jewellery her ample wrist. 'I must have a word with him, then.'

'You'll speak to him on the matter?' Efigenia's eyes widened.

'I will. With age comes a certain right, my girl. It suits you to act the grey mouse now, but in time, you might find even *your* authority extending beyond the slaves, though others won't confess to it.'

'Oh.'

The following morning, Efigenia rose early, feeling as if someone had spooned out her insides, leaving her empty. Her stomach was silent as the grave, but sent ripples of pain through her body. As she stood on her feet, the floor swayed for a second before stabilising again. *Silly girl.* She gave each cheek a hard pinch to elicit a tint of pink—Cosimo did not like the unnatural cosmetics some women used.

A string of slave girls arrived to comb her hair with lavender-infused oil in order to prevent it from losing that golden lustre she so prided herself upon, their own hair cropped short and gathered in unbecoming hairnets. *Poor souls.* Efigenia suppressed a smile. It was not too difficult, for the sickening feeling of emptiness was growing in strength, ruthlessly demanding nourishment in the shape of a thick loaf of bread slathered in grease. *How silly.*

The slaves proceeded to plait her hair, gathering it in a chignon and pinning it to her head with an exquisite comb. After having her skin rubbed with the same oil used in her hair, Efigenia at last stepped into her *khitōn*, then dismissed the other girls. Eyes glued to the ground and arms pressed to their sides, they shambled past her one by one; only upon exiting her chamber did they raise their heads again, erupting in hushed chitchat. Efigenia hardly took any notice of this, though, since the dynamic had been very similar in the *oikos* where she had spent her childhood. Of course, when she had been a giggling girl of five, the slaves would occasionally beam at her or tickle her under the chin, but with each passing year, she had floated further from their unpretentious circle as a result of her mother's rearing. There was a certain camaraderie which the unfortunate servants were able to share on the plain

basis that they were unfortunate, and Efigenia had
long since learnt to regard it with disdain rather than
envy.

CHAPTER TWENTY

EUCLEIDES WAS TWO thirds through a comedy when Lady Milos' papyrus-like voice sounded, and he had to remind himself not to offer her some goat milk to soften her vocal cord, just like so many times before. She had managed to slide into the room without a sound. At this point he was rarely startled to find her peering over his shoulder anymore. If only that dear woman could dispense some of her attention to her son, not me or her financial accounts. But she is dear.

'How can I help you, aunt?'

'I wanted a word with you, a word of caution.' Lady Milos twisted an heirloom ring on her index finger back and forth but otherwise retained her usual unyielding composure. 'I shan't torture either of us with the business of small talk, though you know I prefer your company to that of any other. Rather, I'll speak frankly.'

'Please do.' Eucleides averted his eyes from the scroll
and looked at the older woman.

'I'm concerned about your association with that slave girl. The Spartan girl. It was my daughter-in
law who brought the issue to my attention.'

Eucleides' stomach hissed as if he was falling from a great height. 'I didn't think you knew about that, much less that you thought of it as an issue.'

'Well. What concerns me is not only the terrible influence the slave might have, but the possible consequences. Children.'

'I assure you, aunt, she's not so terrible, not at all, and I'd never dream to...' His words fell flat; they might have soared in the presence of six thousand Athenians, yet this particular conversation was a greater challenge than any oration.

'I don't know her, it's true, just as a mistress should never really know her slaves, whether they serve as more than labour or not. But procreation, my dear boy, does not always follow your intentions.'

'I know that. But even so... I fail to see the issue. I... There have been others, as I'm sure you know, and I never heard a word from your fair lips about it.'

'They were never under our roof. Make no mistake, I only meddle in your affairs for your own good. A flute girl here or there is entirely different than a Spartan woman filled with strange ideas and morals. That one needs to be taught submission, not pampered like a princess!' Lady Milos' voice had grown shrill and she had begun to violently wring the heirloom ring. However, she inhaled deeply and regained her composure, then stroked Eucleides' cheek motherly. 'Be wise. Spartan influences, profane behaviour, demanding offspring...they're the last things this oikos needs. I'll leave you to your studies now.'

Eucleides rose from his chair by the desk and clasped his hands behind his back. The nausea had peaked and was beginning to subside. *She has never known romance. That must play some part in it. Perhaps she has never known anything of the sort.* Pity stung his heart.

'I promise to consider what you've told me,' he said. 'That's all I can promise.'

Lady Milos nodded, doubtlessly interpreting the reply as complete success. Whenever she was told a maybe, she heard a yes or a no depending on what best pleased her.

Nothing more was said on the matter, but Eucleides' thoughts kept straying to it even after his aunt had at last left him to his scrolls. A small and awfully rational part of him knew she was correct in all her qualms. Still, that part slithered to the deepest pit of his mind all too often, giving way to a more fanciful persona. He enjoyed the world as it was when painted in soft colours, the sharp spikes of conflict overpowered by love and pleasure. Others seemed to enjoy it thus, too, at least when he presented them with it, and although he often compromised both the rational and the fanciful parts to maintain balance, he could not help but think that most people would be happier if they paid less attention to the gruesome aspects of life.

Warfare, the Peloponnese, political factions, slaves and masters, relations...all so bothersome at times. He shook his head and began clearing the desk, returning the scroll to its chest.

Alethea's days passed in a similar manner: tasks from dawn till dusk, embraces during the night. She became more estranged from the other servants each time she stole away with Eucleides, but she could not have minded less, since she consistently vowed to remain separate from them. *I must keep my integrity. They're inferior, not Spartan and not born free like I was. If I assimilate then what do I have left? Certainly not my pride.*

The hierarchy of the world was clear as ice in her mind, just as she had been schooled from birth: at the bottom was the *heílotes*, then regular slaves, then other free Hellenes, then those from her own *polis*. Only if she refused to accept her position as slave could she retain that of a Spartan. Then there was the matter of gender: men were said to be by nature superior, but Alethea nurtured a doubt. She finally concluded that if she was right, she was of higher standing than Eucleides, and if she was wrong, she was still no less than his equal since her origins compensated for any disadvantages of her sex.

Regardless, all these technicalities seemed meaningless when they were together. Her kisses were no longer stiff or strange, but came naturally. It was less an act than she could have imagined, not least because she had discovered he did not seem to mind when she spoke freely and curtly. Sometimes, such as this particular night, Alethea had to remind herself not to grow too genuine, and it was a challenge.

She raised herself on her elbow, cheek pressing against her palm. The room was hot and moist as was the season, and her entire body felt swollen, flushed, from loving, from being loved. That word—*love*— was yet much too abstract, too poignant, to describe the pleasant turmoil in her chest. *What is there, then, other than love? Lust? Fondness? I should have acquired a better vocabulary.* She studied the curve of Eucleides' neck in the gloom, his skin covered in thin down, his smell, like earth after rain, thick in her nostrils. There was only one other fragrance she knew better: Apolonio's.

Alethea sank back against the pillow and closed her eyes, images from the hours before flashing by against the dark of her eyelids. Soft hands and angular shoulder blades, bold lips and eyes exploring everything with the delight of a child. *Does it ever change? Will it ever turn dull or unpleasant?* Her scalp prickled with guilt, which she brushed it off in an instant. If she had deceived the boy beside her, the deceit was no worse than the lives she had taken that day on the battlefield—and the relationship was hardly one of fair terms to begin with. Everything, she reminded herself once more, everything was for the sake of her freedom and in the long run for the sake of Sparta. It seemed Eucleides was not influential enough in politics to help her *polis* indirectly, but she could still make him adore her enough to help her escape, after which she could aid Sparta herself.

Time passed painfully slowly. Alethea lay awake, thoughts cluttered and knotted, until morning finally arrived. When it did, life returned to Eucleides' face and she could not help but smile at the way he yawned impossibly big.

'You slept well?' he asked, voice still drowsy.

'Yes.'

Her lover untangled himself from the sheets and rose, slipping a simple tunic over his head.

'Are you...happy?' Alethea propped her chin on her knees, carving little white patterns on her bare ankle with one nail.

Eucleides frowned. 'I believe so. As long as I can stay here in Athens with you. If I have to raid Megara, then I should be unhappy.'

'But you're happy with *this*?'

The sun seemed to warm his face despite the shutters being closed. 'How could I not be?'

Alethea nodded.

'And you?'

'I'm happy to live,' she shrugged. 'I wasn't always, when I first came here.'

A familiar stroke of guilt crossed Eucleides' eyes. 'I know. But life is a wondrous thing, sometimes, don't you think? If I could, I would live *forever*.'

Alethea sat silent. *To live forever. That's not for mortals like us.*

Eucleides' words echoed time and time again in her head like the chime of a bell in a vast stone hall. *If I could, I would live for*ever. The idea made her shudder. What honour was there if not that of a purposeful death? What relief was there if not the prospect of leaving earthly life?

Only heroes—truly spectacular heroes with deeds strung like countless beads on gold chains, heroes rarely kind but always god-like—came to Elysium, and only their counterparts in villainy were doomed to suffer in Tártaros. Therefore, the great masses of humans had nothing to fear but the obscure nothingness in the Asphodel Meadows, which, she reasoned, could be no worse than the life she was currently leading. Even when she was free, Alethea had had no doubts: life was short and dire, a death in battle or in childbirth preferable to withering away in old age, and to have generations remembering your name was a greater achievement than lingering with those new generations yourself.

Eucleides, however, seemed not to mind old age. To be young forever was one thing, but to live forever was quite another. Alethea could easily picture him as an archaic man bent over some equally archaic text, forehead seared with lines, eyes sparkling with joy knowing he could remain there always, enjoying life's pleasures.

'It would get lonely, perhaps, but one could always find new people to cherish and love, if others had to die eventually,' he said once when she asked him about it. 'I'd miss you dreadfully. But I'm not talking sense, am I?' He pulled her into an embrace and the topic was lost.

Alethea tried to shed the emotion picking at her, but it was no use. She was concerned, concerned for someone she had often vowed not to care for in earnest. Despite, or rather because, the concept could never be realised, it was all the more destructive for one so inclined to dream as Eucleides.

CHAPTER TWENTY-ONE

THEY WERE SITTING on the roof, feet dangling over the edge in the tickling early autumn breeze, enjoying the last moments of daylight. A platter of figs sat between them.

'Do you know of the Eleusinian mysteries?'

The question startled Alethea. 'Of course. At least, I've heard things.'

Eucleides nodded and reached for another fig, fingers sticky with grainy sweetness. 'Strange things, I assume. Cosimo knows everything, he knows what happens, but of course he won't tell me, and he really shouldn't. I'd give anything to know—almost anything.'

You would give almost anything to know almost anything. 'I think it sounds morbid. The piglet...' Alethea recalled the conversation she had listened to around the campfire all those months ago, enveloped in Apolonio's arms.

'I thought you liked morbid things,' Eucleides teased, smiles chasing each other on his lips.

'Resilience, not morbidity. But I do like the secrecy of it all. The mysteries reveal something, don't they?'

'Oh, yes. They reveal the path to a new beginning, a better life in the underworld.' His expression was spellbound.

'Immortality?'

'Not in the traditional sense. Death persists, naturally, or we would have a city swarming with people. What it does promise is an immortal soul.'

'All souls are immortal. That's why we perform burial rites.'

'Of course. Only, ordinary people won't have nearly as delightful a time *afterwards*.'

Alethea sank her teeth into the dark flesh of what she realised was her fourth fig. *Have they corrupted me entirely with their gluttony? A delightful time...*

An impulse came over her. 'Would you...would you fear death less if you were an initiate?'

'I suppose so. Why?'

'I don't think one should fear death.'

Eucleides flushed. 'I'm not—are you mocking me? Sometimes I can't tell. Would you go with me, to Eleusis, if I went?'

Alethea stared. 'Now *you* mock me! I can't, anyhow. My hands are stained with blood.' She was right: anyone, even a slave and a woman, could become an initiate except for those who spoke a foreign tongue or were polluted from having taken a life.

'I know better than to mock you, and those men were not murder, but honest deaths in combat. I imagine that's a different matter.'

'When does it begin?'

'The fourteenth day of *Boedromion*, lasting ten days. That's all Cosimo has told me.'

So soon. Ten days... Would the high-and-mighty mistresses allow my absence? And what of my sanity? And yet— 'You won't convince me.'

They said little after that; the sky was too peach-coloured and the fruit too ripe to spoil the moment with further discussion. Nevertheless, Alethea knew Eucleides had indeed already convinced her.

Although the mysteries were of utmost secrecy, what they celebrated was well-known: the descent and ascent of Persephone to and from the underworld, Demeter's distraught search for her daughter, their euphoric reunion. When Persephone returned to the world of the living each year, the crops once more grew and the fruit once more ripened. This symbolised new beginnings and rebirth, fertility in a sense. Just as Persephone had returned to the living, each initiate would escape the tedious nothingness in the underworld and be reborn to a better existence after death.

To participate in the Greater Mysteries, one should first have been initiated in the Lesser, which was held in blooming springtime, but neither Eucleides nor Alethea had any intention of waiting another five years for the next opportunity. Five years was an infinity, as even a single year tends to be to a young life. In five years, they could each be dead since long, occupied with families and children of their own, or, worst of all, robbed of momentum. The number of participants was substantial enough for two more to blend in without anyone taking much notice, and as far as Alethea knew, no one kept a record of names.

Coming the sixteenth day of *Boedromion*, Alethea found herself basking in the cool ocean water at Phaleron, a port situated an hour's walk from the Acropolis. During the two previous days, the mysteries had begun with the bringing of the sacred objects from Eleusis to the Eleusinion sanctuary in Athens. Then the hierophants, the priests, had declared the beginning of the rites by carrying out a sacrifice.

Alethea tilted her head back, her hair spreading like billowing seaweed, her limbs seemingly weightless and infinitely smooth. It was too long since she had last felt like that. Athens' rivers were not inaccessible in themselves, but a young woman who went bathing in public view was an infamy, unlike the Spartan girls who washed in the Eurotas just like their brothers.

I could stay like this always— Her thoughts were interrupted as the purification ceremony ended, the initiates-to-be wading ashore. There were over a hundred of them, a rarely-seen blend of men and women, Athenians and foreigners, *métoikoi* and slaves. Alethea caught Eucleides' squinting eyes and had to smile at the soaked clusters of hair slicked to his face and the plump beads of water trembling on the tip of his nose.

The following day was a festival of its own, celebrating the arrival of Asclepius, god of medicine and son of Apollo, and his daughter Hygeia in Athens. As was custom during festivities such as this, the participants feasted well into the night, sacrificing meat to the gods. Alethea listened to the sizzling of fat dripping onto coal, bracing herself for the fast which would commence shortly: a part of the preparations required for the mysteries.

On the nineteenth of *Boedromion*, initiates marched as one body along the Sacred Way from Athens to Eleusis. It was one of the more spectacular processions Alethea had seen thus far in her life: *khitōns* and tunics of various length flapping around sun-burnt legs in the early autumn winds, people carrying branches called *bacchoi*, chanting like a soaring torrent. Spirits high, they appeared to be carved from the Golden Age of Man, when humans did not have to toil to feed themselves, and grew miraculously old without losing the lambency of youth.

Alethea clung to Eucleides' wrist like a child afraid to get lost in the crowd, drinking in everything she saw.

'I wish I had gone sooner,' he said, radiant.

'Why didn't you?'

'I suppose I was dreading what it might include. I'm not now, though. With you, I could never be truly afraid.'

Alethea licked her lips, lacking response. *How you rush to complete devotion. A dangerous quality.*

At one point, the chanting ceased and, instead, obscenities fell loudly from the initiates' lips. Alethea arched her eyebrows, a smile pulling at her own mouth.

Eucleides flushed. 'In remembrance of Iambe, I should think, the woman who cheered Demeter in all her misery by use of foul words and jests.'

Another hour passed before they reached the city of Eleusis, houses crammed together on the rocky plain. The vaguely familiar sight only held Alethea's attention for a moment before a memory came upon her, a memory of how she had strolled around the army camp during one of those endlessly dull hours, waiting for Apolonio to return from a raid. The tents had been erected on the very ground she now walked over, just outside the city, and she slowly recognised the rocks and trees sprinkled across the plain. Under one of those trees, she had sat scraping her heels in the dirt, waiting, toying with the hairpin Apolonio had once given her, and at some point, that pin had been lost. She had returned searching for it, but in vain. *Maybe, maybe...*

Alethea tugged at Eucleides' *khitōn*. 'Wait. I want to look for something.'

'What?'

'Just wait a moment, will you? And tell me if you see anything bronze-like.'

The two of them inspected the dusty ground for a good while, the other initiates moving along on both sides, before a sliver of blinding light caught Alethea's eye. Her heart skipped with triumph.

There, trampled deep into the soil, lay a piece of dusty bronze, reflecting the setting sun. As she bent down and retrieved it, running her thumb across the smooth metal, she recognised it instantly. The limber mountain cat wrought itself around the top of the hairpin, which was the length of a hand and ended in a knife-sharp point.

After all this time... Yet it hasn't been that long, has it?

Eucleides peered over her shoulder. 'What is that?'

'It's mine. My hairpin. My brother gave it to me.' Alethea's voice sounded peculiar, hollowed by the clawing fingers of nostalgia. She offered the pin to Eucleides, who studied it for a moment before returning it.

'It's beautiful—delightful, really. But how on earth...?'

'We camped here before I was sent back. I told you of it, I think. I must have dropped it.'

'Oh, yes, I remember.' He planted a kiss on her head, drawing in the scent of her hair. 'You miss those days.'

'Yes.'

The procession was constantly moving, threatening to leave any lingering members behind, hence they picked up their feet and continued without another word. Alethea twisted a thick garland of hair around two fingers and fastened it with the pin.

Shortly thereafter, the procession arrived at Eleusis. Having entered inside the imposing stone walls surrounding the sacred buildings, the initiates settled outside the Telesterion—the massive sanctuary dedicated to Demeter, where the heart of the mysteries would take place—to vigil throughout the night. It was a curious sight: countless little clusters of *khitōns*, veils, and *bacchoi* crowding, with the sanctuary's marble colonnade casting long shadows. The sky loomed over them, a heavy shroud of chalked blue gilded with gold.

How absurd. If I had known the last time I was here what I would become, what I would do, I would have despised myself. Alethea swallowed and pushed the thought away. No good could come from lamenting these things. When she had last been at Eleusis, the circumstances had been different, allowing a kind of ideals impossible to fully uphold now.

There was commotion at the outskirts of the crowd, spreading inwards. The hierophants were passing around cheap clay cups so that each initiate might drink freely of the beverage they contained.

'What's that?' Alethea asked.

Eucleides, who was in the process of removing his sandals for comfort during the long vigil, stretched his neck for a better view. 'I don't know. Maybe wine, or a sacred drink required for the rites. Maybe a potion of some sort.'

'A potion?' *I should not drink anything that they give me. Athenian priests carrying poison...*

Nevertheless, when her time came, she slowly brought the cup to her lips, the clay rough and dry, and took first a sip, then another, until nothing remained. The brew was odd but not, it appeared, the poison she had half-feared; meal-like flatness mixed with brighter notes of mint and something Alethea could not quite name. The texture was that of thick soup, clogging her throat, but after the fast, Alethea was only glad of the feeling.

'*Kykeon*,' one of the hierophants declared.

'For what purpose?'

'To help you see.' The man gave no further explanation, but none was needed. Once dark had fallen, Alethea *saw*.

Bodies twirled, flashing twisted limbs, teeth gleaming in torchlight. They were no longer human beings but dark creatures sprung from another world. The milky-white moon dangled loose on the sky; the air vibrated with wailing song and thunderous chanting.

Eucleides saw his bare feet strike the ground until the dust mixed with blood but could not feel them. What he did feel was Alethea's shoulder brushing against his for an instant, then the tickle of her hair on his cheek.

The night seemed eternal. It shifted in a thousand nuances and temperatures, a whole lifetime of sin squeezed into a handful of quivering hours. A discarded *khitōn*, a pool of suspiciously sticky, red wine, beautiful chaos. Amidst it all, Eucleides thought he spotted two impossibly tall women, untouched by the turmoil as they glided across the ground, ethereal light forming wreaths of flowers in their hair. Neither of the goddesses stopped to meet his gaze, and were gone the next time he turned to look.

Eucleides was overcome with an emotion he had never known before, or at least not allowed forth, something too aggressive and passionate to be harmless. *I could dive off a cliff, I could kill a beast and eat it raw, I could do anything.*

Alethea exclaimed, and Eucleides recognised her hairpin in a man's clenched hand. He had no clear perception of what happened next, only that he flung himself forward and heard the sound of the man's knuckles crushing his nose. There was a glimpse of Alethea's hands wrapped around an arm. The pin fell and clattered on the stairs to the Telesterion. Eucleides tumbled to the ground, grappling after it in blind fury.

CHAPTER TWENTY-TWO

DAWN HAD NOT yet arrived when Alethea opened her eyes. She reached up to remove a strand of hair from her face and withdrew her hand as it met with something cold and slimy. She stared at her fingers: crimson smeared with grey, the thick substances half-clotted. It was the same grisly sight as when a sacrificial animal had gone wild and made the slaughter messy. *Dear gods.* She swept her eyes over the scene. The initiates lay on the ground in disarray; at first, Alethea feared there had somehow been a massacre, but soon saw that they were merely drowsy with sleep after the night's intoxication. Apart from rumpled and torn clothes and tousled hair, they appeared unharmed.

One man, however, was the stomach-twisting exception. Face against the ground, limbs sprawled in unnatural angles, he lay with the back of his skull exposed. The dark hair was soaked in red and lay parted. Beneath it, a thin crack in the white bone grinned back at Alethea.

She struggled to her feet, her legs tangling as she staggered backwards. *My hands. Not my hands— they can't be... I never touched him. But I must have. Dear gods.* Without another thought, she turned and ran, faster than she had ever run on the racetracks in Sparta. There was nowhere far to go, though, except for wide circles around the sanctuary. The stone walls were impenetrable and the gates locked so as to prevent any initiates from leaving before completing their part in the mysteries, breaking the vigil.

She stopped behind the Telesterion, where the sleeping men and women were fewer, and pressed flat against one of the shaded columns, hoping to magically melt into the stone.

'A—Alethea?' The voice was hoarse as if worn out with crying. 'Alethea?'

'I didn't do it.' The response was a reflex. *I can't have. I only kill with a purpose. And more neatly than that.*

At first, she barely recognised Eucleides where he stood in his dripping, red *khitōn*, sandals still missing, eyes like an upset owl. Then, he came closer, and relief washed over her as he reached for her hand.

'If not, then I did.'

'You don't know what you're saying.'

'You saw that man—'

'It's not in you, not in a thousand years.'

'I tried to wash my clothes in the well over there.' He pointed with a violently trembling finger. 'It won't go away. It will never go away!'

Alethea stared at him, then at their hands, joined in blood. *What will we do? To murder on sacred ground. That's a crime against the gods...* 'It doesn't matter who did what. My memory is lost.'

'Mine also.'

'Why?' she whispered.

Eucleides shook his head, eyes glassy with tears. 'I think—I think he tried to steal your pin. And that drink, *kykeon*, I think it drives you mad, if only for a few hours. I hope it was madness.'

Alethea did not dare remark on the fact that none of the other initiates had gone this far, despite the fact that they must have been just as affected by the draught. She could recall half-naked bodies and turmoil, but nothing like the man with the cracked skull.

'Should we hide him? I tried but he was too heavy…'

'There's nowhere *to* hide him. And no one needs to know if only we wash *properly*. Even if they saw, they won't remember details or faces, just like we don't.' Alethea spoke with greater confidence than she felt, afraid of what might happen if she allowed Eucleides to break like a piece of pottery. *It wouldn't be pretty.*

'You think we ought to pretend like we know nothing then? They could read it on our faces, I'm sure—'

'Not if you don't let them.'

'And the gods? The Erinyes, and… I don't want to live forever with that cloak of guilt weighing on my shoulders, no, I think perhaps I don't want to live at all.' Eucleides' lower lip was almost as bloody as his *khitōn* from being tugged at.

'Stop it! Just stop!' Alethea drew a shaky breath. 'There will be time for all that, but not now. Now, we only have to take the most urgent measures. Before daybreak.'

They sent both their *khitōns* tumbling down the well's abyss, and hastily replaced them with garments they found discarded on the ground. They drew another bucket of water and wiped away every last stain of brains and blood from their hands and, much to their horror, faces. Eucleides located his sandals, dabbed his broken nose with cold water to ease the swelling, and after a fair bit of forced calm breathing, they sat down as far as possible from the body.

Crisp daylight soon flooded Eleusis, stirring the sleeping crowd. The first shriek cut like broken glass through the dense silence, then another, and another. The initiates shot suspicious glances at one another, their faces like sheets of papyrus scribbled full with accusations. The hierophants were quick to act, swathing the dead man in cloth and tasking three servants with removing him from the temple grounds instantaneously. That way, the pollution, *miasma*—which in a way sullied everyone involved, not merely the guilty—needed not grow. Afterwards, they performed purifying rites over the reddened, sticky ground where the body had lain, and poured libations to appease Demeter and Persephone. The priests made no thorough effort to find the culprits; the deed would be better forgotten, the fact that it had happened under their supposed watch and on sacred ground too alarming to be acknowledged.

Alethea watched from afar with increasing relief. *Perhaps it doesn't have to end in catastrophe after all. Perhaps the only ones who will know are the gods, and they can be swayed to turn a blind eye to the death of an ordinary man.*

If the circumstances had been different, if the man had been a *heílote* for example, she might have chosen to admit her part of the blame; there were no real consequences for killing a *heílote* since the Spartan state systematically declared war on them every year. Still, as it was, she had no intention of being sentenced to death by an Athenian jury in an Athenian court of law. *I've survived too much to end my days at their mercy. And half the crime lies in getting caught—haven't I learned that my entire life?*

She was less certain of Eucleides. Lies did not come as smoothly and effortlessly to him as they did to her, except when he half-believed them himself, and there was the possibility that his burning ideals of the Good and the Wonderful would eat him to the bone unless he confessed all his sins. Unless, of course, his subconscious chose to simply repress the entire incident.

The penalty for unintentional homicide, if one could call it that, was often no more severe than exile, and Alethea knew Eucleides could persuade any jury in Athens to lenience. *But if he talks, he might accidentally drag me into it, and he wouldn't do that.* She realised how little she actually knew what he *would* do, how little she knew who he might turn into when pushed over the edge of insanity.

The vast hall of the Telesterion was biting cold compared to the pools of warmth which lingered outside. Imagery of legendary battles lined the walls: Amazons sprung forth on muscular horses with their bows strung, centaurs galloped with hooves stirring up dust, giants wielded massive clubs, and on one panel, a slim-hipped Paris lounged on his chariot on the Trojan plain. The rich reds and blues, the pitch-black, the artful blends made it look as if the figures moved, brought to life by the sacredness of the moment.

In the centre of the hall stood the *Anaktoron*, a square construction where only the hierophants might enter. Alethea prickled with curiosity and for a moment she forgot the dark clouds crowding in her mind. What might there be inside so secret that not even the sworn initiates, who had already undergone so much ceremonious preparation, were allowed inside?

The core of the mysteries consisted of three elements: the *dromena*, the *deiknumena*, and the *legomena*.

First came the *dromena*, the things done: a dramatic re-enactment portraying the myth of Demeter and Persephone, the actors in masks with bold features. Alethea recalled what Eucleides had told her of the Dionysia, and concluded that this spectacle must be much more extravagant and feverous than the ordinary plays showed to the Athenian public. The so-called Demeter and Persephone screamed and wailed at their loss of one another; Persephone's stiff clay lips received the symbolic pomegranate seeds while the juice dripped down her throat; mother and daughter performed a hypnotising dance of ecstatic joy as they reunited.

The things said—the *legomena*—were mere commentary on the drama. Then, finally, followed the *deiknumena*, the things shown. One by one, the hierophants uncovered a series of sacred objects: replicas of sexual organs painted in odd colours and patterns, and a golden ear of wheat, all symbolising fertility and the growing of crops which in turn symbolised new life.

Alethea had to stifle her disappointment. *Is it those things they guard so zealously? What about the piglets? Maybe that was just a rumour.* Many around her, however, appeared in awe, perhaps owing to the atmosphere and their own expectations.

The initiates were once more bid to drink of the *kykeon*. Alethea and Eucleides exchanged a glance. She could spot the alarm hovering in his eyes just as it did within herself. *But we cannot refuse. It would look too strange. Perhaps it wouldn't even be allowed.*

This time, however, fewer cups were passed from mouth to mouth and only one swallow of the mealy brew was required. Alethea steadied herself and forced it down, suppressing gags now that she knew what it was capable of bringing forth.

The effect was not slow in coming.

Thunder rolled and flashes of lightning seared the temple, streaks of lethal silver attempting to strike down any unworthy mortal gazing upon them. Unearthly noises pierced the dense air like a thousand needles pierces flesh: screeches and moans foreign to the human vocal cords, deafening clatter like an army of ten thousand shaking their weaponry, roars belonging to beasts always whispered of but never seen.

Alethea smothered the panic rising in her best she could. *This must be Tártaros. It must. We've been brought to the deepest pit of the Underworld.*

She could barely discern the other initiates in the dark. Some were frozen in terror, some fidgeted, their raw screams and attempts to ward off evil aligning with the other noise. The hierophants—at least Althea assumed it must be them—drove the people forward and backward in circles like a flock of sheep, thereby creating the illusion of one long wandering.

Then, just as the horror bubbling in Alethea's throat threatened to escape, the escalating noise died down at once and was replaced with the soft music of distant flutes. The cold flashes of silver light warmed to a tranquil glow, which drew towards a point at the far end of the temple hall. As her eyes adapted, Alethea could discern the golden figure of Demeter towering before the initiates, rich garlands of flowers encircling her shoulders and waist, ears of wheat in her hair. The goddess communicated an unmistakable promise, a promise of rebirth of their souls. Alethea felt it flowing strong and vivid in her every vein. She saw before her meadows sprinkled with flowers, the clearest of skies, a pure beauty she had not known she had the predisposition to appreciate.

Although she had not felt any particular aversion towards her eventual fate in the Asphodel Meadows, especially not if the path there offered an honourable exit, now that she had seen this other world it could never be unseen. She knew her soul had been promised a wondrous afterlife, and relished the knowledge despite her principles.

If the other initiates received the same promise, Alethea concluded, they must have quickly transitioned from fearing death to accepting it. She had gone from accepting to truly embracing.

The following evening yet another feast was held, this time a mirthful occasion featuring dancing in the Rharian Fields, where it was said grain first grew. When the clouds cracked with morning light in the early hours, a white bull was sacrificed, and libations poured in honour of the dead.

Alethea stared at the sacred wine being absorbed by the earth. *What an irony. Is it possible to honour the dead, when one has just contributed to their mass?* She said none of this out loud, least of all to Eucleides, who said very little himself. They rarely strayed from one another's side, because doing so felt almost like betraying the secret now entwining them with equal strength as did their affection, but sat in silence while the feast flourished around them and the hierophants chanted over the dying bull.

With the last parts of the mysteries performed, the initiates dispersed and each returned to their deme.

CHAPTER TWENTY-THREE

T HINGS CHANGED AFTER that. The fatal night outside the Telesterion had tied Eucleides closer to Alethea with a thousand invisible, sharp strings that at the same time seemed to pull him farther away from the rest of the world. She *knew*, she had been part of it. Everyone else was like spectators of a play, unaware that he was acting and unable to cross the bar separating bleachers and *orchestra*. Part of him wanted to tear off his mask and show them what lay underneath, part of him was desperate to continue the play for the rest of his life, never faltering a line or a step.

I'm not a violent person. I am not. I prefer words, I always have, I prefer rosy phrases and smiles. And still, though he blamed the *kykeon* for the flashes of burning madness, the brew could not have released that bestial side of him unless it had already existed in some dark corner, draped in illusions.

Athens had lost some of its lustre when he saw it again. The marble on the Acropolis was not quite as bright, the silver-touched olive trees not quite as heavy with fruit, the bustle of the street suddenly agitating. The world seemed a different place.

Indeed, Eucleides no longer feared death, but it was not solely a result of the mysteries themselves. What joy was there in living—in reading and laughing and eating and loving—when one had broken the foremost of humanity's laws, making one a crime against one's own ideals? He kept his eyes to the ground, muddy with the first showers of autumn rain. *Any man or woman I look at could be a grieving friend or relative. Any one of them could be wondering who sent their father or brother to the Underworld without so much as an* obol *under his tongue.*

Entering the *agorá* by the Panathenaic Way, the group turned right to the main square, where temples, *stoas*, and state buildings crammed with beggars, entertainers, and fish mongers. Temporary market stalls were wedged between the established shops with their endless array of offerings: cheeses, onions, cattle, scrolls, wine, pottery, toys, cones of dried fruit and golden-roasted beans.

Eucleides inhaled deeply. The smells were not all pleasant, dung and rotting waste infringing on the more appealing notes, but unlike the stench of Piraeus, he had grown up with it. *Strange that it smells just the same, even after...that. Things don't* look *the same.*

The group consisted of himself, a thickly veiled Efigenia, two male slaves to carry their purchases, and Alethea, who stalked at the front with an empty basket dangling by the crook of her elbow to give the impression of a helpful slave girl. *She only came for my sake, and to escape the house for an hour or two. It's not for Cosimo.*

Word had reached Athens that the fleet was sailing home again so as to not risk being caught and wrecked when the winter winds blew in, ravaging the

Aegean much like the fleet had ravaged the coastal towns. Being defeated by the weather and one's own foolhardiness rather than by the Peloponnese forces would not have been the glorious way to end an empire. Hence, Cosimo's second homecoming was rapidly approaching, and Efigenia had not found it difficult to engage Eucleides in arranging a welcome worthy of a prince.

'Not that one!' she exclaimed as one of the slaves held up a basket of bright red, succulent berries. 'Nothing red. It doesn't please him.'

The layered veil shielded her face completely, but Eucleides could imagine her childishly large eyes somehow made larger by a new tautness to her cheeks. He surveyed the colourful market stall and picked up a honeyed apple by the short stick piercing its core.

'I'll buy you one of these if you like. You didn't have much breakfast, my aunt said.'

She shook her head, veil fluttering. 'No, thank you. I'm content. Thank you.'

Eucleides nodded and returned the sweet to the glaring vendor. They proceeded through the market place, stopping at every other shop and stall to inspect everything from an ivory comb for a gift to a rooster to serve at the welcoming dinner.

With every step, Eucleides felt himself drift further away from the reality of the *agorá*, into a horrible blur of twirling feet and bloodied hands illuminated by flickering torches. Death itself panted in his ear; he could once more taste the *kykeon*. The surge of pain when he reached up to touch his broken, swollen nose only made the memories clearer.

When he could stand it no longer, he touched Alethea's arm. 'Come. You can help me on an errand.' He turned to Efigenia. 'Don't go anywhere. I'll be back in just a little while.'

Alethea latched on to the excuse and they ducked into one of the *stoas*, the shade of the roofed colonnade oddly comforting.

She looked at him properly then, brushing away a hair that had stuck to his lip, and frowned. 'You're not well.'

'I can't stop seeing it all over and over again, except for the part I wish I *could* see, if only to know for certain. It haunts me—'

Alethea nodded. 'We have to cure the pollution, the *miasma*.' She cast a glance over her shoulder to ward off potential eavesdroppers. 'We must find a priest or priestess willing to perform the purifying rites without questions.'

'Yes, yes... All will be better then. I could convince someone.'

'Bring a few shiny coins and be certain.'

'I will. Once we have everything for the homecoming, take Efigenia home, and I'll linger a while. Priests aren't difficult to find. I only hope one of them might see it would be an act of goodness. It would, wouldn't it?'

Alethea gave a one-shouldered shrug, her eyes turned black in the gloom. 'I suppose. If it purifies us in the eyes of the gods, it's good for us, so why not count is as an act of goodness.'

Isn't there a difference?

'How is your nose?'

'Don't worry about that. I'm sure it will heal nicely. And your hand?'

'What?'

'Your hand.' He entwined his fingers with hers. 'Does it still hurt? It looks better than it did when you arrived.'

'It barely hurts now. But I think it will always be stiff.' She grimaced, bending her fingers slightly to demonstrate their immobility.

Eucleides drew her close for a brief kiss before they emerged into the open *agorá*, light stinging their eyes, and re-joined the rest of the little party.

More than another hour went by in search of commodities. Efigenia wanted to buy a hundred things but none she found was quite good enough, while Eucleides thought everything looked satisfactory, and Alethea contributed by cursing the source to the great fuss: Cosimo. Finally, when their feet were battered from walking and the slaves' arms filled with goods, Eucleides separated himself from the group.

Priests were indeed not a rare sight in Athens or in any *polis*, but the task of choosing the right one to approach was not as simple as it had first appeared. The more he trailed around the *agora* spotting sacred figures among common people's mayhem, the more Eucleides hesitated. He made his pick carefully. A man around his father's age, gone almost bald and slack-faced with the turning of the years, became the victim for his quest. A younger man might be too curious, a woman too sensible.

'I need a service performed.'

The man's forehead creased with suspicion. 'Of what nature?'

'Of the purifying kind. A good deed, if you will.' Eucleides dug his nails into his palms, awaiting the verdict.

'Those in need of purification have always done something to sully themselves.' The priest surveyed the young man in front of him with his little pig's eyes and scratched his shiny scalp so that the last trembling hairs fell. 'Where did the pollution spring from? Perhaps your wife has given birth?'

Alethea would lie. I should. But miasma *is different from other pollution, it requires different rites.* 'No, no. I... We need the greatest of purifications. You may take this—' He extracted a handful of glimmering coins from his pocket, quickly estimating two *minae*. '—and know that you will protect Athens from the contagious pollution by means of your services.'

The man squinted at the silver now resting coolly in his own palm, his chapped coral lips parted. 'You speak of bloodshed, then. You wish to escape justice.'

Eucleides forced down the bile rising in his throat. 'Please. Take the money and be reasonable. We will meet you at the Sanctuary of Pandion two hours after dusk tomorrow, my friend and I. Please.'

'Hmm. For the good of the community, then.'

'Yes. For the good of the community.'

Eucleides closed the man's knobbly fingers around the coins, pulled up his *himation* like a shielding hood around his face, and left the *agorá*. *Maybe this is why Efigenia is so fond of her veils. One never has to meet another's eye and thereby reveal the contents of one's heart.*

At the appointed night, Eucleides snuck to the front door, cursing under his breath as he was on the verge of knocking down a precious vase.

Alethea was waiting by the doorpost, having spent the night in the female slaves' quarters to avert any possible suspicion. She stood still as a huntress watching prey, her choppy locks braided back from her face, lips pressed thin.

'Ready?'

'I suppose I must be.'

Hands clasped tightly, they stepped out and let the night's chilly arms encircle them. Finding their way to the Sanctuary of Pandion at the far end of the Acropolis was no more difficult than in daylight. Eucleides knew every street corner like his own pocket, and though they had not been able to bring a torch-carrying slave, their eyes quickly adapted.

The bald priest's silhouette was hunched, his white clothes blending into the marble of the sanctuary. On his arm was looped a rope, which was attached to a much smaller, bleating silhouette.

Dear gods, let him not regret his decision. It is an act of goodness, and I paid fairly.

As they came closer, the man also took a step forward. A sacrificial knife gripped in one hand, the blade reflecting starlight, he spoke. 'You see I have brought both lamb and equipment.'

Eucleides resisted the temptation of letting his eyes wander from the man's face to his knife. *He seeks gratitude. He has it, if not in the flowery terms he wishes for. Not in a moment such as this.*

'Can we begin?' Alethea said, shifting her feet impatiently.

Blood needed cleansing by blood. With harrowing efficiency, the priest slit the lamb's throat and the its life bled out in a single spurt landing in the bowl placed beneath without so much as a stain on its exquisite woollen coat. The priest kneeled and lifted the large, brimming bowl, while the animal collapsed to the ground. He nodded.

Eucleides followed Alethea's example and lowered both hands into the bowl, swallowing hard as the warmth trickled in between his fingers.

The priest proceeded by calling on Zeus Katharsios, who presided over purification from bloodshed, his voice low as if afraid to wake the sleeping citizens. Once finished, after they had washed the blood off their hands in another bowl, he looked at them with a dangerous gleam in his eye.

'I trust you won't tell a living soul what has transpired.'

'That would be foolish. I'm no fool,' Alethea replied.

'Only fools commit heinous acts.'

'I disagree.'

The priest turned to Eucleides. 'Your *friend* should know better than to speak to thus, being a woman.'

Eucleides grasped Alethea's hand. 'We won't quarrel with you. We have paid and you have done good. We bid you farewell now.'

The priest pursed his lips and scooped up the lamb's carcass, placing it across his shoulders with the little hooves dangling below his hips, clicking against one another. 'It's not fitting for a man of my office to carry out this task.'

Eucleides searched for and found three extra *drachmae* in his pocket and gave the silver to the other man. The silent excuse was worth more than words. Then his companion jerked at his hand, signalling their much-longed for departure.

Alethea's short braids bounced against her neck as they half-ran, half-walked down the slope of the Acropolis. 'Do you feel better?' she asked.

'Yes. I must, surely, now that we've done what was necessary. Do you?'

'Naturally.'

Eucleides could detect none of the hesitation in her voice that he felt in his own heart. The *miasma* was, if not wiped out completely, managed; the offended gods would be appeased. The wrath of mankind would not fall upon him unless he confessed, which he could not do, because the consequences were far too severe: exile robbing him of all he held dear in life, Alethea endangered, his *oikos* muddled with shame, and Cosimo's plans of a joint political career shattered. And still, still no purification in the world could undo what he had done. No rites could clean his conscience the way they had cleaned his hands.

Having arrived once more at the doorstep, Alethea pulled him close, their lips brushing, before she hurried back up the staircase to the slaves' dormitory. Eucleides remained for a long while, a tinge of salt and wine lingering from her kiss. *She can't have played any great part—it's impossible. It must have been me.* In his eyes, though he knew well she was no dainty flower, Althea was as unlikely to have committed the murder as the moon was to fall from the sky. In his quest for Great Love, the Beloved lacked faults. His affections would not alter if she *had* slaughtered a hundred in cold blood, but it was not in his nature to assume such a thing to be a possibility.

She'd tell me it's a destructive quality I have. But what kind of person would I be to even ask? If she did it, I'm absolved—but I can't ask. He caught sight of a last rim of clotted blood under one of his nails and removed it hastily. Then, he snuck back to his bedchamber, careful not to touch the fragile vase.

Cosimo arrived three days later, bearing the expression of a man who has done great deeds and is aware of it, waiting for the common little people to raise their voices in accolade. However, he was forced to settle for the simplicity of a warm welcome.

Alethea almost bit through her tongue when she spotted his high cheekbones and blue-veined underarms in the hall. Some part of her had still been clinging to the possibility of him drowning at sea or, even better, getting that swan-like throat ripped open by a Peloponnese soldier. *And now he will stay until next season, when the fleet can sail again.* The hate she had felt for him but almost managed to forget during his absence began to brew hotly again.

The taste of blood in her mouth only grew as Eucleides embraced his cousin with all the sincerity she knew his arms to contain. 'Welcome home.'

'It's a pleasant sight.'

'Yes, yes, I can imagine. Come. We've prepared quite the feast, and I'll not watch you pick your way through it.'

'I merely have a refined taste for delicacies.'

Alethea's sole comfort that evening, small as it was, was that no one asked her to help prepare the dinner nor serve it. Instead, she found a few moments of much-needed solitude, which she spent practising the age-old dance she had once performed at the Hyacinthia. Twirling on bare toes in one of the storage rooms, she imagined herself dancing before an audience of gods and legendary heroes, an illusion shattered every time voices from the *andron* carried through the house. *At least one of them is nice to listen to. If that voice goes away, I'll rather stuff my ears than hear just the rest.*

Once her feet were sore and worn, her lungs exhausted, she sank down and rested her head against the wall. Time appeared infinite yet was passing with alarming velocity. With each heartbeat, Alethea felt as if she was losing another fragment of Eucleides to his cousin and there was nothing she could do to stop Cosimo from wholly taking what had been his for so many years. *At least he hasn't managed to turn him cold and stale in all that time. Perhaps he hasn't tried—even that filthy* gràson *must enjoy the sun sometimes.*

If Cosimo noticed the change of character in Eucleides, which Alethea did not doubt he would, there would be larger issues at hand. A concerned, or rather suspicious, family member with just the right amount of tenacity could pose a dangerous threat to the secret she helped guarding.

Eucleides shall have to keep his heart locked and throw away the key. Or give it to me.

CHAPTER TWENTY-FOUR

D URING HER CHILDHOOD, Efigenia had developed an exceptional skill for observing others and analysing their every whim, and she had perfected this skill while married.

As her husband strode across the room to robe himself after having performed his marital duties, his clammy feet sticking to the cold stone floor with every step, she saw no signs of vexation on his face. Rather, his expression was that of someone who had spent hours on end reading tedious law scrolls or listening to a lecture.

Efigenia pulled up her knees to her chest like a knobby shield, the sheet too sheer to protect her modesty where she sat. *When will be the next time? Within a few days, or longer?* She did not know what she hoped most for: that he would spend every hour of every day in her bed, or that he would never return at all.

'I assume you haven't noticed how strange my cousin is behaving,' Cosimo said, pouring crystal-clear water from a decanter into a cup. He sipped and closed his eyes in relish.

'I...I have noticed. I have.'

'When did it start, then?'

'When he came back from Eleusis with the Spartan—five...six days before your blessed homecoming.'

'I see. It must be her fault. Of course, losing one's character is only what one should expect when fraternising with a savage like her.'

Efigenia glowed at this extraordinarily long dialogue, not to speak of the opportunity of picking a mutual enemy. 'Yes, yes, you're right. Her fault.'

Cosimo turned to face her. 'You should have told me sooner.'

'I...I trusted you didn't need my advice.'

'I never said I did. Well. At least you see the Spartan for the viper she is. Not everyone in this house does.'

'I do.'

Cosimo nodded and emptied the cup, then fastened the gleaming silver *fibulae* holding his *khitōn* at his shoulders. Without another word, he returned the cup to the table and slid out through the door.

Efigenia stretched out her legs before her, sitting exposed in her solace, twisting a garland of hair around her index finger. She reached underneath one of the pillows and extracted a tiny bottle filled with a sluggish brown tincture: deer's blood with fennel and fir ash. One sip was supposed to increase chances of conceiving. Then began the same thought process she went through every time Cosimo left her chamber. *I want him near. It is my duty. I need a child. He may be resigned, but a man shouldn't fawn. And he looks like a celestial deity—silly girl, I should be grateful.* Once the nasty sensation bubbling in her chest had first settled to a simmering and later cooled completely, she drifted off to sleep.

The following morning, Efigenia heard her father's flinty voice traveling up the staircase like smoke curling from a chimney. She started to her feet, shooing away the two women who had been applying lavender oil to her hair, and gazed into the mirror's bronze reflection.

I can't show myself in this state...barely dressed, and...it would only make me a disgrace! Still, her father had never before visited the house—indeed, Efigenia had not spoken with him since the wedding. As long as he received no complaints on her husband's behalf, Thaddeus saw no reason to interfere, hence she concluded that he must either be the bearer of great fortune or the messenger of great tragedy.

Efigenia stared in the mirror again. 'Come back!' she called after the departing slaves, who halted in their step and returned to her side with puckered lips as if sucking on sour olives.

'Finish my dressing only. You may leave the rest of my toilette until I say.'

Once she was presentable enough for this unusual occasion—though still with her hair painfully unadorned and with three balms left to massage into her skin—Efigenia swallowed and descended the stairs.

Thaddeus' crown of downy hair the colour of sand in warm sunlight was the first sight that met her; she owed her complexion to him rather than to her swarthy mother. The second sight was the grief painted with harsh brushstrokes across his face. A moment passed before he seemed to recognise his youngest daughter. Efigenia knew she must look thinner than the last time they met, perhaps older too, but Thaddeus was too sensible to ever draw attention to a woman's appearance by commenting on it.

'Efigenia.' Her name was unwieldy on his lips.

'Father? Forgive me. I should have waited for you to summon me.'

'Yes. But it's no matter now.'

Efigenia tensed and waited. *If he doesn't care, then the news he brings must indeed be grave.*

'I come to tell you of your sister's unfortunate fate. It seems the birth of her child was too great a strain.'

Dead? In childbirth? She had a vague recollection of hearing about her older sister's pregnancy shortly after her own wedding, but had thought little of it since then. Another chunk of envy she had rather not touched upon, a joy she knew she was supposed to feel but could not, and had therefore ignored.

Cosimo, who had been talking with her father before she arrived, cleared his throat and arched an eyebrow. He turned to Thaddeus, his voice sweet as honey. 'It grieves me to hear of your loss. And the child, if I may ask?'

'A healthy boy, gods be blessed.'

'Then let that be a comfort to yourself and the woman's husband.'

'Indeed.' Thaddeus nodded several times, then gestured for a slave who had accompanied him to step forward. The man was holding a large packet swathed in linen, which he now offered to his master.

Thaddeus, in turn, gave it to Efigenia. 'I believe your sister wished you to have this. She thought it might be a pleasant pastime.'

Efigenia stared at the package, too stunned by her father's words to ask what it contained. She did not have to, however, for the familiar shape of a lyre was apparent through the cloth. *Will I ever play as well as she did? Silly girl, no one can.*

'I hope you enjoy music?' Thaddeus asked his son-in-law.

'When it's performed with skilled fingers, yes, I do.'

'I assure you my daughter is skilled enough in this field. Her mother thought the loom was more useful, or course, but she'll play if you please.'

'I'm sure you're right.'

'I bid you farewell now. Daughter—' He touched her cheek briefly. 'Remember your demeanour.' With those words, Thaddeus waved for his slave and the two departed.

Cosimo lifted a fold of the linen and eyed the lyre: a masterfully crafted instrument embossed with gold and with strings sharp enough to cut through flesh. 'You can practice with my mother. She won't mind.'

Lady Milos would not have minded even if half the strings had snapped. She had no ear for music and was content to sit counting *drachmae* with Efigenia's melodies in the background. At first, they faltered a little, but as her fingers picked up the rhythm they had used to know, the tunes flowed like spring water, clear and irresistible.

'You may have to play for me more often, girl, now that my nephew appears to have abandoned my company.'

Efigenia rested the lyre in her lap, tracing a swirling line of gold with her finger. 'He could never do that, surely?'

'Pah! It's no fault of his, the dear boy. I think it must be the slave girl. I warned him, I did.'

'Cosimo said so also, he said she had made him lose his cheery character. He knows best, and that's what he said.'

Lady Milos scoffed and reached for a plum coated in crushed walnuts, chewing with admirable ferocity. 'He does *not* know best—though in this instance I'm complied to agree. That girl has taken her city's strange ideas to our house, and my son is at fault. He should never have brought her here.'

Efigenia shifted her weight. *No, no I wish he hadn't.* She searched her mind for a different subject. 'My sister was a kind soul. I shall miss her.'

'Missing does little good. Your parents have other children?'

'Only me, now. They had a son, too, but...but he didn't live very long.'

Lady Milos' lower lip trembled slightly. Had Efigenia not known her better, she could have sworn she saw the woman swallow tears along with the plum.

'Is anything the matter?'

'Don't fret over me, girl. I'm no child in need of comfort.'

I should have thought. How stupid, insensitive...her own sons... She lowered her eyes to the lyre. 'Should I play some more?'

It was, however, too late; the embankment of the older woman's emotions had burst. 'Little Silvius—my youngest—was only this high, three, I think, yes, three. And Meonides seven. And my poor husband—' Lady Milos fumbled in search of a napkin, which the slave fanning her finally handed her. She blew her nose, loud enough to command an army into battle thinking they had heard the trumpet sound. '—and what was I left with? A single son, begotten cruelly, trotting about healthy as a horse while his sweet brothers were sent to Hades' realm!'

Efigenia could only stare. Never could she have anticipated that the innocent conversation would unravel such a dramatic display. Judging by her mother-in-law's usually so composed and shiny surface, Efigenia had struck a terrible chord, unleashing what lay underneath all the pragmatism. *Stupid, stupid... Now you made her weep.*

'Please... Let me fetch you another plum,' she offered, both as consonance to the other woman and for herself, because seeing another eat often gave Efigenia drops of peculiar pleasure.

Lady Milos shook her head. 'Get one for yourself, if you will. I don't feel very well.'

'No, no, of course. I'm sorry.'

'Don't be, dear. It wasn't you who sent the sickness that took them.'

A few moments passed in silence interrupted only by the flapping of the wooden fan and the occasional trumpet-like snivel. Despite the autumn winds stealing in through the shutters, quite a bit of stagnant warmth was trapped in the *gynaikeion* and Efigenia cringed at the prickling feeling of sweat drying on her lower back.

Lady Milos banished her tears and her voice seemed to shrivel back from soaked to rattling dry leaves. 'You're the one who should be in distress, not I. Your sorrows are far fresher.'

'I prefer to be in distress alone—or one might distress others, too.'

'True. Let them be distressed.'

'I could not.'

Lady Milos gave her a stern look. 'Your mother must have been quite the tyrant, or your father. It's all very well that you should know your place and not fuss too much, but sometimes you remind me of a dove run flat by a cart wheel.'

Efigenia resumed studying the patterns on lyre, imagining it tenderly in her sister's hands, the sorrow Lady Milos had spoken of slowly creeping in on her in a surprisingly subtle manner. *Perhaps I'm not one to mourn. Perhaps I'm too cold-hearted, or too numb... Though too great an emotion would be unwelcomed also.*

'I'm sorry you think of me in that way. I shall do better.'

Lady Milos only shook her head.

Cosimo yanked at Alethea's neckline but the gesture was not as forceful as he must have intended, and she remained with her feet steadily planted. His perfectly sculpted brows knitted and the eyes below flickered with vexation, but his voice was like ice-melted water. 'You will answer what I ask you.' In the absence of a reply, he continued. 'My cousin is dear to me. I don't understand his temporary infatuation with a savage harlot like *you*, but I think you can tell me one or two things.'

I didn't know you could think beyond yourself. Alethea pulled away from his grip effortlessly. 'What is it you want to know?'

'Ever since you returned from Eleusis, he has been like a shadow of himself, like a man bereft of all cheer. What did you do to poison his mind?'

'Nothing,' she spat. 'I've done what I can to bring his *cheer* back.'

'You're the least loving person I have encountered. Perhaps women of your sort are like that.'

'You're not exactly Aphrodite yourself.'

'*Something* happened to my cousin and you will tell me what that was.' Cosimo's jaw was almost too tight for him to speak.

'Why ask me and not him?'

'You know very well.'

Alethea did know. *Because he thinks saying it out loud would take away the last golden sliver of purity he clings on to.*

Cosimo took a step back, the distaste written plainly on his face. He wiped his one hand on his tunic as if touching her had defiled it. 'Perhaps you don't know after all. Perhaps you are not so close to him as you think.'

'You should spend more time with your wife and less harassing me. The two of you can have fun being vile together.'

'Be quiet. A slave only speaks when spoken to.' On that note, he glided away, the two well-groomed dogs strutting at his heels and wagging their tails.

Alethea's glare could have pierced the back of his head—or cracked it like the man in Eleusis'. *If I was his dog, I would bite, not wag my tail like a dimwit. That filthy bastard.*

She clung to the man from behind, clawing at his eyes, digging her nails into his arm, trying to hold him back. Eucleides struggled to his feet with one hand covering his broken nose—and began stabbing blindly with the hairpin as if with a small dagger. On the fourth try, he thrust it deep into the space between the man's shoulder and sinewy throat, blood spurting as the pin punctured a vein. The wound was not fatal, Alethea guessed, but enough to make him howl with pain and stagger backwards.

For a moment, the man swooned, Alethea's weight on his back and the rapid loss of blood impeding his balance. Then, there was the sound of an egg cracking as his head collided with the edge of one of the marble steps leading up to the Telesterion.

She lay squashed under him. With Eucleides' help, she turned the man over and crawled out, hands dripping red.

Alethea drew a sharp breath. Her glance darted around the slaves' dormitory, landing on her hands. She could not discern their colour in the dark, but putting them to her cheeks, she felt only the dryness of her palms—no sticky brains, no blood witnessing of sin.

'Hmm. Bad dream?' Agathe's voice pierced the silence just like the pin had pierced the man's skin.

Alethea nodded, pulling the blanket closer and turning to face the wall. *But it wasn't a dream. It was memory, it must have been. No dream can be that real.*

In the midst of the distraught whirlpool now drowning her was an inkling of relief, for there was another who bore even greater guilt than herself; there was another who had dealt the fatal blow. *If he knew... No. He's close enough to breaking already. If that little doubt, that piece of hope, is taken from him...* Alethea decided in that same moment to keep her lips sealed at least for the time being. She *knew*. The scenes played up so brutally in her head could be nothing but the truth, but, as she often reasoned, the knowledge one kept to oneself became at once harmless.

It was during the early morning hours of soft light and chirping birds that Alethea found Eucleides pacing back and forth on the roof. The city stirred slowly beneath, a swarm of people waking to life after the sweet spell of night.

Dark blue shadows hung under Eucleides' eyes, his hair a bird's nest of tangles. Alethea had not noticed when he slipped out from the bedchamber but suspected he had not slept long before the nightmares pulled him to his feet.

She tapped his arm. 'You're thinking too much.'

'How could I not? A guilty man ought to think about his crime.'

A guilty man. A bolt of realisation struck Alethea to the core. *Of course.* Hesitating only a heartbeat, she placed her hands on his shoulders and mustered all the conviction she could, grateful that they were of a height so that she did not have to look up at him.

'I have…remembered. Not everything, but more. I can see parts—the important parts—clearly now.'

Eucleides' shoulders stiffened under her hands. 'And what do you see?'

'Myself. The guilt is mine.'

'But my hands, and my clothes, they were—'

'You were there. Of course you were stained. You were there, but that was all.' An inkling of pride hit Alethea; she could not help herself. It was the same every time she spotted the complete belief in the eyes of those she lied to, more so when it served the best of purposes.

'Then I haven't…taken a life?'

'No.'

'And you have. And I love a murderess. By Aphrodite, is there no mercy?'

Alethea froze. *Love. No. You can't. Love?* Her lips were dry as withered grass. She had told Apolonio many times how she loved him, though as the years went by, it had become so self-evident that it seemed almost ridiculous to speak it. She had told her mother and Delina a few times, her father once when she was little. She did not mind expressing it, as long as no flowery speeches of everlasting devotion were required, but this was different.

A hundred intense days they had known each other, and although a genuine bond had developed beyond doubt, that bond had sprung from her own ambitions and later from a mutual secret. Furthermore, even if she might name the affection, confessing to it would create an attachment to a place and a culture she must part from if she wanted to see her brother again. Eucleides had come to symbolise Athens, and Alethea could not afford to choose Athens over Apolonio and Sparta.

To her relief, Eucleides had not stopped to ponder her lack of words. Love came as smoothly to him as water over pebbles, and he risked little by declaring it. *Maybe unrequited love doesn't exist in his universe. Maybe he takes it all for granted.*

'Alethea?'

'What?'

'Are you going to be alright?'

'What do you mean?'

'I only know I was not—I'm still not. And now, now that we know, you'll have to carry the burden. I almost wish it had been me.'

'You were crushed to fragments when you thought that.' *Don't tell me I lied in vain.* 'We have rid ourselves of the *miasma*, that's what matters. And I've survived worse, both me and my conscience.'

Eucleides traced her lip with his thumb. 'There's something else. Pericles is sending armed forces to raid the Megarid. It's been decided, it can't wait any longer, they say. Athens must act.'

'You're going with them?'

'It was not my choice to make.'

'I know.' Alethea's stomach turned. Her hand lashed out as if to hold him there with her on the roof forever, morning light like whirlpools in his tousled hair. *Shall I be robbed of everything I love? Or don't love. It seems so.*

She swallowed. 'When do you leave?'

'The troops will be ready within a fortnight, I should think. I...I fear for you.'

'For me? I'm not the one going to war. I wish I was, for both of our sakes.'

Eucleides laughed; it was a half-strangled sound, like the scraping of a rundown olive press left unused too long. 'No woman has ever said that to me before, though I'm sure it might have been true in many cases. No, I mean I fear to leave you alone in this house for so long. As much as I care for them, my family sometimes doesn't know how to treat you well. They only have the best of intentions but—'

Alethea took a step back, a sour taste at once on her tongue. *The best of intentions! Ha!* The streets below now buzzed with everything from cackling hens to loafing young men and scurrying workers, from lowly women carrying water from the *agorá* to slaves escorting the children of wealthier families to their tutoring. It all felt too close, too loud, their curious glances reaching the roof and making her skin itch.

'—but I hope you won't be lonely. If you are, speak to my father. He may be ailed with age and forgetfulness, sometimes capricious even, yet his heart is kind.'

'A rare thing.'

'Promise you will.'

'I promise.'

A growl from Eucleides' stomach startled them both. As if it had signalled an unspoken agreement, they climbed the ladder down from the roof's limestone face in search of breakfast. They had done the very same thing more often than Alethea could remember, yet this particular time, the well-rehearsed movements felt foreign and unnatural.

I lifted the weight of his shoulders, I made him laugh for the first time since that night, and now the fates whisk him away from me within a fortnight. Perhaps Aphrodite really has no mercy.

CHAPTER TWENTY–FIVE

THE KNOWLEDGE OF his relative innocence in the slaughter did not prove the consolation Eucleides had hoped. The blood had not been his doing according to Alethea, at least not solely, but he had *been* there. He had never been as squeamish as Cosimo upon seeing animals killed, yet brutal death was not a sight he enjoyed, and it was a sight that could haunt even the bystander.

Moreover, there was the alteration to Alethea's character as he perceived it: no less loved, yet concerning in her matter-of-fact attitude towards her crime. It did not fit his idea of a lover—but then little in her *did* fit, and he would rather have her level-headed than agonized to the extent he himself had been. *Perhaps it's the Spartan culture, perhaps it's what killing in battle does to a person. Those things would dull one's sensitivity, I suppose. Or, she's far more sensible than I and wholly trusts it was the* kykeon's *doing an nothing else.*

He thought of her eyes when she had told him: unrelenting as ever. What had he said to her? *I mentioned love...* A cold hand closed around his heart, squeezing out the initial warmth. *And she said nothing, not of* that. In the moment, he had not reflected upon it. Being drilled in hearing the word *love* returned, he had assumed it would be this time too, not until now realising it had not been. This was a foreign phenomenon, an absurdity, a possibility never before presented to him.

Other girls had never even hesitated—whether this was because there was indeed love brewing in them or because they knew their inferior social position and thus felt compelled, Eucleides had never asked himself. Ten, fifteen such uniform replies he had drawn easily from rose-petal lips, always presuming that *if* there was no such reply, he could just as easily re-direct his own affections towards some more receptive paramour. Now, though, nothing seemed more impossible, and for the first time he was frustrated by how love can come so easily when called upon but seldom goes away when dismissed.

Eucleides decided to consult the man who had played his sole advisor for many years and been rather successful.

'I really don't see the issue, cousin. The solution is simple: take another mistress, if whatever comes out of her mouth is so important.' Cosimo drew his arm back in a wide arch and sent the ball of knotted leather flying across the courtyard, a floppy-eared dog sprinting after it the minute if left his hand.

Eucleides leaned against one of the columns. 'But don't you see? I can't. If I did, it wouldn't matter if that woman loved me, because I wouldn't love *her*.'

'It's no news to me that you love the wrong person.'

'It is to me—if it's true, which I don't know if it is.'

'Of course it's true.' Cosimo bent down to coax the ball from the dog's jaw, scratched the animal's neck, then threw again. 'Spartans are not the sentimental kind, and it's high time you realised it.'

Eucleides sighed. 'I know that, but one doesn't have to be sentimental to love. Maybe I'm interpreting far too much. Maybe she just thought the moment was poorly chosen. It was, I suppose.'

'What kind of moment?'

'Oh—never mind that. But you've never suffered like this?'

'Not that I can recall. Why bother? I think you'll find yourself with greater concerns on your mind soon enough.'

Oh dear gods. Eucleides stood erect from his leaning position, cold dread racing up his spine. Cosimo's forebodings were never a good sign. Indeed, his eyes were grim, and there lay genuine anxiety in the way his hands twitched when not petting the dog.

'It concerns the Megarid.'

Eucleides' insides revolted. 'I know they're sending a force. I was there, remember?'

'Yes. What you don't know is that you'll depart in three days' time.' The words were pronounced slowly as if it hurt, but were only made worse by it, much like pulling out a splinter.

Three days. Three days is nothing, nothing... 'Why was I not informed?'

'You just haven't seen the plaque yet. It's pinned up in the *agora.*'

Eucleides stared. He had not visited the *agorá* since the day before yesterday, but spent the hours lost in Hesiod's *Works and Days*, not knowing what news ran through Athens. The realisation that time was even more precious than he might have guessed made him shudder.

'I have to pray, and I have to tell Alethea, or she might despair. Perhaps there's no need to fear that, but I have to tell her nonetheless.' Eucleides made a start to leave, but Cosimo's fingers encircled his wrist.

'*I* will despair. Now, if you would only take your mind off that woman and listen to me.' The uncharacteristically desperate note lodged deep in his voice made Eucleides attentive. 'Be courageous, but not reckless, clever rather than bold. It's only a raid, or so those cursed *strategoi* claim. Unless the Peloponnese assemble their forces like the *panoùgroi* they are, you may stay quite safe.'

Safer than you were at sea, I'm sure. I shouldn't make such a fuss. Despite these rational thoughts, instincts screamed louder, and Eucleides gripped both Cosimo's cool hands in his own. 'I don't want to destroy their crops and make them starve, burn their farms and—' he began. 'It's cruel and it's brutal and I won't have anything to read or anyone to embrace. And Alethea... You must promise me to treat her better than you have!'

Cosimo's lips puckered almost unnoticeably. 'She's a slave, and one of them, which is worse.'

'Promise me?'

A moment of tensed breaths and thick air passed. Eucleides refused to blink.

Then the other man nodded. 'Only for you, I shan't bother her. Nor will I pamper—only a fool would—but she'll have no great complains.'

'Thank you. Thank you.'

Three days passed with dizzying velocity, each hour flickering by like ash in the wind, before Eucleides had the chance to truly treasure them, though he tried his utmost by filling each moment with all life's earthly delights and pleasures. However, there was a limit to the number of honey-basted pieces of bread he could eat, the number of comedic plays and stimulating discussions he could indulge in, before he had to leave.

Farewells had never been his strongest suit. Luckily there had been few in his life, giving him little practice. Hence, the throng of family and slaves assembled in the hall on the morning of the third day baffled him. *They must think it strange of me to dread an expedition most men would long to go on. It won't even be very for long.*

Lady Milos' pillow-arms literally pulled him out of his reflections as she drew him close in the intimate way that she had reserved for her nephew ever since he was a child. She squeezed with admirable strength, her clusters of bracelets cutting into his own arms.

'Goodbye, aunt. Please, don't fret in vain,' he pressed forth.

Lady Milos took a step back and smoothened her crumpled *khitōn*. 'I never do. I know better.' Her voice rose to a pitch.

Next came Efigenia; the quick glance she gave him brimmed with more than she would say. 'We will pray for your quick return.'

'Take care of yourself—properly.'

Efigenia nodded. He considered planting a kiss on her forehead but refrained.

Cosimo's embrace was cold and warm all at once. Neither he nor Achaikos spoke a word, but Eucleides could see the anguish lurking in their eyes, even behind the confused fog always present in his father's.

Having checked off each of his family members with increasing difficulty, he at last arrived at his final trial: Aletha. She had sunk into the line of slaves but failed to blend in completely where she stood with her arms crossed and her chin jutted forward. It was perhaps not an ideal farewell, before the eyes of everyone, but Lady Milos had ordered all the household staff to be present, and Eucleides had kept postponing their last encounter.

Now, Alethea took a step towards him, her voice low enough to ward off eavesdroppers. 'This isn't how we send people off to war in Sparta, but I'll say it nonetheless. I'd rather have you live a coward than die a hero.'

Eucleides nodded, swallowing. 'Is there anything else you want to say before I go?'

There was a moment's hesitation, just enough for him to catch the guilty flicker in her face. *She knows what I mean. She wants to say it, surely.*

'No. No, go.'

'I'll see you in a while, then.' On that note, he turned on his heel and left behind what felt like half his heart and all his hope.

Nikephoros, the ash-grey mare Cosimo had so delightedly named—no doubt with thus far unrealised visions of his cousin's great victories on horseback—turned her pointy ears towards the noise, nostrils emitting steaming breath.

Eucleides reached out, careful not to slide off her slippery back, and lightly patted her coarse mane. He had never understood horses the way he at least thought he understood humans. The animals were far simpler to please for the moment and yet far more difficult to charm completely. *All the apples in the world couldn't win that creature's true loyalty.*

The Athenian cavalry was one boisterous mass of heavily armed men, weapons, horses scratching the Attic soil with their hooves, and slaves running about between their owners fetching cups of diluted wine or whatever else the man in question might order.

Eucleides did not know the exact number of *hippeis*, nor could he count them as they all appeared the same to him in their uniform armour and faces shadowed by Boeotian helmets, but he would not have been surprised if they amounted to a thousand. Moreover, the troops consisted of almost ten thousand citizen *hoplites* as well as the light-armed infantry and three thousand *métoikoi*; in addition to these came the countless slaves and servants. Eucleides had brought two men of his own, but had dismissed them for the moment. This number of soldiers was abundant in order to raid the Megarid but it certainly provided the show of force and relief of tension which Athens had been in dire need of. Indeed, Pericles had taken a plunge, leading the army himself, the plume of his helmet fluttering behind him in the wind like a gigantic scarlet butterfly.

The butterfly might as well have lodged in Eucleides' stomach. As he looked around him, he saw nothing but lunatics yearning to destroy and ravage, although this was hardly the truth.

A trumpet sounded. The slaves were dismissed, the horses pulled into formation. The *hoplites'* greaves chafed against each other as they shuffled into place. The raiding of the Megarid began.

Despite his customary two ephebe years in military training, Eucleides had never seen chaos of this nature before. Alethea had recounted to him several times what she had heard and seen during her time with the Spartan army, but nothing could have prepared him for the utter mass destruction of perfectly good land he now took part in. Crops and olive groves cut to stumps and roots staring back at the soldiers, accusing, farm houses burnt to their foundations, clouds of black smoke rising from the dismal remains.

Eventually, Eucleides submitted to the unavoidable task, mechanically raising his arm to slash down cattle or galloping Nikephoros over the Megarian harvest, allowing her hooves to trample grain beyond rescue. He watched others do the same and found some obscure little comfort in that. *It's not my choice, only my duty. That's what Alethea would say, regardless of whose side it benefitted. And it's all for Athens. Glorious, wondrous Athens.* With this sentiment safely imprinted, the brutal activities became marginally easier to endure. The days passed in a monotone manner. The area was vaster than Eucleides had anticipated and laying waste to it took surprisingly long considering the scale of the army. No attempt was made to capture Megara, though. Such an endeavour would have been foolhardy, since it would have required valuable manpower to stay behind and keep the city under submission. Pericles hoped, it was rumoured, that the raiding in addition to the trade embargo, which had been the result of the Megarian Decree a year and a half ago, would suffice to make the Megarians succumb to Athenian rule.

Life in field was to Eucleides a near torturous existence: the food plain and dry on his tongue, the wine on the verge of sour, the company dull and the bedrolls too uncomfortable to offer a solid night's sleep. Every evening, when he dismounted Nikephoros and withdrew to his tent, he yearned for the familiar scent of his scrolls as well as the taste of ripe figs and lush bread and the view from the roof. *How can anyone enjoy this kind of life? Maybe Alethea would...*

The thought of her stung like a needle with barbs being twisted in his chest. It was not hurt or disappointment—not the most prominent pain, at least—but pure missing. His qualms about loving one who had not immediately and expressively returned the emotion were wiped out; her absence had convinced him that none of that mattered as long as he was allowed to be near her. *If she'll let me, that shall be enough. Perhaps with time... As long as she'll let me be there, I can be joyful enough.*

He did not fully comprehend just how fundamentally different such a relationship would be from the Great Love he had spent the last seven, eight years searching for, different even from the delightful little affairs he had busied himself with in the process. It simply did not matter, because to linger forever in Alethea's company with a certain measure of affection seemed twice as appealing to him now as exchanging love serenades with any other.

Furthermore, Eucleides was of the firm belief that hands united in manslaughter, vile as the act had been, could not be so easily wrung apart. The dead man from Eleusis only haunted his dreams occasionally now, as opposed to the nightly visits which the wandering spirit had used to pay him, wailing and glaring. Though he hesitated to acknowledge it, the rough experience of raiding helped in this one aspect, dulling the sharp edges of what had happened. He had grown accustomed to violent sights. *This must be why some claim they feel nothing when killing in battle.* The realisation was sickening.

Eucleides had lost count of the days, and knew only that less than a month had passed when Pericles withdrew the troops behind the Long Walls again, releasing the soldiers from active duty for the time being. Few had been injured in the handful of minor skirmishes with the Megarians—too small to be called even that—and fewer still had perished.

Nikephoros trotted through the Dipylon Gate with the enforced dignity of a mare who would rather run free than take part in the procession back to Athens. Eucleides was not of the same opinion. He had had quite enough of the world outside the walls, however enchanting it could be to read about.

From the Dipylon Gate the Panathenaic Way stretched and curved through the *agorá*: the easiest way home to Collytus. The street swarmed with the usual clutter of labourers and craftsmen, travellers and slaves, goats and hens, all contributing to the noise and smell Eucleides knew so well. A few of the passers-by caught his glance—but none in the way of a young woman farther down.

The woman was clutching an *amphora* from which olive oil trickled as the vessel bounced against her hip when she walked. A choppy nest of hair was tied back from her face, revealing a set jaw and above it a knotted scar. Alethea kept her eyes fixed on the wobbly *amphora*—her carrying technique seeming only a little improved from when she had dropped one from the second floor on that first day—then looked up for a moment and halted.

Eucleides' heart flipped in his chest. No matter how much he had thought of her, imagined taking her in his arms, seeing her again here on the dusty road felt like diving off a cliff into the unknown, and everything he had thought to say was at once trapped in his throat

The two of them remained stiff as statues staring ahead stupefied, moulded from different clay and by different sculptors. Finally, as a man on a donkey behind him shouted something indiscernible, Eucleides dismounted and continued forward by foot. *If only I could see her eyes clearer, maybe I could tell what she's thinking. But no, no, that never quite worked before.*

Alethea waited on the spot, still clutching the *amphora* like a mother holding a small child. Her tongue flickered over her lips in a flash of pink.

Eucleides stopped before her and let his hand holding Nikephoros' reins drop to his side. '*Khaíre.*'

'Hello to you too.'

'I've returned in one piece just like you wished me to.' The words felt too smug in his mouth. *Maybe she never did. Maybe I just remembered what I wanted to remember.*

Alethea nodded slowly. 'I can see that. I'm glad. Truly.'

A few moments passed, nothing more being uttered, the bustle of the Panathenaic Way failing to drown Eucleides' own ear-deafening heartbeats. *I have to tell her what I've concluded: that it doesn't matter if she'll say it, that all I ask for is her company. I have to tell her* now. He swallowed and opened his mouth, but did not get the chance.

'I do love you, I do, I swear it, only it's not so simple. I have so much to lose, don't you see? You don't. But I love you, cursed—' She squeezed her lips shut as if taken back by her own outburst, the *amphora* almost slipping from her grip.

What happened next was beyond all bounds of decency and perhaps because it was, it was also inevitable. Eucleides, in a fit of pure ecstasy, abandoned Nikephoros' reins and scooped Alethea off the ground, the *amphora* being crushed against the stones below in a flurry of oil and knife-sharp potsherds. She emitted a startled shriek and he quickly put her down, his arms buckling under a heavier weight than he had expected. Once safe and steady on the ground again, she held him close, and he revelled in the silky touch of hair against his cheek, the curve of her neck where his chin fitted so perfectly. The sky could have crumbled down on his shoulders, and Eucleides would hardly have felt it.

People stopped in their tracks to cast curious glances; a few fired snide comments.

Alethea pulled back slightly, visibly trying to hide a smile. 'How sentimental you're being. Come.'

'What about your oil?'

'Efigenia can manage without it. She's oily enough all on her own.'

If Cosimo's return from the fleet had been a success in the *oikos* save for his mother and a majority of the slaves, Eucleides' far surpassed it, though his absence had been both shorter and a less dangerous endeavour. Three thorough embraces and one shy '*welcome*' were given and received, after which his family members set to the task of kindly cross-examining him on every last detail of the raids.

Alethea almost slid back to her favourite storage room, where she would sometimes hide and wait for his relatives to resign, but Eucleides took her by the hand and presented a *klismos* identical to the others', half-blind to and half-defiant of the strange social collision her presence as an equal was. *Let them stare. It's unconventional, but after what she told me I couldn't have it otherwise.*

And stare they did, everyone except Achaikos, whose gaze was far away, each one giving the comical impression of competing in who could look the most aghast.

That night, cold and quiet and heavy with rain that never fell, was the sweetest bliss Eucleides had known for a long time, in stark contrast to all the lonesome nights preceding it. A crust of clouds coated the sky, filtering the moonlight to a soft mother-of-pearl daze; the stars were only barely visible and appeared broken loose from their constellations. The chirping of crickets and the rustle of the wind was the only sound hanging in the air, as is often the case on Mediterranean nights.

Alethea turned in Eucleides' arms where they lay on the roof, having ignored the coming of autumn's chill in favour of the naked sky. She propped herself on her elbow.

'If anyone had told me half a year ago that this is where I would be now, I would have called them mad.'

'Would you have been happy, had you believed them?'

'No, furious. But I'm not now.'

'Good. I know your fury well enough to dread the very mention of it.' Eucleides smiled. *Dread and adore both, strangely.*

'I don't think you'll face it too soon.'

He drew her closer, and all the grimness of war, the nastiness of murder, diminished.

Golden autumn crept smoothly towards biting winter, the days passing in a haze of crisp mornings and warm touches. The months of *Maimakterion* and *Poseidon* came and went. On the eighth day of the latter, Athens paused its usual labouring to celebrate an agricultural festival in honour of Poseidon and Athena.

Alethea's own labours seemed easier with each passing day. Perhaps it was the making of a habit, perhaps Eucleides sought every possibility to lighten her burden, elevating her to a strange position where to him she was above everything and to the rest of the *oikos* she was a lowly slave with undeserved privileges. The other slaves, especially the women, cast envious, even bitter, glances, and Alethea could not blame them. After all, some of them might themselves have nourished a hope of obtaining the rare status she now held in the household.

Life was no longer just barely endurable but, sometimes, treading carefully on the verge of pleasant, despite the ever-present pestilences in the house. Cosimo had grown a little less bothersome. Alethea presumed it was because he had finally, somehow, convinced a stunning, red-head *hetaira* to become his exclusive mistress, or so the rumour went.

However, Alethea constantly found herself asking whether this would be *it*, whether this existence was indeed what her fate had come to. What of her freedom? What of home? What of all those things she had thought of when she had kissed Eucleides on the roof for the first time, the motives and schemes of escaping by means of his gullible nature? They felt dreadfully far away—they remained, but were joined by another, foreign feeling: true infatuation.

The Peloponnese army will return in spring, when the next campaign season starts. Maybe then...yes, then would be a better time to escape. I wouldn't have to go far to find my peers. Thus, she managed to extend her time in Eucleides' company a few months more while dulling the guilt.

What she could never dull was the clarity of Apolonio's face re-appearing in her thoughts and dreams alike, his face hard as granite, asking why she had not yet returned to him and to her *polis*. Her chest ached for him, her stomach queasy, her head in fits of painful longing. Still, she remained in Athens without struggle. *When spring comes, I'll try to leave.*

CHAPTER TWENTY-SIX

THE SKY, IRON grey with patches of veil-like clouds, hung heavy over the city. The temperature had dropped further during the night and Eucleides desperately wished he had picked a thicker *himation*.

Pericles' eyes matched the sky so well that it appeared the gods had crafted it as such solely to strengthen his appearance. His beard was greyer than the last time Eucleides saw him, the brackets of lines around his eyes were deeper, the full lips had lost their pink hue. War had worn on him like ungentle handling wears on a marble bust, yet he was no less composed, no less imposing. An embodiment of the democracy he so relentlessly pushed forward, the aging man seemed to tower before the spectators, higher now than any of the countless previous moments Eucleides had looked upon him.

The Athenians were impatient. With grim mouths and bodies tensed under their warmest clothes, eyes too tired to press forth any more tears, they waited for their leader to speak of the sons and brothers they had lost to sharp spears and arrows. Would he condemn the savagery, the bloodthirsty Spartans and their allies? Would he perhaps smother them with false reassurance that their sacrifices would soon be over? The dead had been lost through raids from both parties, and once the real battles began, their number would increase rapidly.

Pericles' voice cut through the dense silence like a knife through flesh. 'That part of our history which tells of the military achievements that gave us our several possessions, or of the ready valour with which either we or our fathers stemmed the tide of Hellenic or foreign aggression, is a theme too familiar to my hearers for me to dwell upon, and I shall therefore pass it by.'

The crowd's faces shifted in surprise, then brows furrowed and Eucleides heard knuckles crack as the man next to him clenched his fist. *Won't he praise the military prowess of the deceased? He must.* But Pericles proceeded, and instead directed his accolade towards Athens itself: the golden yolk of Hellas, the home of learned men, the government from which greatness had sprung. With every word he spoke, Eucleides realised the genius behind this odd choice, because the speech did not merely lament the sacrifices the audience had made, but convinced them that every drop of blood had been spilled for the sake of a glorious *polis*.

Pericles continued for a good while before reaching what seemed to be the peak of his oration. 'In short, I say that as a city we are the school of Hellas. I doubt if the world can produce a man, who, where he has only himself to depend upon, is equal to so many emergencies, and graced by so happy a versatility as the Athenian.'

Eucleides wrung his hands. *Is it true, or is it just to raise the spirits of the masses? Maybe it* is *true, but...*The more time he spent in Alethea's company, whether it was conversing or simply watching her perform mundane tasks, the more he began to doubt the greatness of Athens. From everything she told him, his city was far from the progressive champion of liberty he had always been taught it was. Sparta was a place of brutality, and yet it treated much of its populous with more respect than did its civilized counterparts.

He did not understand the ideals she elevated above everything. They went beyond patriotism, beyond what he felt for his own *polis*. The Spartans' strange customs, their contempt for even the slightest of decadence, the girls' wild dancing and the boys' ruthless rites of passage, all these things still made Eucleides wince. Yet he absorbed every word she uttered like a well-fed man scraping crumbs from the floor for some reason he could not explain. A creature so divinely imperfect could not be mistaken, and the place which had fostered such a gleaming Stymphalian bird could not be completely wrong.

And so, despite the views he had been nurtured with since he was born, despite what the iron-eyed man on the platform said of Athens, Eucleides felt the ambiguity creeping up on him. A city strong as bronze, or one shiny as silver—which deserved the most admiration?

'And now, when you have duly lamented, everyone his own dead, you may depart.' Pericles' gaze swept over the crowd, perhaps searching their expressions for the hint of a doubt, but found none. They had been swayed. Like weeds bending for the wind they bent for his rhetoric. As they slowly disbanded, their eyes wandered over the public buildings with renewed appreciation.

Eucleides tarried behind a moment, still caught in his own thoughts. The chill seeped in through the slits in his garments so that it felt as if the blood in his veins were freezing to ice.

'What occupies your mind, son of Achaikos?' The voice was less formal now, but as cogent as ever.

'I only reflect upon the qualities of Athens, as you presented them. It was a most memorable speech; the skill of your tongue is rightly envied.'

'If I'm correct, you're rarely short of words yourself. And these reflections?'

Pericles' infamous affection for his mistress and companion, Aspasia—could it mean he would understand? *It's not the same... She's not the enemy, she doesn't sow grains of doubt in his head by merely existing. At least not as far as I know. And to question our foremost leader would be foolish.*

'Oh, nothing. Nothing to bother someone as busy as you with.'

Efigenia tapped at the door leading from the hallway to the *andron*, her entire body bristling with anxiety. Never before had she been so bold as to ask entrance into these seemingly sacred quarters where Cosimo and Eucleides often dwelled with their illustrious acquaintances, conversing and eating. However, she had not so much as glimpsed her husband in four days' time, which was a concerningly long absence even for him.

No answer came from within the *andron*. Efigenia adjusted the *fibulae* holding her *khitōn*: silver orchids crowning her pointy shoulders. *What if...what if all is not well?* She squeezed her eyes shut until she saw nothing but white, banishing the images of Cosimo's limp body from her inner sight, and knocked again, this time with the knob of her parasol.

Though silence still reigned, the door creaked open at the pressure. Efigenia pushed it further, forcing deep breaths in an attempt to calm her hammering heart, then proceeded through the empty room into the second and third.

Not a dead man, but a fusion of reddish gold and frosty white, plump limbs entangled with lean met her. There was a strange spark in Cosimo's eyes, triumph, perhaps, while Xenia's held an indifferent gaze.

No. Please no. Silly girl—there's a reason why I'm not supposed to be here. The flustered lovers had not noticed her slight stature, nor did they interrupt themselves as she fled the quarters, emerging in the open courtyard. There, she dropped down on the bench where she had shared confidence with Lady Milos, crumpling the fabric of her *khitōn* in her hands until her knuckle bones shone through the skin. Like a marble sculpture, drained of all colour save for the red circles on her cheeks and lips purple from the biting cold, she remained a long while.

I knew it, of course I knew, from the day we married. Anything else would be strange indeed. Still, it was one thing to *know*, and an entirely different thing to have the sight of it forever carved under her eyelids. She stared at her hands. Her nails had taken on a plum-like hue by the cuticles the past month, and she doubted the weather was to blame. *That woman* had brimmed with life, her complexion basted in lingering summer sun. And Eucleides' darling slave—Efigenia was still reluctant to acknowledging her original name—was not always sunny, but nonetheless a small explosion of all the things Efigenia had pained herself never to become. The longer she sat on the bench, hands still vehemently clutching linen, the more she wondered how two people so far below her on the social ladder, so far outside ideals or virtue, could have had so much greater success in the house than she. She could not yet fathom that the true issue was said definition of a woman's success.

'What are you doing out here?' The Doric dialect carried clearly. The speaker approached the bench.

Tears burnt Efigenia's eyes as she rose to face the intruder, threatening to deluge at any moment. 'You laugh at me, I'm sure. You think I'm weak because I trot after him like...like a puppy, trying to do what I'm supposed to. You scorn me because you think all this—' she gestured at the pearls in her hair, dropping her parasol to the ground, '—because you consider this too feminine to be of any worth.'

Alethea stared at her, lips slightly parted, a blush rising on her cheeks. 'No. No. I don't think you can be weak, seeing as you're still alive under this...this suffocating yoke! I only wish life hadn't forced you to shrink smaller than nature made you.'

'But your own ways? Sometimes...sometimes I think you're just like the men.'

'I was reared a Spartan—perhaps that's all. Or perhaps it's because you think austerity is for men alone.'

Is it? Isn't it true, then? She never ceases to startle. Efigenia bent down to retrieve her parasol, the tears having sunk back though constantly on the verge of erupting again. 'My mother always said—'

'I don't care!' This time, it was Alethea's voice that quivered, to Efigenia's surprise. 'Wear all the gold and pearls you want, take your warm baths. It's all sick luxury, but I loathe it because it's Athenian, not because it's a womanly habit. Never think that of me.'

Efigenia could only stare in awe. No more than half a year had passed since this older woman had sat by the hearth, being showered with dried fruit and nuts to introduce her into the *oikos*, and now she was practically shouting at her mistress. Furthermore, the words spewing from her lips like an endless string of beads were bolder than Efigenia had ever heard before, and they struck a chord of truth. The solemn, unapproachable Spartan with her harsh ways and scandalous demeanour suddenly reasoned with her, even just a little.

'Then you don't laugh at me?' Efigenia asked, still suspicious.

Alethea shrugged. 'You can be a spoiled brat. But that's a different matter.'

The entire courtyard was covered in a thin sheath of silvery frost reflecting the blinding winter sun which was perched high on the sky like an egg. Efigenia regretted taking the parasol with her rather than the warming, less stylish *énkyklon*. As she did so, she began retreating, once more cementing the illusions that had been threatened by the argument. *I almost let her see me cry. Silly girl. She's a slave, after all.*

'You can go now. And remember not to speak to me like that again. Remember your place.' She turned and walked towards the colonnade.

'You know I'm right,' Alethea called. 'You just won't stop striving for perfection—for your own or for others' sake is a riddle to me.'

Efigenia did not turn, but kept walking, her bare arms speckled with goose bumps.

CHAPTER TWENTY-SEVEN

RUMOUR REACHED EFIGENIA before any of the family members sought her out with the news. Slaves' whispers carried quick, gossip being their coin and solace.

The birth of Cosimo's child was expected in the late summer that year, and although one could not yet spot any significant difference on Xenia's curvaceous figure, the pregnancy was thought to be three months gone already. A nuisance, people said, for the poor *hetaira* who risked not only her life and her attractive parts—both were as crucial to one in her position—but might find herself lacking her rich clientele for the final few months of her condition. As soon as the baby was born, it would be exposed, left at nature's cruel hands, for the cases when the result of liaisons such as this was reared were as rare as sphinxes.

Efigenia sat numb by the loom, fingers turned to stone, the ivy-green shroud she had been weaving hanging unfinished with loose threads like a choppy fringe. *A nuisance. For her, for him. And for me?* She knew the answer already but did not dare to think it: proof that Cosimo was capable of siring children, hence if the marriage remained fruitless it stood clear whose fault that was. A smack of humiliation, a stamp marking her failure to satisfy her husband.

Indeed, the pregnancy per se was not what hurt the most—Efigenia knew jealousy like she knew her own hands or the strings of her sister's lyre and was rarely taken back by it anymore—but the titters and snickers, the long glances passed between slaves. A respectable woman was better unspoken of than praised, much less made part of a juicy little story. Efigenia recalled a piece of Pericles' funeral oration, which Eucleides had recounted to her with a sorry grimace: "*To a woman, not to show more weakness than is natural to her sex is a great glory, and not to be talked about for good or for evil among men.*"

Efigenia forced her fingers to return to the loom, but it was as if all the skill she had acquired during the decade under her mother's stern supervision had abandoned her entirely. The threads knotted and tangled, the loom weights dropped to the floor, the shroud slowly turned into an unrecognizable rag.

Her mind strayed to baser things. *Bread would be good. Thick, soft bread with goat's cheese, or honeyed sesame cookies, or...* Though the pangs of painful hunger had long since faded, having been brushed off time and time, the ever-present hollow feeling increased. Efigenia pressed her palm to her stomach in an attempt to curb it. *Don't be piggish. Look at that sloppy work!* She pulled at the loose threads and began to unravel the shroud, first slowly, then faster and faster until the yarn blurred and her fingers burned with friction.

The ivy-green pile at her feet almost looked offended. She rose and regarded it for a moment before calling on a slave to clean up the mess and bring her a cup of water. The liquid cooled the blood scorching her veins as well as her head; it cured the hollowness in her body for the moment.

Alethea would know what to do. She would...she would... Efigenia did not know. Spartans did not keep *hetairai*, nor did they expose babies for other reasons than sickliness. Rather, it was wives who took lovers with the *polis'* blessing so that they would not run short of children. *Maybe* she *wouldn't mind at all. But then she doesn't love her husband even a little, it seems. I do. I do, I do, I must.*

Despite, or perhaps because of, her uncertainties regarding Alethea, Efigenia sent the slave to find her. A good while passed; the other woman still had a habit of delaying when summoned by her mistresses, though she was meticulous under almost any other circumstances. Efigenia folded her arms and clutched herself, pacing between the loom and the small table while she waited.

'You called.'

Efigenia turned, swallowing at the languid tone of Alethea's voice. 'Yes. Yes, I called. I would ask you something.'

'What?'

'You...you know of...' If she said it aloud, it would suddenly become utterly, irrevocably true.

'Your husband's bastard baby? Yes, I heard. Queen Pasiphaë was luckier than that *hetaira*, though I hope the baby will turn out prettier than the minotaur.'

'You cannot say such things!' Efigenia balled her fists but hid them in the thick folds of her clothes. 'I could...I could have you whipped for comparing my husband—your master—to an animal.'

Alethea glared. The expression had lost none of its affect even as the slashed scar on her face had healed to a pale-pink seam. 'That's not why you called on me.'

'I just wanted to know... What would you have felt? Would you have done anything? I won't, you mustn't think that. It's not my place to interfere with his choices.'

'If it had been my husband, and my city, I would have condoned it. But Athens isn't Sparta—you have enough sons already—and Cosimo isn't as innocuous as my husband.'

'What do you mean?'

'I mean Crysanthos can be managed, for all our controversies. I am lucky in that way.'

'I don't think I will get any sensible advice out of you. I don't know why I sent for you, a *slave*. You cannot understand.' Efigenia returned to clutching her arms and turned her back to Alethea, hiding slight the tremor of her lip. 'You may leave.'

'What if you were to become pregnant as well?'

Why is she always crueller than I think she'll be? Is it a Spartan custom to rub salt in the wounds? 'My hopes have not been realised before.'

'They needn't be. It would only have to look like it.' Alethea took a few strides into the room and her voice was tinged with conspiracy. 'There are always ways to get what you want, and as long as it serves a fair purpose, what's the harm?'

'Why are you telling me this?'

Alethea scoffed. 'You know why. Because for almost a year I have watched that man prance around, while the rest of us, particularly you, crawl at his feet. A child, a son, would strengthen your position.'

Efigenia's heart fluttered with hope. *It would, it really would.* 'You think his affection could grow?'

'No, but he would be forced to a finger's-width of respect.'

'And he would have to keep me, too!' She could not help but smile. 'And I would have a baby to dote on, to fill my days, and we would be a *proper* family.'

Alethea crinkled her nose. 'Don't get your hopes too high, Mousey.'

'It was your idea.'

'Anything to alter the twisted power balance in this house a little.'

That brazen woman is imagining things. But if she can be of some help... Efigenia smoothened the non-existing crinkles in her *khitōn*. She mustered all her courage and met Alethea's eyes. 'How would we manage it?'

'You expect me to do the dirty work, then?'

'You're the slave. And...' She swallowed her pride. 'And I don't think I could do it on my own.'

Alethea shrugged. There was something both brusque and ethereal about her where she stood in all her unadorned simplicity. 'Babies are exposed differently here. They're perfectly healthy. Find one.'

'And the...the nine months before? I could never lie to my husband that many times—'

'You won't have to, unless he is suddenly a changed man. I doubt he'll be near enough to feel your belly.'

The words were like a pair of hands choking her, yet Efigenia knew the truth that lay in them. Cosimo was not the kind of husband to busy himself with the details concerning his wife's pregnancy, or even to bother being suspicious. Of course, he had no reason to be, either. One last wave of scruples flooded Efigenia. *A faithful, good wife would never do this. She would breed her own children with success, or resign with bent head. But the disgrace—* She decided.

'You may help me find a pillow or something else of suitable size.'

Efigenia chose her moment with utmost care. Having interrogated Eucleides as innocently as she could, she knew Cosimo had enjoyed a day of unusual success at the gymnasium, followed by a calm evening and a dinner to his liking. She also knew he would visit her that night; the half hour he dutifully spent in her bedchamber every tenth day had become routine. Of course, there was little use in telling him it was too seldom to stand any good chance of conceiving.

She orchestrated her appearance meticulously. She took care placing her hair in seemingly effortless curls draping her face as if belonging to an *oread,* a mountain nymph; the *khitōn* had been sewn for the occasion and had not a stitch of red in it.

This has to be perfect, it has *to. This time, this time he* will *smile like the sun.* With a thousand butterflies beating their wings against her ribs, Efigenia stood by the bedpost, her hands clasped before her.

Cosimo closed the door swiftly behind him, reaching to disrobe himself before turning to look at her. When he did, seeing the poorly concealed anticipation glittering back at him, he halted in his movements, one fibula still clasped at his shoulder.

'What's the matter with you?'

'What is it you want most in life, husband?'

'Political renown and influence. Respect. *Arete.*'

Of course. Efigenia made a new attempt. 'I mean...I mean from our union?'

'A son, then. A daughter, too, if she turns out charming enough to marry well.' Cosimo slowly dressed again, his forehead creasing at her odd turn of speech.

'Then you shall have it.'

'You've been mistaken before.'

'I won't be this time, I promise I won't. I'll give you your first child,' she beamed.

Cosimo raised an eyebrow, his cheekbone catching the specks of golden light from the lamp. 'It won't be the first of mine to be born.'

Something inside Efigenia snapped like a lyre string played too roughly. 'You cannot mean that whore's offspring! You cannot count it as a true child of yours!'

'Hold your tongue and hold your promise, and I will say nothing of your tone towards me.'

Efigenia managed to nod, stiff with fright. *How could I say something like that?* The fear, however, did not so much concern keeping her promise as it did keeping her tongue, in fact, it would be an easier task than when she had truthfully thought she *was* with child. Then, the outcome had been subject to nature's cruel fickleness; now, she only had to depend on her own and Alethea's abilities.

Cosimo eyed her, she thought, with newly-found interest, whether sprung in her outburst or her supposed condition, Efigenia could not tell. To her puzzlement, this interest did not feel quite so gratifying as she had expected.

'You...you have no obligation tonight, then. The goal has already been achieved.'

It was the first time she had ever even hinted at rejection but her husband did not seem to notice. Rather, he nodded as if he had decided on leaving her chamber long before she had suggested it.

At the door, he turned. 'You may never use crude words again. Understand?'

'Yes. Yes.'

Then, he was gone.

Efigenia glanced down at her stomach. Sometimes she was under the illusion that it had ballooned, just as she sometimes imagined her thighs thick and flabby like the lumps of fat cut from sacrificial animals, but rationally she knew it was more concave than anything else—and it certainly did not look pregnant. *Well... I can enlist the Spartan's help tomorrow. Not tonight. She's bound to be with her lover at this hour.*

'You told him?' A half-smile played at the corner of Alethea's mouth.

'Yes.'

Alethea fumbled with the pillow, which she had acquired through sparse sewing skills. She tied the last strap holding the stuffed piece of wool to Efigenia's stomach, allowed the *khitōn* to fall back into place, and stepped back to inspect the little fake belly. It looked even more real than she had hoped: from afar barely noticeable, upfront it was the unmistakable bulge of early childbearing.

'There. We'll adjust the size as time passes. Happy?'

Efigenia glanced down at herself. 'Yes...yes. You truly think it might work?'

'If it doesn't, it won't be my fault.'

'But it was your idea!'

'And I've done my bit, no?'

The young girl reached up to adjust the shiny butterfly comb in her hair, flashing underarms kept impeccably white, hidden from sun. After a long moment, she appeared satisfied with the comb and spoke again, this time in a more formal tone. 'You want something in return, I suppose?'

A thousand things which you cannot give me. But I'll settle for something else. 'A charming set of clothes.'

'Clothes? You?'

'*Yes.*' Alethea rolled her eyes. 'There's an occasion I have to dress up for, unfortunately.'

'And what...what is that?'

'A gathering with Eucleides' acquaintances. Protagoras, Paralus and Xanthippus, a few others.'

Efigenia gaped, her pouting lips forming a perfect little *o*, and Alethea could not blame her. That she, a slave and a woman, not to speak of a Spartan one, should accompany a promising and wealthy young Athenian *anywhere* as anything but a servant was incredulous enough; that she should accompany him in the presence of the city's utmost elite of politicians and thinkers was better suited to a comedy and reality. Nevertheless, Alethea was curious to know what it was he fawned over, what sort of people these men were whom he had spoken so highly of all this time, and Eucleides had been unable to refuse when she asked.

'But—but you can't possibly—'

'I can.'

'You're not even a woman of good standing!'

'Maybe that's why I can,' Alethea shrugged. 'It doesn't matter. I need something pretty to wear.'

Efigenia pressed her lips to a thin line and surveyed the older woman from head to toe. A triumphant gleam lit in her sienna eyes. 'You're bigger than me, and not just taller, but in the flesh, too. You could never fit in my garments. Maybe you should mind what you put in your mouth.'

Don't you ever just shut up? You do, but not at the right time. 'At least I'm not all skin and bones. Now, won't you do as I ask and remember what *I've* done for *you*?'

Efigenia clenched her little fists, then a deep, trembling breath passed through her body like a wave, and she nodded, expressionless. 'You shall have it. And silver jewellery—it suits you better than gold, I think.'

Her mistress was right, Alethea discovered as she clasped the silver earrings to her earlobes. They looked like lilies made of liquid moonlight, contrasting against her dark hair as if against the night sky, and though she had little experience of gold, nothing could have been as sublime. *How morbidly vain of me. But no one needs to know what I think.*

Efigenia had been correct also regarding the clothes; new ones had been bought in haste, and in secret, since Althea preferred to be a surprise to both Eucleides and Cosimo, for vastly different reasons. The first she would dazzle and delight—something she had done too seldom, she sometimes thought— the latter she would disturb beyond reason. *He won't be able to stand all this finery wasted on such as myself. That alone makes luxury endurable.*

Cosimo had grumbled enough to make her smile upon hearing she would attend with himself and his cousin, his face turned sage. Eucleides had merely reminded them both that Alethea's presence was no more of a controversy than Aspasia's. This was completely false: Pericles' sworn companion and mistress was far from a Spartan slave in both education, status, and charm. She was the exception of Athens, a lone star, and owned every shred of society's half-acceptance to her wits and to her lover. *Will she be there? Dear Artemis, let her be there or I'll have nothing but men's smug voices to listen to. Some say she even writes Pericles' speeches for him.*

Alethea threw one last glance in the mirror Efigenia had agreed to lend her after much ado, popped a few grapes in her mouth, fearing their hosts might not provide adequate refreshments, and descended the staircase. To her surprise and, she had to confess, disappointment, neither of the other two were at the bottom waiting for her. She passed a good while sitting on the lowest step before Eucleides and Cosimo emerged from the *andron,* still perfecting the way a strand of hair fell or the exact positioning of a sandal strap.

Alethea rose as did her eyebrows. 'And I thought *I* had made an effort.'

Eucleides halted in his step. 'You look splendid. Doesn't she?'

Cosimo continued towards the door.

As they followed him, Eucleides leant in to whisper in Alethea's ear. 'I didn't want to dress up *this* much, but he said it would be best, and I'm sure he's right.'

'Do you think I'm overdressed, too?'

'Oh no—beauty can never come in too heavy a dose. I'm sure they would have welcomed you in grey woollen rags, too, but silver and white is a lovely combination.'

'Perhaps. Thank you.' She returned his smile.

Dusk had not yet fallen, so there was no need for a torch bearer until they would embark home again from Pericles' imposing house, which was not far away.

A slave opened the door for the trio and escorted them through a grand but simply furnished vestibule. The slave halted and nodded at the fifth doorway they passed, upon which they entered.

The room was large enough to impress a prince, yet furnished so as to create the illusion of an intimate retreat. Warm light from countless terracotta lamps licked the rich, Egyptian-blue wall hangings; skins of oxen and of a lion lay spread out on the marble floor like islands in a white sea.

A man and a woman—servants, Alethea presumed—stood flat against one of the walls, hands clasped, awaiting their master's orders. Each held a jug in one hand and balanced a plate stacked with little dark green rolls in the other.

Alethea squinted. *Filled wine leaves, if we're lucky. I shouldn't have eaten before we came.*

Six men were already half-laying on *klinae* in a wide, uneven circle around the room, and although Alethea only knew half of them by sight, she suspected she knew all of them by reputation. One was the unmistakable, pug-faced Socrates, another was Xanthippus, the square-jawed son of Pericles, and the young man lounging with a cup of wine leisurely balanced between two fingers she at once recognised as Alcibiades.

Two of the remaining three men, both dressed in *khitōns* the colour of cream gone bad, were engaged in a discussion of some sort, their hands constantly gesticulating as if trying to describe shapes by moulding the air. The thinner one appeared to be winning the argument; his glossy eyes possessed a refined passion.

The sixth and final member of the company presented the most eye-catching sight: one arm was significantly shorter than the other, and his ears were almost twice as large as one would deem natural—yet in contrast to these deformities, his face was one of the most attractive Alethea had seen. There was no beauty in it, beauty being too pure a word to apply, but rather too sharp and too soft attributes creating an irresistible combination.

'We're not late in coming, are we?' Cosimo said, glancing around the room. 'The finest of citizens should not be kept waiting by the likes of us.'

Oh shut up, or at least pick either *flattery or irony.*

Alcibiades laughed and flicked his wrist so as to swirl around the wine in his cup. 'Gracious of you to be concerned. Don't be—we've suffered no boredom yet.'

'Please, sit.' Xanthippus' voice was surprisingly high-pitched and sallow. 'My father and his...your hostess will join us soon, if they can be bothered.'

As the group of three obliged, placing themselves on the empty *klinae*, Alethea whispered in Eucleides' ear. 'I bet I could *smell* that man's dislike if I tried.'

'He never approved of his father's relationship. His loyalty to his mother is admirable, but not always agreeable in social situations.'

'Nothing is as valuable as loyalty. Can be impractical, though.'

Xanthippus waved for the slaves with the refreshments to come forward and serve. Alethea sipped at the diluted wine which was still bleak compared to what she had grown up with, despite the probable exclusiveness, and directed her attention to the food instead. To her quiet delight, the green rolls were indeed wine leaves, basted in a tangy, sticky marinade and stuffed with a crush of raisins and almonds. Alethea devoured two, three rolls before she noticed several pair of eyes upon her. *They probably never saw a woman eat. Or maybe it's the scar. Or a hundred other things.*

The first to speak was Socrates. As he did so, he moved closer, and Alethea could not help but notice the pungent smell surrounding him, like an unwashed street dog misplaced in the fine salon. Rumour had it he did not live very different from one, either. Alethea distinctly recalled one time when he had stopped her at random in the *agorá*, where he had been loafing about barefoot, to ask her what she thought virtue was.

'I think I've seen you once, young woman, but we were never introduced.'

'My name is Alethea. I'm...a companion of Eucleides, son of Achaikos.' *And I wish I didn't have to reference two men's names to make my own mean anything to you.*

'Ah! A companion. Much like our dear hostess.'

'Maybe.'

As they spoke, Alethea felt Alcibiades' heavy gaze rest upon her—it had been, she realised, from the very moment she walked through the doorway. He said nothing, but was doubtlessly searching for a patch of bare skin previously hidden, or an inviting twinkle in her eye. Ever since it became known among the elite of Athens that Xenia was with child, he had been less besotted with the *hetaira* and had instead begun selecting his new primary pick from the hoard of girls who trotted at his heels desperate for both kisses and the more useful silver that came with them.

Eucleides tapped her arm, 'Let me introduce you to Polykleitos and Phidias, both sculptors of great renown.' He nodded to the two men who had previously been engrossed in discussion.

The man with the glossy eyes offered a placid smile. 'Phidias. And I believe I heard your name already. You must feel quite out of place in this kind of circle.'

Alethea gritted her teeth. He was right, of course, and it was no secret, but she would rather he had left it unsaid. 'And what has this *renowned* sculptor sculpted? Art is often overly admired without reason.'

Phidias' smile remained, joyless. 'Athena in the Parthenon and Zeus in Olympia are among the works I am best known for.'

'I see.'

No one could deny the grandeur of the statues he had mentioned with such confident calm, and Alethea cursed her own question which, though meant to mock, had given him the perfect opportunity to remind everyone present of his mastery.

At that moment, a woman entered the room and conversation stopped instantaneously, as if Zephyr had blown it out. Her face was a perfectly oval framed by soft waves of walnut-coloured hair, her lips like fat bumblebees under a prominent nose. She gazed out on the rest of the company with glittering amusement in her heavy-lidded eyes. She was no longer in youth's bloom, yet the faint lines diminishing conventional beauty seemed only to increase the woman's lucid expression.

Aspasia strode across the lion skin. 'I see our last guests have arrived. Welcome.'

Eucleides beamed at her. 'Thank you, a thousand times, Lady.'

'Now, is this the girl you spoke of? No, she must be—I have rarely seen such a face.'

Alethea's cheeks flared. 'I hope it doesn't displease you.'

Aspasia's laughter rippled low and melodious like a mountain brook trickling over hills and valleys. She dropped down on a *kline* and crossed her legs, their contours clearly visible under the many layers of thin fabric.

'It does not. You're no Helen, though. Pardon my frankness.'

'There's nothing to pardon, Lady. I appreciate frankness. And no, we don't have many Helens in Sparta these days. The closest thing is my husband. Vain and lovesick.' Alethea bit her tongue. She had not intended to mention Crysanthos—she hardly ever did—yet the words had slipped out.

Aspasia tilted her head. 'Is that what you think Helen was?'

'In my home, the girls and boys both worship her, but I never understood why.'

'You can't blame her rash actions when Aphrodite was the true culprit.'

'Or Paris. *He*, at least, was vain and lovesick.' Alethea glanced at Eucleides, looking for the amused accord so often in his eyes in moments such as this, but found only strained courtesy. *Maybe I should never have spoken of my husband. I don't even think of him that way, not any longer, he means nothing. But you don't seem to grasp that.*

Socrates, who had begun unwrapping one of the wine-leafrolls and proceeded to inspect the stuffing as if it was an intricate map over the heavens, crinkled his nose. 'I suggest we move on to other topics of conversation. As I like to say, strong minds discuss ideas, weak minds discuss people.' He poked at the wine leaf one last time before neatly folding it and putting it in his mouth.

The man with the peculiar appearance—Alethea still did not know his name—sighed. 'You think yourself so wise, don't you? You can't know everything.'

'On the contrary, my friend, I know only one thing: that I know nothing else. The rest of you don't know anything else, either, but you don't know even that. Thus, I am wiser than the lot of you.'

The evening progressed in a similar manner, with the pug-faced philosopher agitating his company just as Aspasia charmed it and Alethea tried to navigate in it.

As they made their way home, she grabbed Eucleides' hand. 'You know I possess no devotion to my husband other than what my *polis* assigned me.'

He squeezed her fingers, the torchlight illuminating his cheekbones. 'I know. You convince me more with every day that passes, I just—I wish I knew what *our* future held.'

'I can't tell you. I'll just have to convince you a little more.'

CHAPTER TWENTY-EIGHT

ATHENS SIMMERED, FILTHIER and more crowded than ever, its inhabitants trapped between the blazing rays of sun and the stagnant alleys. The former country dwellers had gone from temporary visitors to residents in every sense but the fact that most still had no permanent lodgings, if they had lodgings at all. The city bent under the weight of their presence, threatening to burst. At first, nothing about this was remarkable. It was still only late spring, but still, the previous year had been just as hot and nearly as crammed with people at this time. Then came the burning rashes and the fever.

The first victims suffered without causing much commotion; a few men and women dropping dead after an unidentified disease was nothing to stir an entire *polis*, since few survived infancy and even fewer reached old age. However, as the number rapidly increased and the mysterious symptoms became more widely known on the street, no one could escape being reached by rumour.

Alethea accompanied Efigenia on one of her quests of purchasing odd foods which she claimed the child in her womb craved and usually proceeded to spit out in a napkin. These excursions had become more frequent lately, and to Alethea's surprise, Cosimo did not appear to mind, providing his wife went like a respectable woman: heavily veiled and with a small entourage of slaves as well as a trustworthy male relative, meaning Eucleides, who in turn let them wander freely. This particular time, they had ventured outside to purchase quail eggs.

The man managing the stall was far from well, and Alethea could see the inflamed red hue of his eyes at a considerable distance. *He looks as if possessed by evil spirits or cursed by Hecate herself.*

Efigenia pressed a *drachma* in her hand and nodded towards the man. 'Buy ten, no, twelve, and the prettiest ones.'

Alethea sighed but obliged. The quail eggs were all equally pretty as far as she could see, with their turquoise sheen and dark flecks. She pretended to study each of them in detail though, hesitant to meet the man's sickly scarlet gaze.

'Twelve of those. The prettiest, if you can tell any difference—I can't,' she said.

The man opened his mouth but no reply came. His tongue was swollen to twice its normal size and his calloused hand grasped at his throat as if trying to quench a burn.

Alethea took an automatic step back. *Whatever that is, it's no merciful ailment.* She clenched her hand, the coin digging into her palm.

The man emitted a half-choked sound, his pupils floating around in feverish stupor. Finally, he managed to form just-discernible words. 'The eggs— the eggs are worth their—their price.'

'I'm sure,' Alethea said. 'But you're unwell.'

'No—no, I can work—'

Poor man. More anxious about his earnings than his life. Well, I won't have his disease rob me of mine. She backed further and jerked at Efigenia's clothes, pulling the girl with her as she went. The slaves were quick to follow; they were no fools and knew a hazard when they saw it.

'Let go of me! You may not behave so—' Efigenia started, but soon closed her mouth behind the veil and allowed herself to be led off. When they reached the other side of the *agorá*, she stopped to brush non-existent dirt from her arms. 'What about my quail eggs?'

'He's not the *only* salesman in Athens,' Alethea said.

'But...but we've already been outside too long. Cosimo will wonder.'

'Then tell him you changed your mind. I truly do not care.'

'You should know better than to be so...so rude!'

Alethea clenched her jaw. 'Let's go home.'

'Yes. Yes, you may walk with the others.' Efigenia gestured at the other slaves, two of them women and the third Zesiro, who trailed behind her at a uniform distance of two steps.

Alethea considered for a moment. *I've lost all sense of obedience and order, it seems, since leaving Sparta. But then obedience to an Athenian brat is no worthy way of life.* She gave a one-shouldered shrug and surged ahead of the rest of the party for the duration of the walk home.

Eucleides' brows came together like a single strip of dark wool when Alethea recounted the incident with the vendor. He was oddly quiet, propping his chin in his hand, elbow on desk. In that moment, he reminded Alethea of the old man she had imagined him to be when he used to talk of living for*ever*.

'What?' she asked. 'It was unpleasant, but many things are.'

'It's not that in itself—though I'm sorry you should have to see anything unpleasant, ever. No, it's the rumours. Haven't you heard?'

'No. Not a lot of people talk to a savage slave girl. Tell me.'

'They say there have been tens, hundreds of people like that man. They say it's a plague, brought on by Pericles' insistence that everyone should live inside the walls, or the wrath of a god.'

'I hope it's the latter. A god we can pray to, but your politicians are impossible.'

'Pericles is a great man and a prolific leader.'

'Even if there's a plague?'

Eucleides grew silent again, and Alethea regretted her words. *He admires that man too much for his own good. And I'm too blunt for* mine. She reached for the tray on the side table, which was laden with bread softer than down feathers and honey stickier than resin, and offered him some of it as a peace gift of sorts.

Eucleides accepted the bread with a smile and the lustre returned in an instant, chasing away the pensive old man.

'What are the symptoms of this...plague? If that's what it is.'

'I'm not entirely sure. I've heard tales of reddened eyes and burning rashes, fever and revolting bowels. Awful things, really.'

'Just like the quail-man, then, though I don't know if he suffered from that last one.'

Eucleides laughed. 'Fortunately for you.'

'I wish your cousin's wife could manage her own business, not drag me with her.'

'You did accompany her of free will,' Eucleides pointed out. 'But I know she's become a little...a little difficult since discovering her pregnancy. We must make allowances.'

Alethea bit her tongue. The lie she had taken part in crafting and now maintaining was just as much a lie to him as to Cosimo and everyone else. She had never before had any great scruples about omitting the truth when another story was more beneficial to herself or those she loved, but this was another matter: she in no way loved Efigenia, and Eucleides had never done either of them any harm. *It's only that he's too close to the one who has done harm, far too close. He might spill the knowledge by accident if he had it.* Hence, she concluded, it would be best to keep him ignorant if possible—after all, he would love the child even without sharing its bloodline, and the hurt in a lie rarely originated from the truth itself but from the discovery of the lie.

Alethea dismissed the thought from her mind and reached for a piece of plain bread, wishing for the hundredth time that the wheat would turn into a Spartan loaf of barley.

'When do you think we'll know? Whether it's a plague, I mean, or just coincidence.'

'I've never practiced medicine or prophesising— I really can't tell, though time will. Won't you give me a kiss regardless?'

They did not have to wait long. Athens had been a goblet spilling over with people and bustling with too much life; within a fortnight the city was littered with corpses instead. Ironically, the rapidly rising death toll helped relieve some of the crowding which had contributed to the outbreak, but it was too late.

The smell of flesh decaying in summer heat was immediate, mingling with the more habitual stench of the living to create a peculiar blend. Relatives who dared touch the bodies of the deceased did their best to rid get rid of them before the rotting had gone too far, and the funeral pyres burned like hundreds of fireflies throughout the nights. Occasionally, two persons would walk down the street with a limp, third member carried between them by the feet and shoulders. Upon reaching the first pyre they caught sight of, the pair would hurdle their dead comrade into the flames where another was already burning to ash and bones, before scrambling away, throwing stealthy glances over their shoulders.

Just as any epidemic, the plague altered patterns in the whole of society. No one was immune, therefor everyone felt death's cold fingers tickle, or imagined they felt it. What was the use in leading a life dictated by laws and morals when that very life threatened to slip away any moment? What was the use of making wise investments or restricting one's emotions if one might not live to reap the fruits?

Alethea had never before seen anything like the near-anarchy released in Athens within days. On the evermore rare occasion when she dared venture outside to the infested public, her eyes grew round as she beheld the filth, the promiscuous lechery, and the violence. *So much for the refined Athenians... They even neglect the gods. What do they expect to happen? Of course they won't be spared if they've already given up on praying.*

Indeed, faith was dwindling, but many of the priests and priestesses had chosen the opposite path, spending every waking hour sacrificing sheep or chanting their pleas. Apollo, god of medicine and sender of the plague which devastated the Helenian camp during the Trojan war, was the main recipient of their prayers, as was Zeus, Athena the protectress, and Asclepius.

In spite of their efforts—or perhaps because of the masses' lack thereof—the plague prevailed.

CHAPTER TWENTY-NINE

THOUGH THE SICKNESS did not seem to discriminate between the physically vigorous and the already weak, the *oikos* did not gape in surprise when the first member—slaves included—to be struck was Achaikos.

'It's simply not fair!' Eucleides said, tears welling in his eyes. 'My father is a kind man, and what would the world be without kind people? He must recover. He *will*, surely?'

It was Lady Milos who, when he was not fit to protest, took him in her crushing arms. She smelled strongly of orange blossom oil, and Eucleides had to hold his breath.

'Life isn't fair, my dear boy, much less death. Believe me, I know. We shall have to wait and see.'

'I don't know if I could bear it.'

'You will if you have to.'

I suppose I will. But it would *be unfair, and the world would be even crueller than I've already tried to accept.* He remained in his aunt's embrace a little while longer, then rose and climbed the stairs to his father's bedchamber.

Achaikos had only developed the scarlet eyes; the discoloured patches on his skin and the excruciating fever, which sufferers claimed felt as if they were being burnt alive and made some spend their last days naked in tubs of cool water, were yet to come. His temples were damp with sweat, his breathing shallow. When his son entered the room, he made a futile effort to sit up.

'Who goes there?'

'It's me, Eucleides, your son.'

The exchange was routine, but Eucleides suspected Achaikos' failing memory was only made worse by the disease.

No slaves were in attendance in the room at the moment. *Who can blame them? None should be forced to perform tasks where death spreads like dust in the wind.*

Eucleides drew a pallet to the bed and sat down. 'How are you feeling?'

'Feeling? I—' The words came like thick porridge from his throat and the sweat on his temples beaded as he tried to speak properly. 'If the gods would end me, I should be...grateful.'

'You mustn't say such things! Come now, father, you will be perfectly well.'

A confused flicker crossed Achaikos' face, his pupils darting. 'Who speaks?'

'It's me, Eucleides.'

The conversation carried no further; Achaikos had drifted into a twitching slumber and his comprehension would hardly have been better had he been awake. His son left him there, realising the fruitless situation, and went instead to join the scattered mass constituting the *ecclesia* on the Pnynx Hill.

The crowd was half its usual size. Some struck by plague, others terrified behind barred doors, others still simply neglecting their civic duties in favour of debauchery, the assembled group was barely half of what it had been.

Eucleides took a seat on the bare rock and exchanged concerned glances with a few of the men around him. Cosimo was nowhere to be seen; the otherwise so ardent young politician had only ventured outside the *oikos'* four walls twice since the plague broke out, both times to call on his mistress. Eucleides doubted it was due to concern over her health, but he knew there was no use in asking. Cosimo had always dreaded ill health above most things and the situation in the city sometimes prompted him to strange behaviour.

One who *was* present was Pericles. The *strategos* barely spoke but stood tight-lipped. When the *ecclesia* was dismissed, having reached no conclusion as to what ought to be done, Eucleides approached the older man directly.

'I know none of this was your doing. Perhaps it's a poor comfort, but still.'

Pericles' granite gaze met his. 'But it was my doing, son of Achaikos. Either that, or a god is punishing the entirety of Athens, which I do not believe, since our priests would have seen the signs.'

'Does that mean you regret your tactics?'

'I don't know. Truly, I don't know. Perhaps I saved them a year of life—or perhaps they despise me, wishing they had been killed in their homes by the Peloponnese rather than wasting away like rats under the plague's heavy yoke.'

Achaikos frowned. 'Cosimo... Get him for me, will you? I would...I would speak with my son.'

Eucleides stared at the old man, an icy wave rippling through his body. '*I* am your son. Cosimo— your nephew—is not at home this very moment. What was it you wanted to speak about?'

'You...ah...yes, yes. My son. Yes. Oh, nothing.'

'Are you sure?' He swallowed hard as the damp pool of pus spread further through the bandage on his father's leg. The injury from the fall down the staircase had still not healed, and even the smallest deterioration of his health could be fatal. Achaikos appeared not to have heard him, eyes misty again and jaw slack.

Eucleides rose. *How much longer will he last? No, no, I shan't think such things.*

Cosimo had, it turned out, just returned from the gymnasium and was sipping a cup of water in the vestibule. When he saw his cousin approaching, he handed the cup to a slave and dabbed the corner of his lips with two fingers.

'There you are!'

Eucleides eyed him. 'I've been speaking to my father.'

'And what ails him this time?' Cosimo's voice dripped with boredom.

'He asked for you. He mistook you for his son.'

For a fracture of a heartbeat, triumph flickered in Cosimo's eyes, one shapely eyebrow twitching upwards, then, his face was a solemn mask, and Eucleides could spot nothing of the expression which had been there. *I imagined it. Of course I did. This whole matter has made me tired and hallucinating.*

'I'm sorry to hear the poor man has grown so forgetful. But he realised his mistake?'

'Yes. Yes, I reminded him.'

'Good. Well, won't you join me in a game of dice?'

'I...I suppose I will. You'd never take advantage of a sick man?' The question was a sharp needle, strange in his mouth, but the words refused to be silenced.

Cosimo froze. 'I don't know what you're alluding to, cousin.'

'Nothing, nothing. Forget what I said—it was foolish of me. Now, let's play.'

Cosimo was victorious in the game, though none of them had much luck. Eucleides could sense the other man stealing glances at him but could not bring himself to return them. There had always existed a tiny, suppressed tension between them when family relations were mentioned. Despite being both older and more ambitious, it was Cosimo who would eventually become dependent on Eucleides' goodwill. When Achaikos died, their positions would alter significantly: they would no longer be two young men living on fairly equal terms but one rich and the other penniless, regardless of how generous Eucleides was prepared to be. The fact that Cosimo would have been Achaikos' closest male relative and therefore heir, had the old man been without sons, only made matters worse. For many years, they had contained the tension within—Eucleides had hardly paid it a thought—but now that the master of the *oikos*' health was so rapidly deteriorating, it bubbled to the surface.

Once they finished, Cosimo left the house again in search for Xenia, passing Alethea in the vestibule. The Spartan sent him the usual glare, then proceeded out into the courtyard where Eucleides still sat rolling the dice from one hand to the other. She crossed her arms and sank down next to him.

'Do you remember when we sat here the first time?' Eucleides managed a smile.

Alethea nodded. 'You wouldn't tell me what your dream was about.'

'You weren't too talkative yourself, if I recall correctly.'

'No. Will you now?'

'What?'

'Will you tell me what's bothering you?'

Eucleides watched her wide pupils resting steady on him and knew in an instant there was no refusing her. *The things you could ask of me...* 'My father's condition bothers me now, naturally, but back then it was rather our past. He *is* a kind man, a good man, but the wine would twist his mind and make him another when I was younger.'

'He beat you often?'

'Only when drunken. Yes...often. It was no fault of his, surely, I tended to get in the way just as often, and it was his right given by nature. It just wasn't very pleasant.'

The young woman beside him turned her gaze to Aphrodite and Adonis' flighty embrace by the fountain, picking at her cuticles, a sad little smile curling at the corner of her mouth. 'No, beatings rarely are. But I always thought they were a necessity for creating a strong character. That's why the boys in the *agōgá* live as they do, because hardship is beneficial.'

'I think I'd rather have a weak character and a joyful childhood than the reverse.'

Alethea leaned in to kiss his cheek. 'Then I'm sorry.'

Your words are softer with each passing day, those spoken to me, at least. I wonder if you know that. A short silence came and went, during which they simply sat thus, each finding a small comfort for their own troubles.

Then, Alethea withdrew slightly, an inquisitive gleam in her eyes. 'Your cousin looked especially grim when I saw him just a moment ago.'

'I'm sorry to hear it.' Eucleides had to sit on his fingers to keep from wringing his hands, knowing she would grasp at every chance to point out Cosimo as a villain. 'It was nothing.'

'Well. I know that tone of wishful denial.'

He hesitated. 'I think he ponders what might happen if, well, if our fears are realised. If my father succumbs to the disease.'

'And what's that?'

'The house, the money, the lands—they would all fall to me. I would never see my cousin or my aunt beg in the street, I'm sure you know, but I don't think that knowledge satisfies Cosimo.'

'Of course it doesn't. Nothing satisfies that bastard.'

'I wish you would not call him that.'

Alethea cocked her head. 'I thought that was what he was? I hope you haven't forgotten you told me of his parentage. Lady Milos was—' She rose and approached the fountain, letting her fingers brush against the cool water surface.

Eucleides sighed. 'No, no I have not forgotten. I'm sure the whole issue was only my imagining.'

Achaikos did not last long. Three days later, Eucleides' own heart nearly stopped as he put his ear to his father's chest and heard only dense, horrible silence. He soon learned to stifle his grief, however, because it appeared he was the sole member of the household who truly felt it. Alethea and Efigenia only grieved for his sake; Cosimo and Lady Milos mourned the security they had doubtlessly felt when their standard of living had been dependent on one too dim-witted to deny them anything. Lady Milos was more hopeful than her son, embracing Eucleides with motherly pride as he assumed his father's property and the fortune which had accumulated over many years of investment in the Laurion silver mines.

'You'll take good care of your poor aunt, won't you, my dear boy?' she said more than once.

Eucleides nodded.

'I knew you would. You won't *believe* what marvellous jewellery I saw the other day—not too expensive, I think.'

The funeral rites were hastily dealt with for fear that the body might still spread the disease. Lady Milos and Efigenia washed and anointed it. Under normal circumstances, relatives and friends would have come to pay homage on the second day, lamenting in the most dramatic ways, tearing their hair and beating their breasts, but such a gathering was not convenient in these times. On the third day, Achaikos' ashes were taken to the *Kerameikos*, the potteries' quarter where the cemetery lay, and the mourners offered libations before the urn was lowered into the gaping ground.

Eucleides watched one of the slaves fill the grave. His mother had died shortly after birthing him, and his father had never remarried. He had not been the most level-headed of fathers nor the most tender, but as the last patch of the urn disappear under a shovel-full of dirt, a thousand thorns tore Eucleides' chest from the inside and out. *I know too little to manage a household and the lands belonging to it. I'm not ready, far from it. And how I'll miss your idle humming.*

Cosimo squeezed Eucleides shoulder. 'Congratulations, little cousin. You are quite the wealthy man.'

'How can you say something like that? I wish things were different, as you know very well.' Eucleides tried to shake Cosimo's hand, a sour taste on his tongue.

'Oh, believe me, no one wishes it more than I.' The smile was not the glow that could melt stone, the glow that had always been reserved for Eucleides, but a frozen mask.

CHAPTER THIRTY

ALETHEA RUBBED THE linen rag over the mirror's spotty bronze surface, freezing as she caught sight of her own reflection. A scarlet hue had crept into the whites of her eyes and the lids glistened like raw beef. The mirror fell to the floor, metal clattering horribly against polished stone. Her hand flew to her forehead and was almost burnt by the touch.

No. No, no, no... It can't be. I'm never ill. For all the dubious things I've done, plague can't take me. Impossible. Another part of her was vaguely aware of how the denial resembled the things she had always told Eucleides not to think. To believe oneself above the wrath of gods and the power of nature could only be called either hubris or ignorance, neither of which was a favourable path to walk.

Clenching the rag to a ball in her hand, Alethea backed towards the door as if the sickness sat in the mirror itself and she might escape by leaving it there on the floor. When she reached the doorpost, she turned on her heel and ran through the hall and down the staircase, feet pattering against marble, hand sliding down the rail. Just as she reached the bottom step, she smashed into a man's chest, the forceful collision sending her staggering backwards, nose throbbing dully.

'Careful!' Zesiro barked.

Alethea put a hand to her sore nose, having regained her balance. 'I could say the same to you.'

'I don't run around like a madwoman. *You* do.' He squinted at her, his own eyes a perfectly healthy contrast of white and black, the dotted lines of dark blue running below them a constant reminder of his native land. 'You're struck. Struck by the plague.'

'No, I—'

'You have the eyes. And the blisters on your arm.' Zesiro touched his lips and the base of his throat with two fingers; Alethea assumed it was a sign against evil.

'I don't have any blisters.'

'You haven't looked.'

Alethea looked. There, a spatter of pink and yellow sullied her skin, minuscule blisters rising ominously from the flat rash underneath.

'You can't be here. Others will catch it. You must go!' His voice was a torrent. 'It's not right to risk the lives of others.'

'No. No, it is not right.' *Has that dilemma ever affected me? Maybe. It depends.* However, she knew she would do as the Aetheopian said, because regardless of right and wrong, Eucleides would be at the highest risk if she did not, and there was no danger for her in the plague-ridden streets which she had not already met by contracting the disease.

She nailed down Zesiro's gaze with her own. 'I will go. And you will refrain the young master from looking for me. For his own good, tell him that.'

Zesiro emitted a strangely melodious laugh. 'You think they listen to me? They don't. We don't give orders. Only pretty women do.'

'Women are slaves more than any others.'

'Slaves who can influence.'

Alethea shook her head in sheer frustration. 'Just...please. Just tell him, whether he listens or not.' She swallowed and surged past him, steering her course to the storage rooms for a few necessary supplies. Her flight was as improvised as could be, and a satchel with figs, bread, and wine would have to suffice.

Zesiro called after her. 'It wounds my heart. That you go. But it's the right thing.'

Alethea did not get very far with her satchel and worn-out sandals before her fears were realised. In fact, she had not yet reached the Panathenaic Way when Eucleides' voice made her heart skip a beat.

'You're insane!'

Her knuckles whitened as she clenched the strap from which the satchel hung from her shoulder. 'Why can't you ever do what I ask you to?'

'I do that plenty, but not when you think to elope to a slow death in the street! If you truly are ill, you should be cared for, not allowed to abandon all reason!'

There was an edge to his voice Alethea had rarely, detected before. She turned to face him and was taken back by the flushed fury high on his cheeks though he had never been prone to visible blushing. *And I thought I was doing you a favour. Perhaps you* are the insane one, who would risk your health. Still, some small part of her knew she would have done the same had the roles been reversed.

'By Aphrodite, why won't you ever let anyone care for you properly, let alone pity you?'

'Even hate is preferable to pity. And I *do* let you care, but if I allowed you near me, it would be poor retribution.'

'I stayed with my father until the end—' Eucleides swallowed as if the memory was physically painful. '—and I lived. Five slaves have already perished and yet I live. Perhaps the gods look kindly upon me.'

'Then do not tempt them.'

Two men—labourers, judging by their coarse tunics and broad shoulders—walked past them, carrying a swaddled body between them. One of them gave a nod at a coiling plume of smoke further down in the city and muttered a few indiscernible words before proceeding with his companion towards the funeral pyre.

'Come back with me,' Eucleides pleaded, his eyes soft once more. 'Come back with me and cease this nonsense. You know very well I should rather be struck down than be without you.'

And how I love you for it. You fool. 'If I do, promise me one thing.'

'Anything.'

'If I die, don't throw me on the pyre here. Not in Athens. I don't know how you would manage, but take me back home to Sparta. Please.' The bold request dropped from her lips without warning, yet the moment she spoke it, she knew it must be so. Perhaps it was mere imagination, but Alethea was convinced she could feel the fever burning behind her temples hotter than before.

Eucleides eyed her. 'If it will console you, I swear it, but you mustn't think of yourself as gone already. I could never bear it, and... No, you *will* live.'

Alethea slowly reached out a hand, her palm clammy with sweat. 'This city,' she almost whispered, 'this city is doomed. If it goes on for much longer.'

'I don't believe it, but if it is, Sparta will be the overlords of Hellas.'

'Music to my ears. I would rather have us both alive, though. I've grown selfish.' She realised the truth in her own words with nausea: before, she would not have chosen any earthly blessing in the world over her *polis'* hegemony.

Hands dangling between them as if taking a light-hearted stroll, they walked the short stretch back to the house. Flies buzzed in the air, a canopy of black speckles swarming around corpses left to rot. Alethea shivered, not so much because of the presence of death itself or because of the stench, but because the poor souls would wander around aimlessly in agony, lacking the proper burial rites. *Maybe they'll never reach the Underworld, but be stuck here forever, still feeling the plague gnawing to their bones, unable to make themselves heard. And all the rest of us chin-deep in pollution.*

Zesiro was the first to meet them in the vestibule. He quickly made the sign against evil once more, and his eyes were those of a man having both failed and been failed, but he said nothing, and there was nothing to say.

Alethea allowed herself to be led the familiar path to Eucleides' bedchamber. Passing through the *andron*, she caught sight of Cosimo slumped on his back on a *kline*, one arm thrown gracefully across his brow, the dim light illuminating the delicate curve of his throat and the sharp line of his collarbone.

'Asleep?' she hissed.

Eucleides threw a glance at his cousin and nodded.

'Good. He'd be enraged.'

'I'm sure he would see reason.'

'Really?' She could imagine the toxic remarks rolling off his tongue about how they would be better off with her on the street. In this particular matter Alethea did not wholly disagree. It suddenly occurred to her, however, that Cosimo's life would also be at greater risk with her present, and this prospect gave some small consolation.

Two days of pure deterioration ensued. Two days she spent slipping further down the trail of illness, until she knew precisely what the dead slaves and Eucleides' father had meant when they prayed for Hades to put them out of their humiliating misery. The fever, which escalated rapidly, was not unlike what she had suffered when riding the cargo mule on her way back to Sparta; the heat in her head made her so delirious that she sometimes had no idea what she was saying, and she saw the world through a quivering, red filter. No amount of clear, cool water fetched straight from the well could extinguish the dryness in her throat, no balms or baths could soothe the feeling of a thousand sunrays grilling her skin. On the fourth day, the blisters began to burst, emitting sticky pus which, unless carefully removed, dried into the already itching rashes underneath.

If I'd been slain on the battlefield, or died on Cosimo's trireme, or at Eleusis, or... Any one of those ends would have been better. Or in childbirth, honourably. Not like this, not in my own vomit.

It was rarely that she *did* find herself in her own vomit, since Eucleides had personally taken on the task of wiping her clean and dabbing her forehead, occasionally assisted by Agathe, his fingers clumsy at this task that he had only performed once before, for his father. His own eyes were turning red as well, but it was simply the result of keeping them open for too many hours at length, and sometimes the result of tears. Alethea wished first for her pains to cease, second for his eyes to dry, and third for everything else she had used to pray for. She dared not touch him for fear that the bursting blisters on her arms would magically wander to his smooth skin and settle there.

There came a day when their seemingly timeless existence confined together in the bedchamber was disrupted as Efigenia's pointy little face peered through a slit in the door. The girl pushed it open with all the dignity she could summon, and entered like a streak of white gold in a world of gloom.

'Oh, there you are,' Eucleides said, the cheer in his voice more forced than a stubborn donkey.

'You have us worried. We...we haven't seen you in a long time now—several days.'

'I thought keeping the door closed would be safest. The slaves have brought refreshments, more than we could need.'

Alethea watched the exchange from her lulling state between the sheets. They burned against her skin, but she was not tempted to expose her battered body to Efigenia's prudent eyes. *She would either flee or make a curt remark. I couldn't blame her.*

'I should like to speak to the Spartan alone, if you don't mind. If you do mind, I shall go at once.' She added the last bit with hasty reassurance.

Alethea looked at Eucleides, secretly hoping he would indeed mind, but of course he did not, and she found herself trying to focus on her mistress' features without much success.

'Well?' she croaked, voice rasping in her throat.

'I am afraid.' Efigenia clasped her hands in front of her, hard, the sharp bones in her shoulders poking through the *khitōn* as she tensed. 'I am afraid my husband might discover...you know.'

'What?'

'Please do not make me say it...you're making a fool of me!'

'*What*?' Alethea frowned. The fever clouded her mind, making it truly difficult to remember what in Zeus' name the girl was referring to. *Infidelity maybe? No, impossible...ah, yes, that belly of hers...funny story...*

'Be serious.'

'Don't talk so loud. My head hurts.'

'You have to help me, you simply have to.'

'Do I...do I look like I'm in a state to help *anyone*?' Alethea grimaced for emphasis, though the agony was genuine as she accidentally rubbed a blistered wrist against the bed.

Efigenia's lips parted, then closed and parted again, this time trembling. 'I know...I know you might die, and believe it or not, it's no joy to me. I can be shallow sometimes or speak harshly, zI know. But I need your help dearly.'

'I don't think the plague cares if you do.'

'But...but you don't understand. Yesterday, Lady Milos said he was not as ardent a father as he should be, so he put his hand here—to quiet her, I think—and for a while he said nothing.' She pressed her palm against the strapped-on belly, which did give in to the pressure just a little too much compared to the firm bulge one might expect to find on a pregnant woman. 'I told him...I told him it was just a layer of fat. I swear it isn't *that* though, I swear.' Tears sprung to her eyes.

'Cosimo...Cosimo is...' Alethea begun to flit into unconsciousness before snapping back. 'Cosimo has more than air in that...head of his. Clever. But he thinks you're not, so he would not think you capable. That's...the trick. They constantly underestimate us.'

Efigenia drew a quivering breath. 'I wish I were not capable. I wish I was not such a horrid wife.'

'Now my head hurts again. Don't start.'

'What if he wants to feel it kicking? What do I do then?'

'You think he will?'

The girl hesitated for a moment, then shook her head, thin coils escaping the twirled ivory comb digging deep into her hair.

Alethea shifted her weight trying to find a more comfortable position, but it was futile. 'You have several months left. You'll just have to act better.

When...*if* I get well, I'll help you adjust the size of that thing,' she said and gave a weak nod at Efigenia's belly.

Having extracted all the advice she could, the streak of white gold retreated towards the door, blurring, and moments later, Alethea was once more in the company of a bleary-eyed Eucleides.

'What did she want?' he asked.

'Womanly advice. You wouldn't understand.' *Half true, at least. Or entirely, perhaps.*

Eucleides drew in a breath as if to investigate the matter further, but seemed to change his mind and merely caressed the back of her hand resting in his. 'I'll let you sleep now. Do you think you can do that?'

'Not while my skin is burning.' She offered a half-smile. 'But I'll lie very still and quiet and pretend to if it lightens your heart.'

CHAPTER THIRTY-ONE

ALETHEA WAS RIGHT: Cosimo had not taken any lasting notice of the slightly odd feeling of Efigenia's stomach. He had never felt a pregnant belly before, and this lack of experience combined with lack of interest came to his young wife's fortunate rescue. However, Efigenia watched him grow more irritated with each passing day—planting plenty of concern on her part that she might be the underlying cause—until finally she could stand it no longer.

It was almost nightfall; they had taken their separate dinners of which one was non-existent, the other horrendously expensive, the food picked apart on the plate and thoroughly surveyed. Despite the late hour, the city was still simmering with life enhanced by death, the pale rose quartz-sky infused with pillars of black smoke from the funeral pyres always burning.

Efigenia mustered courage and reached for her husband's hand as she followed him through the passage from the dining room.

Cosimo halted. To her immense relief he did not withdraw his hand from hers, but it lay limp and dismissive. 'What now?'

'I...I only wanted to ask whether I have done anything to displease you. You haven't been very bright in spirit of late.'

'There's a plague ravaging our city. Brightness is hardly the natural sentiment.'

'No, of course not... But it's not my fault, then?'

'If you *must* know, my dear cousin spending every waking hour tending to his harlot is what displeases me.'

That's it! Not my fault, not my fault... Efigenia bobbed her head up and down. 'It displeases me also. What if he were to catch the disease?'

Something gleamed in Cosimo's eye, reminding her of a dog sniffing a faraway juicy bone. 'I suppose he might. It would be a dreadful thing.'

He turned from her, leaving, but Efigenia could not suppress the question now tickling her. 'Who...who would inherit his fortunes? The fortunes he himself inherited so recently?'

'I would. Go to bed. You're far too chatty tonight.'

His wife lingered several minutes before adhering to this instruction. She stood with her arms folded, watching the flat of his back grow smaller in the distance as he departed to his chambers. *"I would." That's what he said. I should have known— the closest living male relative, yes... All the silver from Laurion, glittering in his hands...* The image sent shivers down her spine. It was delightful, for would not her husband, when he had all the wealth he could desire, deck her in clothes worthy of a queen? She thought he might, if only to display said wealth in a socially acceptable manner.

The very next moment, dread struck her. The man who had shown her the most kindness ever since she arrived in the *oikos*, the man whom she loved like a brother though she had never dared tell him as much, dead so that she could live in even greater splendour than she already did? It would be unbearable. *And surely, surely Cosimo would never wish for such a thing either? Doesn't he love his cousin beyond that kind of monstrous idea? Or maybe...maybe it was I who now planted it in his mind, maybe he only meant he was displeased because it bored him to spend the days on his own.*

The whirlwind of thoughts kept spinning in Efigenia's head until she could no longer disentangle them and had to press her fingers to her temples to try and ease the ache.

Alethea whimpered and twisted where she lay, her skin and head burning, her stomach cramping as the sour bile continued to spurt from her chapped lips despite her bowls having been emptied long since.

A dark silhouette stood by the doorpost. Slowly, it floated across the floor, and as it approached, its face cleared for Alethea's sight.

'Brother?' she whispered hoarsely.

The figure gave no reply, but Apolonio's stern eyes looked down upon her with all the intensity possible.

'Brother? Don't...don't be cruel...say something.'

Apolonio extended a hand, pressing his palm against his sister's blistered cheek. Alethea almost flinched, expecting a thousand needles of pain at his touch, but found his skin startlingly pleasant against hers. No cool water, no soothing balm or fan had had any easing effect so far, yet Apolonio's hand was an all-consuming salvation. There was something more to it than the coolness. It was a symbol; Alethea was certain of it.

'I have to come back, don't I?' Her voice was barely audible now, her sore throat exhausted. 'I have to come back because you're the only one. And home is the only place. All this disease, oppression, lavishness... It's no good...' Another stomach cramp rode her body. When she recovered enough to return her attention to her surroundings, there was no trace of her floating visitor. 'Apolonio? Brother...? No, no...!'

Alethea had lost him again, and somehow it felt even more crushing than the first time, when they had parted at Eleusis over a year ago. Her cheek, where his hand had pressed just a moment ago, became sticky with tears.

But no... Perhaps I have not lost you again. Perhaps I have found you. If this was your message to me, then I will find you. Just you wait. Thus, in a feverish state yet with clearer resolve than ever, she knew the course her life would have to take: the course home, back to Sparta, back to Apolonio, away from this infested nest called Athens. Here resided her love, and here resided the root to her every unhappiness. At her destination resided a different type of love, love of the river and the mountains and, above all, of her life-long companion. At her destination resided a hundred possible sources of happiness.

CHAPTER THIRTY-TWO

COSIMO? Are you in there?' Eucleides stuck his head into the room and entered.

The bedchamber was empty save for one of the dogs who lay with its damp black nose resting against its pawns in one corner. He was just about to turn and leave and resume his search for Cosimo elsewhere, when something in the corner of his eye sparked his curiosity. There, what appeared to be a thin scroll poked out from underneath the bed. Kneeling, Eucleides extracted it and carefully unrolled it, eyes skimming the writing. The words were unlike anything he had ever read before. Each black letter was like a needle to his skin. *Impossible.* He had never doubted the legitimacy of his father's marriage to his mother—he had never been given any reason to do so—but if this document was genuine, it had been nothing more than the relationship between a wealthy man and his concubine. It claimed a previous marriage of his mother to a Corinthian man, a marriage which her relatives would not be able to testify was a pretence, since they had long since left Athens.

'What are you doing here?'

Eucleides' head snapped up. 'There you are. I—'

'What's that in your hand? Give it to me. Now!' Cosimo strode across the room and snatched the scroll from Eucleides' hands.

Eucleides frowned and stood up so that he would not have to crane his neck to look at the other man. 'You know what it says, then?'

Cosimo's face was a perfect mask of stone but his reply came just a little too late. 'No. No, I do not. Why?'

'I think you do, and I think you should tell me where you found it, and why you kept it hidden rather than show it to me.'

'That's of little importance, cousin dear. I know it's difficult for you but we simply have to face the facts: you were not conceived in a lawful union. You have my sympathies.'

Eucleides could only stare. *Something isn't right. You're behaving too...too...* 'Did you craft this forgery? Did you write this?' He latched out, taking back the scroll. This time, his gaze went straight to the end of the text, where the sentence stopped abruptly, left unfinished.

Cosimo blew out a whiff of air. 'Don't be ridiculous.'

'I am not.'

'I hope you realise what it is you are accusing me of.' His face was a hand's width from Eucleides', a blue vein pulsating at his temple. 'Perhaps your Spartan whore put you up to it. That wouldn't be surprising at all.'

Eucleides shoved Cosimo back with both hands. 'Don't call her that! Haven't you done enough to anguish her, not to speak of your wife? And now you want *my rightful* inheritance? After all these years, all the years I've excused you and supported you when others said—'

'She really *has* infected your mind! Don't you know that all you have is my doing? Your social standing, your friends in the *ecclesia*, everything. Where would you be without me?' Cosimo hissed, his voice reaching an odd pitch.

Far happier, I should think. What wouldn't I give to turn back the clock, to rid myself of all the time I've spent folding under you? He said nothing, though, but let the scroll—doubtlessly a forgery, the more he thought of it—drop to the floor, then stalked out of the bedchamber.

Day by day, Alethea regained the health she had thought was lost forever. She could hardly believe her luck when the torturous blisters healed and her bowel movements returned to normal. *How I used to take these reliefs for granted! I won't ever again, I swear by Asclepius.* As the plague seeped from her veins and she regained her strength, devouring the plates of lamb stew and the cups of fat milk that Eucleides eagerly presented her with, it felt as if her survival was a sign. A sign that what she had realised in her feverish haze had to be translated to action, a sign that the reason she was still alive was so that she could return to Sparta. It would not be so difficult now as it had been once; with Athens in chaos and with Eucleides completely on her side, escaping was a very real prospect. However, there was one last thing Alethea needed to obtain first: vengeance.

So many months had passed during which she had nurtured an ever-deepening hatred for the man who had abducted her from the coastal town: the way he could sweet-talk one second and dismiss everything the world had to offer the next, the way his impeccable appearance never failed him, his hubris, his marble-like skin and his physique, which was far from Spartanly robust. She hated when he showered his dogs with affection and his wife with cruelty, she hated how nothing was ever quite good enough and how he picked his way through every meal. Most of all, he hated what he had done to her. Throughout all these months she had been twice-fold agitated by the fact that neither of the two people whom she might have shared this sentiment with understood; they had both been blinded by some strange attraction Alethea could not grasp.

But now? Perhaps now they're starting to see. Efigenia's fear of being discovered was rubbing raw against her nerves, no doubt adding to the accumulation of nasty emotions she associated with her husband whether she liked it or not. If the repulsive beddings—because that was what they were, Alethea knew, though the girl would never acknowledge it—and the constant cold comments did not suffice to tip the scales, then that fear just might.

And Eucleides... He'll see that it's either him and us or his bastard for a cousin. She had noticed a rare blend of fury and despair in his eyes when he told her what Cosimo had done and said, not only regarding the inheritance and the forgery but all the little slights over the years. There was no knowing how far Cosimo was willing to go to put his hands on the money at stake, but considering his attitude towards wealth, in itself inherited from his mother, Alethea did not doubt her lover had reason to fear for his own life. Whether she was right or not, well, it hardly mattered. If Eucleides believed it, and his belief drove him to compliance with the scheme taking shape in her mind, it would only do him good in the long run.

As Alethea pondered how the situation in the *oikos* had gradually changed, a sweet warmth spread in her stomach. If she could just manoeuvre with a little skill and luck, she might be able to reap not only her own long-awaited revenge but liberate others from her abductor's claws as well—and then they could finally leave Athens.

Before she knew it, she had launched herself into a whirr of fantasies quite unlike her, fantasies of the wondrous future she hoped to obtain through a horrid deed, a horrid deed that would perhaps be closer to heroic in this particular case. *Surely, the gods discriminate. Surely, they know the difference between killing a stranger on sacred Eleusinian temple ground and demanding a perfectly justified repayment for harm done? We received purification once already. We can get it again.*

Efigenia had never before been summoned by a slave, nor had she expected to be as long as she lived. Nonetheless, she complied when Alethea asked her to the *bibliotheca*, not least because she had never entered this room of wise men's works. She had been on the verge once, but her husband had caught her and redirected her back to the *gynaikeon*.

Both Alethea and Eucleides were waiting for her as she crossed the threshold and let her eyes wander over the five sturdy chests presumably containing scrolls. The slave girl was perched on the desk, feet dangling, while her lover sat on the *klismos*, playing with her fingers. They looked like pieces from two different puzzles who somehow fit perfectly together, and Efigenia's insides twisted with envy.

'What...what is it you want from me?' she asked.

Alethea looked up. 'Ah. Come closer. I'll be honest with both of you. I have a request—a desire. I'm afraid you won't like it one bit, but you must listen carefully.'

Efigenia did as asked and came closer to the desk despite her ominous feeling. *Whatever it is, it can't be good.*

'We all have a mutual enemy, whether you know it or not. A viper not fit to lick the soles of a beggar's sandals,' Alethea continued.

Eucleides tugged at his lip. 'A month ago, I would have opposed those strong words, but I'm not so sure as I once was. It grieves me.'

'And you, *Lady*?'

Efigenia gaped. 'I...I...no! I cannot allow a slave to speak thus! Eucleides... Please, won't you tell her?'

Eucleides remained quiet.

'But you're *wrong*... My husband has never done damage to anyone...' *Silly girl. A proper wife wouldn't even be here.*

'Ha!' Alethea heaved herself down from the desk and folded her arms. 'Let's see, shall we? He abducted me, took me away from all I held dear, made me his servant, treated me with contempt ever since. He forged a document to rob his cousin of his inheritance and I bet he wouldn't hesitate to take more extreme measures if he had to. And *you*? You he has raped—or at least you haven't had much option—and diminished and the gods only know what else. Look at yourself! You're all skin and bones and fear!' She drew a deep breath; the speech seemed to have exhausted her.

Efigenia studied the floor through a hot mist of tears. 'I know. Don't you think I know that?'

'Then, there is the matter of your *pregnancy*. Don't worry. He knows.' Alethea nodded at Eucleides, who buried his face in his hands.

'What...what are you saying?'

'I am saying that you have two alternatives. Either you do as I ask and go on to have a much-improved life, or you can oppose it and all of Athens will know of your deceit, including Cosimo. I'd rather you cooperated willingly, though.' Alethea closed her eyes for a brief moment, presumably mustering niceness. 'Please. It would be better for you, too.'

'You still have not told me what it is you want.' *But I can figure it out, I think. Oh dear god*

This time, it was Eucleides who spoke, his expression blank but his voice tormented. 'She wants him dead. And she needs us to help her. And I...I can't refuse, not any longer.'

An unwieldy mass of questions flickered through Efigenia's head. What kind of person would she be? Was death not too harsh a punishment? Who was she to judge? How could it be done, and what would follow? With the questions came an equal number of images, images of every time she had felt like a beetle trampled under Cosimo's foot, every time she had forced herself to beam rather than twitch when he touched her. She had loved him and hated him for a year and a half, and she realised she would waste away if she continued to do so much longer, her sixteen years turning into sixty. *And if he found out I tricked him... What would he do to me? Do I really want to know? No, I don't. And I'm* not *a silly girl.*

Efigenia swallowed. 'Tell me what I need to do.'

The plan was simple. Eucleides would reconcile with his cousin, which presented no great obstacle, since Cosimo was eager to think himself free of suspicion. When the opportunity arose, namely when Athens had recovered enough from the plague, they would attend a *symposion* together. Eucleides would break the locks on the door before they left, and distract the hopefully drunken Cosimo when they returned. Alethea would perform the deed itself.

Efigenia's part was perhaps even simpler: to stay out of the way, and to rid the house of some precious necklaces and earrings—she was the only one except Lady Milos who had access to the jewellery box—so that a burglary ended in violence seemed plausible. The missing jewellery, the broken locks, and the feigned alarm they would raise were all aimed at having that effect.

'And...*afterwards*? What happens to me then?' Efigenia whispered.

Alethea offered a strangely warm smile. 'That's almost the best part. Afterwards, you come with us away from this hellhole. That will be your reward: a chance to start anew without a husband or a father controlling your every move. We say your pregnancy ended in miscarriage, and no one will ever know it was a sham.'

'But where will you go?'

'First Delphi, to ask for counsel from the oracle, then Sparta. But don't worry. We can drop you off along the way, maybe in some sanctuary. Of course you could stay in Athens, but as a childless young widow... Your father would only have you married off again. You know that, don't you?'

When Efigenia left the *bibliotheca* an hour later, her world had turned on its axis. She almost could not comprehend what had just transgressed. The plan was madness, the act was morbid, the aftermath would be an unbelievable mess. Alethea claimed they, meaning she, was going to figure out the details in the days to follow, yet Efigenia felt as if standing at a dwindling height with an abyss below. *I never thought she'd do something as lunatic as this, something so rash. But then I never thought I would, either.*

CHAPTER THIRTY-THREE

THE NIGHT WAS painfully serene. A blanket of dark velvet enveloped Athens, the stars aligning clear and bright. If they could sing, their music would have been the soothing ripples of a harp. When Alethea leaned back to gaze at them, she at once remembered the stories of how they came to be there—Orion the huntsman, Heracles, Pegasus. She shook her head in frustration, cursing the night for its lack of proper atmosphere. *Doesn't it know these are the hours of death? Shouldn't the moon be embedded in heavy, dark clouds, shouldn't there be biting wind or pouring rain?* It appeared not. After all, the weather was not always so compliant to the situation as the tragedians would have one believe.

Alethea turned her attention to the iron dagger's point, sharp enough to cleave a strand of hair. She had acquired it in the *agorá* a few days ago, veiled to disguise her face. The weapon almost looked decorative. The knives she had used performing different daily tasks in Sparta had been twice the size, and it rested unsettlingly light in her hand, but she had considered every part of the deed in great detail. *I only hope the others have, too. If they buckle and waver, if they are caught in some silly fit of old affection... It's true what I told Eucleides that time:*

loyalty is admirable, but if one chooses the wrong loyalties, it can be terribly impractical. She slipped the dagger back into its sheath and returned it to the deep pocket sewn between the folds of her *khitōn.* Then she exhaled slowly, attempting to drain the tension from her muscles, and descended down the staircase, the clicking of her sandals loud as thunder in her ears.

The courtyard lay abandoned by all life save for a few fluttering moths and crickets. Alethea tripped across the stone tiles, past the fountain and the bench, until she reached the opposite side of the colonnade. Like a perfectly symmetric forest of marble trees, the columns seemed to tower higher than usual, the starlight too faint to disperse the dense shadows between them. There, by the fifth column from the far-left corner, Alethea melted into the marble forest, out of view from whomever might pass through the courtyard, resting both palms and cheek against the cold stone. *All I have to do is wait.*

Waiting, it turned out, was easier said than done. She had no means of measuring the time other than counting under her breath. Shortly after reaching seven hundred, the numbers tangled in her head and she had to start from zero again. *What if they're stuck at that cursed symposion? What if Eucleides hasn't remained sober enough? What if...*

Muffled voices interrupted her thoughts.

'I feel nauseous.' Cosimo emerged on unsteady legs into the moonlit open space, his companion following a few steps behind.

Alethea bit her tongue. Eucleides' arms were pressed close to his body, his movements rigid. If Cosimo had not been drunk beyond his senses, the false good humour in the younger man's voice would hardly have fooled him.

'That doesn't surprise me. Come.'

'That man was a...terrible sum...*symposiarch*. Unfair, too.'

'It was his right to dictate the amounts for each guest. He was kinder to me, I suppose.'

And thank the gods for that. Alethea was realising with every passing moment just how haphazard the plan was, but then a certain haphazardness served most crimes favourably. If they had bribed the *symposiarch*, such a thing might have been revealed afterwards; now, they had achieved the desired effect simply by picking the right drinking party and trusting in the fact that there were many who would gladly take the chance to torture Cosimo with wine, despite his occasional honeyed flattery.

Eucleides' shoulders tensed further as he escorted their prey towards the fifth column. 'Here. Lean against that and I'll help you untie your sandals.'

Cosimo accepted the peculiar offer without protest. Like a dozing child, he stretched out one foot to the now-kneeling Eucleides, head lolling against the stone behind him.

Alethea could smell him from the other side of the column separating them. She held her breath as she reached into her pocket, pulled out the dagger from its sheath, elevated her arm and—

The iron clattered against stone. Alethea almost choked on thin air. Never in her worst nightmares had she imagined dropping the deadly weapon in the most critical moment. The thought was too ludicrous to even think, yet it had happened.

Cosimo flinched at the sharp sound and his eyes darted over the floor, trying to locate the fallen object, but he was as unsuccessful as Alethea in the dense dark.

Eucleides was still kneeling, stiff with shock. 'Never mind that. Probably just one of the dogs.' The words came slowly from behind his teeth.

Alethea considered her options during a single heartbeat: to leap forth and blindly search the floor with her hands would give their victim plenty of time to grasp the situation; to remain idle and let the moment slip away felt impossible. Her dressing pins were neither sharp nor large enough to perform the deed with, and she dared not entrust the matter entirely to Eucleides.

Cosimo took a wobbly step forward. Without quite knowing what she was doing, Alethea leaped forth and hooked her arm around his neck from behind in an attempt to strangle or at the very least hold him still so that Eucleides might find the knife. The young man emitted a gurgling little sound of surprise and grabbed her arm with both hands, trying to wring her from him.

Eucleides' eyes were round like globes and a moment passed before he moved. It was painfully obvious that he had never before hit someone properly, except perhaps at Eleusis, and the blow landed on Alethea's wrist rather than on his cousin's face. Cosimo seized the opportunity and flung Alethea from him with a force she had not thought he possessed, the side of her head smashing against the column behind them. The blood rushed in her ears. Three, four heartbeats passed while she struggled to make sense of her surroundings and briefly examined her limbs for broken bones. She fumbled to wipe the blood-smeared hair from her eyes and blinked frantically, trying to discern anything, the stars and the moon being her only source of light in the black of night and the red of blood. The pounding in her cheek brought back memories of the day she had acquired her scar, only this pain was duller and stretched into her skull.

What she did see sent cold rat's feet of panic skittering up her spine: Cosimo's knees pressed down upon Eucleides' wrists, making it impossible for him to move, and though her old captor was far from sturdily built, the entirety of his weight was enough to disarm his opponent beyond all hope. Cosimo's arm was lodged against Eucleides' throat, slowly choking whether it was his intention or not.

'Is this...this your repaymun...repayment to me? After...everything I've done for you?'

Eucleides' reply was naught but a wheezing sound.

'Spartan whore co...corrupted you! You let her! You would—cold blood...'

Light steps padded against the bare stone, then the scrape of metal followed by the sound of flesh being pierced, and Cosimo's words turned into rattling. Thick, dark liquid trickled over his pale lips and throat, accumulating in a little pool on his cousin's face and collarbone.

By Artemis and everything sacred— Alethea's heart hammered violently as she finally managed to get on her feet and cross the space separating her from the others. She grabbed hold of Cosimo's neckline to pull him away from Eucleides, but it was hardly needed, because the force in his body was seeping out with the blood dripping from his mouth, until he crumbled to the side.

Alethea threw herself forward to examine Eucleides for fatal injuries, and cursed loudly over the lack of proper light.

'I—' he wheezed. 'I just need—'

'To be quiet. And drink fat goat's milk with honey, I think.' *At least that* sounds *soothing.*

Cosimo's body twitched over and over again where it lay. At first Alethea thought it might be the kind of twitches she had seen in soldiers and animals, when the last inkling of life struggles against death's embrace before giving way. Then she saw Efigenia's owl-wide eyes and her stick-thin arm moving the dagger mechanically in and out her husband's body until his skin must have started to resemble a needle pad.

'Stop it! Stop!' Alethea hissed, taking hold of Efigenia's arm to stay the dagger before it once more pierced its target. 'You'll make a mess!'

'There—there you go—you...' The words came strangled and choppy, quickly turning into a blend of sobs and giggles. Had she not looked so tiny and almost transparent in her unusually plain garments, her conduct would have been intimidating to the most seasoned of warriors.

Eucleides had risen to his feet, his face was struck with horror, and was successful in wrestling the blade from Efigenia's hands. And so there they stood: three figures in a poor state staring at a fourth, which was hardly even a figure anymore, each trying in vain to comprehend the magnitude of their actions, each fervently doing their best to remember the latter part of the plan.

'Can we...can we still say it was burglars?' Eucleides wheezed.

'Not if she's seen. Look at her. She was supposed to keep out of the way!' Alethea nodded at Efigenia. 'It was supposed to be clean enough to keep bloodstains from our clothes, and she's soaked.'

'Could you really have done it that clean?' the girl whispered. The sobs and giggles still came in a trickle.

'I would certainly have tried. And we could have rid ourselves of my clothes much easier than yours. We'll have to burn them.'

Eucleides frowned, 'Light the hearth in the middle of the summer night? Someone would notice, it would all seem too odd.'

I know that. *Maybe this was* too *haphazard. Maybe we've thrown ourselves into a perilous pit of stupidity and error.*

Alethea crossed her arms, hugging herself tight. 'It can't be mended now. You go upstairs and change and calm your nerves. Hide the *khitōn* and we can take care of it in the morning. Have you done away with the jewellery? Good. I'll go back to Eucleides' bedchamber and feign sleep, and he'll sound alarm in just a little while.' She turned to Eucleides. 'Those marks on your throat might actually help convince people, though of course you shall have to tell the story skilfully of how you only barely survived the brutes who broke in and killed your cousin. We'll leave the body, naturally, and the knife too. Then you can tell them the perpetrators dropped it in their haste, whereas if we tried to hide it and it was discovered...' Althea drew a deep breath. *I don't think I've wasted my voice to that extent for years. But* someone *has to take care of this mess.*

Eucleides nodded, slowly. 'I can do that. I may not be a very good liar, but I do tell stories well. I can do it.'

'You have to.' Her eyes softened for an instant as she beheld his courageous attempt to keep his own nerves under control. 'I don't like this part more than any of you do. But there is no turning back now.'

Efigenia was holding out the lower part of her *khitōn*, spreading it like a fan before her, eyeing the damp patches of crimson. 'Look at me,' she whispered, her voice as soaked in misery as the linen was in blood. 'I look as if I've bled to death in childbirth. I never will, and he'll never know—' A giggle broke off the sentence.

'Shh! Please!' Eucleides pleaded.

'He will be...vexed with me for ruining my clothes. Very vexed...'

'Please don't. Come now, won't you go upstairs?
Go back to sleep, if you can, hide that thing. Please?'
'If you want me to.'

CHAPTER THIRTY-FOUR

EUCLEIDES HAD WOKEN the whole house a mere hour earlier, rambling and shouting and nearly crying, telling everyone the well-rehearsed story of the burglary. Alethea thought the tumult of genuine emotions that must have been in his chest only added realism to the act. Eventually, Zesiro had covered Cosimo's body with a sheet and ushered everyone back to their beds, since nothing more could be done before daybreak.

Eucleides' legs dangled over the edge of the roof, heels kicking against the limestone. The contours of the city below were sheathed in darkness; the bright spatters that were funeral pyres were not nearly as frequent as they had been the previous month when the plague raged at its peak.

Alethea treaded carefully so she would not startle him, the warm stone strangely comforting against her bare soles. She squatted down next to him and crossed her legs, resting her elbows on her knees and her hands by her ankles, filling her lungs with night until she thought she might burst.

'It's surreal. I—I can still feel him pressing against my throat, still hear his voice. And his dogs, I think they wonder where he is,' Eucleides said, speaking slowly as if in a trance. Only a couple of hours had passed since the murder, but his voice had recovered to a great extent.

Alethea tilted her head back, searching for the constellations on the black canvas sky. 'Well. It will fade, just like the man in Eleusis faded after some time.'

'You told me yourself that you were the one to kill him.'

'Yes. And Efigenia did it this time, and it was I who orchestrated it. Your role was no worse than at Eleusis.'

'But this is still different. I knew it was going to happen, I was there when we planned it, and I consented without being under the spell of the *kykeon*. And he was as far from a stranger as it gets. How can I ever forget?'

'You don't have to forget. You only have to see the necessity in it and not let it burden you so.'

'Does it not burden you?'

Alethea gave an abrupt laugh. 'If it had been anyone but *him*, it would have. But no, in this mess, I feel like an ingot of iron has been lifted from my shoulders.'

Eucleides said nothing for a long while. It appeared that the drastic turn of events had switched their roles: now it was she who spoke and he who sat in silence.

Finally, he turned to gaze at her in the dark, the whites of his eyes like chips of bone. 'I do not think they will accuse me, or you.'

'No, I do not think so either. Why would anyone doubt what you tell them? This house has plenty of riches for burglars to seek, and he had plenty of enemies for the law courts to consider before their eyes could fall on us.'

'Precisely.' Eucleides' hand was pleasantly warm as he cupped her cheek in his palm. 'The story won't crack, just so long as we don't.'

'Then you must promise me not to. Efigenia is...Efigenia is trouble enough.'

He gave a slight, quick shake of his head. 'Stop fretting over me, please. I am not as soft-hearted as when you found me.'

No, no you aren't, and somehow it almost saddens me. Alethea pressed her forehead to his. 'Are you sorry for it?' she mumbled.

'Perhaps I should be. Can I ask you something?'

'Anything.'

'Why a knife? Why not poison or something equally...easy?'

'Two reasons. Firstly, if he had just dropped dead, it would have been obvious that someone in the *oikos* did it, and the physicians could find out what poison was used. This way, there was a reasonable explanation and less sneaking. Secondly, I wanted to feel it. You must despise me.'

'I could never.'

They stayed there for better part of the hour, the night growing even more dense around them, reaching its zenith. Neither of them saw any use in attempting to sleep; their dreams would be more exhausting than being awake, if they at all managed to drift off.

When morning came, there was another matter which had to be dealt with: the hurricane of questions that was the astounded Lady Milos. After being awoken and greeted with her son's massacred body and her nephew's shocking account of the past hours, she had somehow managed to go to bed again. Now, however, it appeared she was fully taking in what had happened.

Eucleides had never seen a face twitch like Lady Milos' did as he carefully lay out his words before her, silently praying she would not see past the guile.

Her cheeks shifted from ash-grey to cherry-red and back again. Only her eyes remained the same, set in disbelief but as dry as the deserts in Africa.

'What of my son's body?'

'I believe we ought to make arrangements for the burial. I don't think you want to see the body. I'm afraid it is quite macabre, aunt.'

'Oh, yes. Must the burial be expensive?'

'Not abundantly. But we cannot shy away from the public—it mustn't look *shabby*.'

'Well, then, dearest. I shall indulge in a nap. I never do, but the incident has taken a toll.'

You always indulge in a nap, and the incident hasn't taken that much of a toll on you. But I won't argue. Eucleides studied his aunt's face, which had returned to its normal colour. The initial shock might have been staggering, but the woman had recovered remarkably quickly. Perhaps she mourned her son no more than his perpetrators did—perpetrators now planning their victim's burial—and Eucleides wondered whether she would have stopped them had she known. *Surely, she would have. No mother can wish for the death of her child, regardless of the crackles in the so-called love between them. But perhaps I won't have to worry about the poor lady's heart. Though there's something else that will wound it.*

'Aunt?'

'Yes?'

Eucleides drew a deep breath. 'I intend to make a journey. Soon. In fact, I'm leaving Athens once the proper rites have been carried out and the trial is over. If there is a trial. Alethea—you call her Doris, I think—will go with me.'

Lady Milos' face began shifting in colour again and her nephew immediately regretted revealing his plans to her so soon.

'Leaving? Leaving Athens, leaving *me*? With your...your *mistress*? What will become of your pitiful—'

'I have no choice!' Eucleides forced a note of harmony into his voice, clashing badly with the whirlwind in his chest. 'I feel the memories would be too painful if I stayed. Besides, it was Cosimo who drove the politics we conducted—I have no role in the *ecclesia* without him, at least not if I am to follow my heart. And I would very much like to do just that.'

Lady Milos surveyed him, a suspicious gleam in her eye, 'And where would your heart take you?'

'I don't know yet, Aunt. I will seek council from the Pythia, and if Apollo has no words of wisdom for me, I have no doubts I will find out for myself.'

'It all sounds like wishful dreaming to me.'

'Maybe. If it is any comfort to you, I'm leaving the better part of the fortune in your capable hands. With the silver from the mines and my late father's savings, you won't be bereft of anything. Does it please you?'

He did not have to wait for a reply; it was as if the sun itself had come out from behind a cloud and illuminated the old woman's doughy face. The mere idea of being able to purchase all the glistening gold bracelets and emerald earrings she could ever desire seemed to more than compensate for her son's brutal death and her nephew's impending departure.

'It does me good to hear it. A much-needed consolation indeed. And Efigenia?'

'What of her?'

'She will be returned to her father's *oikos*, I presume. I shall miss the girl, I won't deny it.'

'I heard Thaddeus is on the island of Serfios in business. He may not be home in over a fortnight—until then, she'll stay here.' *And that will give us some time to prepare our own journey, or rather, escape.*

'Good. Yes, good.'

Eucleides nodded. 'I'll leave you to your nap.'

Efigenia stared at the *himation* she had been weaving with such fervent fingers. Cosimo would not have any use of it now; he would never have to be pained by the tiny knot in the yarn that his wife had accidentally woven into the hem. A strangled sob escaped her at the thought, turning into laughter as she struggled to contain both the joy over what felt like the greatest freedom in the world, and the horror over what she had done to obtain it. *How angry he would have been that I spoiled both mine and his fancy clothes with all that blood.*

'Efigenia?'

'Lady?'

'You don't look well at all, my girl. I presume the shock is wearing on your nerves.' Lady Milos waddled up to the loom where her widowed daughter-in-law sat, and sank down on a *klimos* next to it, the wood creaking under her weight.

Efigenia fumbled for words. *She can't know. That's what Alethea would say.* 'Yes, yes, the shock. It wears on my nerves.'

'So I can see. Well, I was quite stunned myself when I heard. A strange business, to think the jewellery box was not even broken. What a clever burglar!' Lady Milos' eyes, like little black beads, peered at Efigenia.

'I... Yes, very clever. I hope you manage to replace the riches.'

'With one expensive mouth less for this *oikos* to feed, I'm sure I will.'

'Oh. Good.'

'A few more things did strike me. To kill one man so morbidly and only give another choking marks, well, it certainly displays a variety in method.' She began twisting the heirloom ring on her finger back and forth. 'And your miscarriage was really rather...clean.'

Efigenia stared at Lady Milos, then down at her own stomach, where the bulge had vanished. She had, being preoccupied to say the least, forgotten to display any alarm at the supposed miscarriage. 'Yes...yes, Lady. It was very...very neat. My loss caused it. I did not want to trouble you.'

'I see.'

Tensed silence fell over them like a wet blanket. *She knows. Of course she knows.*

Their eyes met for a long moment.

At last, Lady Milos stood up. 'The law courts would not take my word, regardless. My nephew tells me he's leaving Athens, taking that crude slave girl with him. I'll miss him awfully, naturally, but he has entrusted me with the majority of the household assets, so I shall not live in squalor.'

'It pleases me to hear, Lady.'

'Yes. Well, I'll leave you to your weaving, my girl. And do scrub your nails.'

As the goose-like woman departed, Efigenia cast a hasty glance at her hands and discovered the thin line of dried blood along her cuticles. *Foolish. Foolish, foolish...*

It appeared that they had committed a hundred mistakes, all of which now lined up before her. She had not thought to smash the lock on the jewellery box, but had used the key that her mother-in-law trusted only her with. She had then tucked away the gold and precious stones at the bottom of her clothing chest, where they would have to stay until she found a way of dispersing with them.

She had stood dead quiet by the top of the staircase, listening to the low hum of voices from below, biting her tongue bloody as she waited and waited. When waiting became too agonizing, she had scuttled down the steps without a single sane thought lodging in her head. Only one instinct drove her in that moment: the unbenevolent urge to perform the grisly act with her own two hands, before Cosimo's life had already been spilt and there was no revenge left for her to take. Alethea believed it was *her* revenge, yet Efigenia could not ward off the zealous voice thundering inside her. It was unlike any emotion that had taken her in its grip before—or perhaps it was all those emotions she had not allowed herself to feel that now came bubbling to the surface. The clatter when the knife collided with the floor had been the last drop. If she had not done it, she doubted it would have been done at all.

The handle had been warm from Alethea's grip. Efigenia barely dared think of what had happened next. It was too bizarre. Still, it had happened and now her cuticles were coloured with her husband's blood. *Will it ever truly wash off? Maybe if I scrub and scrub for the remnant of my life. Only I don't want to spent my days doing that.* Her emotions were tangled and twisted, indiscernible at times, and she suspected they would be for a good while. However, there was one sentiment that had not touched her even once: regret. Regardless of the remorse and the disbelief she felt, the relief overpowered every wave of it just when she thought she could stand it no longer.

Efigenia was free, or at least she was on the path to freedom. While her father was out on his travels, word would not reach him, and she would not be forced back to his household until he returned. Though she did not know how much time she had at her disposal, she hoped to be long gone before her relatives demanded her back so that they might trade her off in another marriage alliance.

What ignited the greatest fear in her was the thought of smothering herself for another husband, both in the marital bed and outside it, whether he was a decent man or not. If she became a priestess—if the fates willed it, if the opportunity presented itself—no one could blame her for abstaining from remarrying. Furthermore, she would be protected from much of the dangers of the war still engulfing Hellas. Naturally, not even priestesses were guaranteed a haven from either war or rape, but they certainly occupied a position of relative security and privilege, being allowed greater independence than any wife. *Independence.* The word tasted strange on Efigenia's tongue whenever she tried whispering it to herself. *Freedom* sounded absurd enough, but independence was so far beyond everything she had ever known that it might as well have been spoken in a foreign language. *Would I like it?* There was no way of knowing other than by finding out, and although the plan that their trio had crafted was sketchy at best, it was hardly worse than the risk they had undertook when committing the murder itself. In leaving Athens, Efigenia was leaving all she had, yet she stood to gain more than that.

As long as I don't wind up in Sparta. That would be dreadful. She had heard plenty of gory stories about the tyrannous city state in the Peloponnese, and seen enough of what the inhabitants were like through her acquaintance with Alethea. Although the Spartan woman—Efigenia found it difficult to think of her as a slave after their shared crime and deceits—was not the baffling stranger she had been some time ago, her ideals and behaviours were still of a type that Efigenia would rather not live surrounded by. *If Eucleides goes with her to that place, I'll miss him, yes, I'll miss him horribly. But I won't follow, no... I will only follow them as far as I must go to find solace. Happiness, even, if it doesn't escape my grip again.*

CHAPTER THIRTY-FIVE

THE CHARGE OF murder had to be made by a citizen with a personal relationship to the victim, in essence a close relative, since the crime had not been committed against the state or the public. Cosimo's closest male relative being Eucleides, it was a peculiar situation. He claimed he had not recognised the brutal burglars and therefore did not know whom to accuse. Other relatives could be consulted, but few were willing to speculate in and investigate a matter that appeared without resolve. Eucleides' doe-eyed face and genuinely devastated voice worked well; his peers believed his story without flinching, and despite being anxious to convict the perpetrator, they knew it was a hopeless task to search the entire *polis* for two unknown men who had allegedly been masked during the break-in. Protagoras' schooling had been efficient. Alethea thanked the gods for this and for the lack of witnesses, as well as Lady Milos' quiet cooperation. In truth, she could not have wished for a more favourable aftermath.

In lack of a guilty party, the *Areopagus,* the part of the Athenian law court system that tried intentional homicide, convicted the weapon, as was custom. The knife—the blade wiped clean though specks of blood remained on the handle—was hence exiled and taken far from Athens. This measure was supposed to save the public from the contagious pollution a murder resulted in; it was a desperate solution but the symbolism of it sufficed to calm the Athenians. *How stupid, really. A weapon doesn't kill, a person does. But all the better for us.*

To Alethea's surprise, Eucleides and Efigenia were every bit as eager as she to leave the city. As far as she knew, the young widow had never possessed any great love for it, and Eucleides' had rapidly turned to aversion through all he had experienced within the Long Walls this past summer. He was still Athenian at the core, but his outermost layers shifted, and Alethea suspected she had made him a man who no longer knew what kind of life he wished to live. *I must help him find his way, then. Could he thrive in Sparta?* She doubted it, however much she wanted to believe it. Eucleides had changed, true, but that kind of transition was too fundamental even for a murder to bring about. Efigenia was even worse suited for the Peloponnese, with her fondness for luxuries and her dainty illusions. From now on, she would have to manage without ivory combs regardless, but perhaps she would not have to go so far as to comply with Spartan frugality. Nevertheless, she could not be left behind, not if she was to avoid her father hauling her back in and trading her off to some other man. An escape was necessary.

Alethea had her sights set on home, and she intended to get there with as little ado as possible. She had already thought up a plan, just as she had told her accomplices. They would visit the oracle of Delphi to seek her advice on what their respective futures might hold.

The oracle, the Pythia, was all of Hellas' well of knowledge. For centuries, the woman occupying the post had prophesied the fates of princes and warlords, beggars and merchants, kingdoms and villages. Her instructions were never plain and her forebodings came in the shape of indiscernible tongue-twisters which the priests then interpreted for the visiting consultants. It was said that Apollo himself induced the Pythia into trance, explaining why she only received consultants during the nine warmest months of the year, since the god abandoned his temple in wintertime.

She, if anyone, must have answers to our uncertainties. We'll bring a sacrificial kid and some gold and all that's required.

On the fifteenth day since *that night,* their little group of three set out from Athens: Eucleides and Alethea on the coach box, Efigenia safely tucked away under the carriage's covering, the kid for Delphi resting there as well, occasionally emitting a trembling bleat. They had brought with them the most necessary things, a term that held a vastly different meaning for each of them. Alethea's luggage consisted only of what she would have needed to survive in the wilderness; Eucleides had filled the carriage with beloved scrolls; Efigenia had taken her sister's lyre and her most flattering clothes, although her various beauty concoctions had been left behind. Lady Milos' jewellery, supposedly stolen by the burglars, would be used to pay the oracle. Not a single slave was accompanying them, but the privacy they needed for the quest did not allow for that kind of luxury.

The two horses trotted on tirelessly, their pointy ears turning from side to side, listening for sudden noises, their glassy eyes serene as they heard none. The road was uneven and narrow, the carriage wheels bumping over countless stones, but Alethea's heart warmed with every *stadion* they put between themselves and the Long Walls. The proper autumn winds would still be a month or so in coming, but a pleasant breeze whisked her hair and tickled her neck, and the feeling of freedom only increased with the endlessly blue sky stretching out above. It felt as if she had not seen that much sky in ages.

When they were a safe distance from the city, Eucleides handed Alethea the reins and leaned back to remove the woollen blanket that lay spread over their luggage in the carriage.

A pointy little face emerged, hair like a cloud of gold around it. Efigenia at once began untangling the strands and with much difficulty smooth down the cloud, then climbed to the front of the carriage. The space was made for two rather than three, but none of them were broad-shouldered.

'This is...this is madness. I...I never should have—'

Alethea reached into the satchel containing their provision and handed Efigenia a pomegranate and a piece of bread, 'Here. Eat. He can't see you.'

'But I...'

'What do you think is going to happen? Nothing, I promise you that.'

She nodded, slowly, and took the knife Alethea handed her next. Her eyes widened as she cut the fruit open and sank her teeth into its red, bubbly grains.

I wish you'd done that a long time ago. Just look how you needed it. Perhaps you'll be like Persephone, only you'll ascend to the world of the living rather than the reverse.

Eucleides, who had taken the reins again, squinted at the afternoon sun. 'Maybe we should have left earlier in the morning. The gods only know what dangers roam this landscape.'

'Bandits and robbers. Perhaps a mountain cat or two, but no soldiers, I think. Not at this time of year,' Alethea said.

'Was that intended to ease my concerns?'

'I'm only telling the truth as it is.'

'I know. Are you frightened?'

'I was frightened in Athens—almost always, though I'm not sure you noticed. But now? No, I'm not frightened. I feel like a bird let out of captivity.'

Eucleides smiled, pressing his lips against hers for as long as he could without giving the horses free rein.

Althea savoured his smile and his kiss equally, for it was the first time since *that night* that she had seen him almost as glowing as before.

Efigenia had begun devouring the *artos,* her cheeks and fingers sticky with pomegranate juice, her eyes glazed with disbelief and joy all at once. 'Why are we not traveling more comfortably? We could have afforded it, could we not?' She threw a glance at Eucleides and hastily added: 'I'm not complaining, I swear I'm not.'

'We could have, I suppose, but I did not want to make too much of a show, considering...well, considering the circumstances. Are you feeling alright? You can borrow my *himation* if you're freezing.'

Efigenia laughed. 'No, not in this heat. But thank you.'

Alethea looked at her in awe. She had rarely seen her smile, and certainly never heard her laugh. It was a strained sound, like rusty machinery, yet wondrous beyond comprehension. Eucleides did not appear to have noticed, but then he was quite preoccupied with recovering his own mirth.

When night fell, they set up camp by the road. Having cooked a plain evening meal over an open fire and dined in thoughtful silence, they took to their beds: Efigenia curled up under the covering on the carriage, Alethea and Eucleides on a bedroll by the side of it.

'I can stay up and keep guard for the first few hours,' Alethea offered.

'I'll do it. You need rest.'

'And you don't?'

Eucleides tilted his head, his lips twitching in a smile. 'Why don't we both keep guard? It will be much more fun than staying awake alone, surely. Besides, we've had so little time for one another.'

That's true. And I've missed you. Alethea moved so that they were sitting facing one another, and clasped her arms around his neck. The campfire had died down to ember, the faint red light caressing their skin. She thought to kiss him but was unable to tear her eyes from the dark shield of thick eyelashes, the softly curved chin, the contour of his neck, the birthmark on his shoulder.

'What?' Eucleides said, his voice a half-whisper.

'Nothing. I just... Have I ever told you how much I like your eyelashes?'

'Never. Jealous?'

'Be serious!'

'I'm sorry.' He traced her faded scar with his thumb, continuing to her jaw and collar, 'Might one even say you love them?'

Ah. So that's where you want to go. Very well— I could never mind, not anymore. 'One might say that.'

'And what else?'

Alethea watched the ember reflect Eucleides' dark eyes. 'You. And you love me also, and I know it very well. Happy now?'

'As happy as can be in a place like this. My Stymphalian bird.' He pulled her closer, her legs encircling his waist. Alone on the plain save for a heavily sleeping Efigenia, Alethea felt infinite.

CHAPTER THIRTY-SIX

FOR ANOTHER FOUR days they travelled northwest before reaching that renowned city of Delphi: a place coated in mythological mist and incomparable reputation, thought to be the navel of the world. It clung to the slope of Mount Parnassos as if Apollo had glued it there himself for fear it might tumble down. The cluster of houses was similar to that of any other *polis*, tightly crammed and built of limestone and brick, the streets swarming with life. The eye-catching difference lay at the heart of the city. A high, sand-coloured wall encompassed the innermost sacred quarters. The road zig-zagged from the gates up the mountainside, passing monuments and treasure houses where *poleis* from all of Hellas stored their assets, leading to the imposing temple of Apollo. It was on this road the consultants would soon walk in procession carrying symbolic laurel branches. The temple itself towered on an elevated platform, its colonnades starch-white against the sky, its frieze striped in crimson and deep blue. Behind it towered an equally impressive theatre, which made Eucleides' eyes shine as he beheld it.

It was the fourth day of the month of *Boedromion* and they would have to wait three more before the Pythia would receive her consultants on the seventh day. There was the issue of housing: if they sought a host in Delphi, they would leave further trace. Efigenia still had to go as unnoticed as possible until they found a suitable place of sanctuary for her, and camping on the mountainside in the outskirts of the city was no more uncomfortable than the life they had led since leaving Athens.

'But it's not seemly that I should do that when there are other options available! A woman of my standing should never...'

Alethea rolled her eyes. 'A woman of your standing should not have come to begin with. But what alternative is there?'

'We...we could say that I'm Eucleides' wife and that you're our slave...?'

'Oh, yes, what a marvellous act to maintain for days. No, *thank you.* I've done enough acting. You're sleeping in the carriage.'

Eucleides said nothing since there was no point in taking sides when the matter had already been decided. They set up a provisory camp just outside the city, and tied the horses to an out-jutting cliff. *If Cosimo was here he would insist we found proper lodgings for him, preferably a palace. No. I cannot think like that. Cosimo isn't here.*

Not a single day had passed since *that night* without similar thoughts. Every time he noticed or heard something that would have made his cousin laugh or frown, the realisation washed over him like ice-melted water: he had heard that laugh and seen that frown for the very last time during the *symposion.* Then, there had only been twisted hatred and shock in Cosimo's eyes. The expression was carved in Eucleides' memory, not only from the night itself but from all those following it, when the events had played up over and over in his dreams. It was unlike the nightmares sprung from the incident at Eleusis; this time, he was certain of what had happened and what had not, he knew the extent of his guilt, yet he did not regret it. Dreams would cease their torment, as they always did, but if Cosimo had lived, the torment would have continued for another forty years and not only in Eucleides' head. *It's best this way. I cannot allow myself to think otherwise. It's best this way.* Whenever a qualm came upon him, he merely had to cast a glance at Alethea or Efigenia to extinguish it like a burning log in snow. He had come to love even his cousin's widow ardently—he imagined this was what it might be like to have a younger sister—and now, when he saw her flourishing, he realised just how much it had hurt to see her constrained. *And what will become of her? And of me? Well, the oracle can tell us that, or we wouldn't be here.*

The priests of Apollo required all consultants to state their business before approaching the temple. Eucleides had force patience while two tawny men in grey shrouds interrogated him. It was a simple question they wanted to ask, he told them, as simple as could be. Surely, they could not suspect any malicious intentions?

Eventually, the tawny men looked satisfied, having cross-examined Eucleides through and through. 'Very well,' one of them muttered. 'You may remain in the city and put forth your question to the Pythia when the time is ripe.'

Alethea held the laurel branch as high as she could, signifying an offering to the deities. Beside her walked Eucleides, carrying two more branches, and Efigenia, leading the bleating kid by a rope. The girl and the baby goat had become quite attached to one another, each small and bright and easily overlooked. Both in front of their retinue and behind it were numerous people on similar errands: men and women from every imaginable place and background flooding to the city in search for answers, brimming with hope and dread alike.

'How does she do it? I know it's Apollo, but she must do *something* to be worthy?'

Eucleides nodded. 'She fasts, she purifies herself in the Castalian Spring, just like we did this morning, and drinks holy water. Then...well, I do not know what happens after that. I do not think one is allowed to inquire.'

'No, no I don't either.' *I wonder what it's like, to have that much power even over men. She must be—*

An unmistakable pair of cat's eyes locked Alethea's gaze and cut her thoughts short. She froze in her step. Whisks of unruly hair the same dark nuance as her own, olive skin dappled with scars and blemishes, a square jaw. *It can't be. Impossible. But it is.*

Apolonio walked at the end of a small retinue, doubtlessly a Spartan envoy judging by their red tunics and military gear, their Corinthian helmets tucked under their arms. His steps did not falter, but neither did he avert his eyes from hers a single moment.

Alethea forced her legs to cooperate and continued walking, unwilling to share her discovery with Eucleides until she had had a chance to decide what action she would take.

They proceeded up the road, the laurel leaves fluttering in the wind, until they reached the temple. A golden statue of the god guarded his sanctuary, three times as high as a mortal, holding an elegantly wrought bow in one hand and a lyre in the other.

'Now what?' Efigenia whispered.

'Now we wait for our turn,' Eucleides said. 'How is the kid?'

The white little goat bleated in response. Alethea almost felt sorry for it, having spent the past eight days in its endearing company, but she had far more pressing matters on her mind. *I have to talk to him, I have to touch him if only to make sure it's no hallucination.*

'What occupies your thoughts?'

She shrugged. 'Nothing. Nothing. I only wonder what council we'll receive.'

The consultants drew lot, but it was no secret that delegations from *poleis* and those who offered the greatest sum of gold were guaranteed precedence, whether it was their importance or their wealth that had bought it. Hence, the Spartan envoy were the first group to enter the temple, bringing with them a beautiful sacrificial kid, though if Alethea knew her kinsmen right, they carried no coin.

She counted the consultants that came and went and reached seventeen before the turn passed to herself, Eucleides, and Efigenia. It seemed that those who entered the temple were then escorted out a different way than they had come, because she did not see the Spartans again. *Have I lost him a third time? First at Eleusis, then when he came to me in my fevers, and now… No. I refuse it.* She resolved to find him as soon as darkness fell, as soon as the matter of the consultancy was done with and she could leave Eucleides and Efigenia at their improvised camp by the carriage. Now, however, she required every bit of presence for the procedure that lay ahead. The oracle did not care if her visitors had just had their hearts put aflame with longing.

At last, their turn came. First, their guide sprinkled the sacrificial animal with spring water at an altar dedicated to Hestia. Alethea held her breath. If it did not tremble as it was supposed to, the consultancy could not proceed, for it was a bad omen. Fortunately, the kid quivered from the hooves and up, and she felt a surge of relief run through her. She exchanged a glance with Eucleides, who smiled.

The priest raised his arm and plunged the knife into the animal's throat with precision sprung from years of practice. The blood spurted out until there was no life left in the little creature, its legs buckled and it collapsed on the altar like so many of its peers had done over the past decades if not centuries. The internal organs, in particular the liver, were examined for signs that could aid the Pythia in her forebodings. Efigenia grimaced at the steaming pile of gleaming organs, where milky-white blended with brown and purple. She had likely seen similar ceremonies before, but not with the same frequency as the others, locked up inside one *oikos* or another since birth.

'Hmm. You may proceed to the oracle,' the priest declared after surveying the intestines.

'Thank you,' Eucleides replied.

Alethea clasped his hand in her left and Efigenia's in her right as the three of them climbed the steps to the temple and entered Apollo's legendary realm, led by one of the elderly priests. The words inscribed above the entrance rang in her head: *gnōthi seauton,* know thyself.

There was a certain odour inside the temple, a certain mist in the air that was too thin to quite discern. *It must be the fumes. The fissure from beneath the rocks, from Python.* The legend of the gigantic snake Python, whom Apollo had slain at the spot where his sanctuary now stood, was a common enough bedtime story used to frighten children. Still, it was far from just a story, and no one dared question the truth of it. The fumes from the beast's carcass played a central role in inducing the trance, and despite the Pythia being the only one who could enter the divine by breathing them, Alethea felt dizzy herself.

At the farthest end of the hall stood a large bronze tripod, and mounted on the tripod sat a surprisingly small figure. In one of her outstretched palms rested a dish of what appeared to be water, in the other a laurel branch. The Pythia wore a short, white robe signifying her supposed virginity. A purple veil framed her head; she had lifted the shield of fabric from her face for this occasion alone. Wrinkles were set deep in her skin like a shrivelled fig and her hair hung in brittle strands white as bone—yet her eyes held all the wisdom of the known world, specked with only a dash of madness, which was perhaps necessary in one performing the services she did.

The oracle's priestesses and female attendants were not present, but by her side stood a group of identically dressed, elderly men.

One of them made a gesture with his hand. 'You may put forth your question. Speak clearly. You may only ask once.'

Aletha looked at Eucleides, realising they had not decided who would speak. He gave her a slight nod and she took a step forward, her stomach in fluttering uproar. *I have to get it just right. I'll likely never have a chance like this again.*

'Revered Oracle. My companions and I come to seek your advice and take part of the knowledge given to you by the god Apollo. What will our future bring, what are our fates?'

The oracle closed her eyes. At first, the trance was a calm condition—Alethea could only compare it to Delina's violent seizures—then the prophecy came tumbling from her withered lips in incoherent, delirious chanting. The Pythia's voice was low and vibrant, rising in strength with every syllable until it thundered in Alethea's ears. It stopped abruptly and complete silence issued before the priest who had prompted them to ask their question cleared his throat.

'It is I who will interpret the Revered Oracle's sacred words for you as they were given by Apollo. The others may confirm what I tell you. The Revered Oracle has prophesied three things. One of you shall have fame extending beyond that of kings and more riches than queens. Another will know great misery. The third belongs to Hades.'

Alethea stared at him. 'Does she not say which fate belongs to whom?'

'The Revered Oracle speaks only what is necessary and what the god shows her. You may only ask one question. The session has come to an end—she must now receive another consultant.'

Like a flock of sheep, the group of three was ushered from the temple, a cascade of sunlight blinding them as they stepped out on the platform again. The ragged contours of Mount Parnassos against the evening lavender sky looked sharper than they had before, while the bustle among the treasury houses below felt more distant.

I'm not so sure the world makes more sense now. The opposite. Perhaps it was better to know nothing than to know just enough to truly wonder. Neither Eucleides nor Efigenia said anything, but Alethea knew what they were thinking. Who was the lucky one? Who was it who would ripe the astounding rewards the Pythia had mentioned? One's loss was another's gain, and as much as Alethea had prayed that they would all be designated equally prosperous fates, she could not deny the tiny part of her that hoped fortune might be hers. *Misery or Hades... I'd rather have none of those. Fame and riches... I can do without riches, but fame for me would be fame for Sparta, and—*

'Do I...do *I* belong to Hades?' Efigenia asked, clutching her bony elbows. She had forgotten to bring a parasol from Athens, and her alabaster skin had turned rosy under the sun the past few days.

'Surely not!' Eucleides squeezed her hand. 'She cannot have meant you.'

'There is no way of knowing that,' Alethea pointed out. *And it itches me as if she had stuck that cursed laurel branch under my clothes.* 'But the Pythia is never wrong, is she?'

Her lover shook his head, 'Never. Not in any of the stories I've read, be it tragedies or memoirs. It's not always like it seems at first, but she's always right one way or another.'

CHAPTER THIRTY-SEVEN

ALETHEA STOLE A quick glance at Eucleides' face. He looked as harmonious as a child exhausted from playing, his chest heaving with every deep breath, the back of his hand resting against his cheek. She planted a kiss on his nose, careful not to wake him, then left him to his dreams.

She had located the Spartan camp earlier that evening, and as she made her way through the outskirts of Delphi it was without doubt in her step. Other envoys sometimes resided in one of the finer houses in the city, but Alethea had expected nothing less of the Spartans than that they should sleep on the bare ground with the sky for roof and their red cloaks for beds. Just as she had thought, she found the five men a *stadion* east from where the mass of houses grew thick, camping on the mountainside.

Four men lay sleeping while a fifth, familiar figure sat erect, apparently keeping watch. *He knew I would come for him, or perhaps he intended to find me first. That's why he offered to stay up. We're two apples from the same tree—he knows me almost too well.*

Emitting no sound, Alethea treaded closer until she was less than an arm's width from her brother's back. She stretched out a finger and tapped his shoulder.

'You should be more on your guard.' Her voice was a mere whisper, yet Apolonio started as if she had shouted in his ear without warning.

'Alethea!'

'I did hope you'd still remember my name.'

'I would sooner forget my own.' Apolonio drew her close, wrapping his arms around her.

Alethea closed her eyes and buried her nose in his tunic. The familiar scent made her eyes sting with tears, both of joy and of anger over the hundreds of days in his company that had been stolen from her. In that moment, it became clearer than ever that no man or woman could hope to replace him in her affections, neither in this world nor in the next, because none could make her feel as absurdly complete.

Apolonio withdrew the slightest and whispered: 'I thought—I thought they killed you. I thought they killed you in that raid. That's what the *heílotes* claimed.'

'They lived? They got away when I didn't?'

'Only long enough to get back home. We finished them off as punishment. Terrible at taking care of their mistress. They said the fleet must have burnt your body along with the city.'

'They were mistaken, then, or maybe they were wrong on purpose. It doesn't matter. No one has burnt me yet, not as far as I know.'

'I can see that. You look...'

Alethea mirrored his smile. 'You too, brother dear. You look just like you were meant to. Thriving.'

They sat in silence for a good while, studying each other's faces, identifying every well-known curve and angle and faded freckle. At last, Apolonio broke the spell.

'If not death then what? What did they do to you?'

Alethea drew a trembling breath. 'They made me...they made me...they made me *serve* them. I wished it had been death many times over.'

'I'm glad you live. But I wish it had been *their* deaths.'

'In a way...' *I can tell him all about my sweet vengeance later. There will be time for that.*

As far as Alethea could tell, the other members of the envoy were still sleeping. Perhaps they dreamed of home, or perhaps of victory in the war that was dragging on without any clear direction. Night hung heavy in the air, the sky weighing on their shoulders, the moon barely visible behind a veil of clouds.

Apolonio licked his lips. 'Whose deed was it?'

'The most pathetic, loathsome man that walked this earth. Athenian,' Alethea could not contain herself any longer. 'If you had seen that grossly *perfect* chestnut hair, those delicate limbs—'

One of the soldiers stirred, turning on his back and rubbing the sleep from his eyes.

Alethea's heart skipped a beat. *I can't let them see me, not yet. The situation is too fragile, the man might think I'm an enemy. I have to speak to Eucleides and—* On instinct, she threw herself behind one of the stones poking up from the mountainside. The soldier had not seen her, but muttered something to his young companion about salted pork and Apolonio gave a succinct reply. From behind the cliff, Alethea saw them change positions: it was the other man's turn to keep guard and her brother's turn to drift off to Morpheus' lands of dreams. *No, no, not yet... I'll have to come back tomorrow. Yes, tomorrow, in broad daylight, once I have everything sorted. And then, then we'll go back home.*

When dawn broke, Eucleides gave Alethea a nudge and she stirred next to him.

'If you go and fetch some water in the public well, I'll try and mend that rein. The rock cut it last night.'

Her voice carried a note of teasing. 'You want me to do the woman's work, then?'

'I thought you might enjoy stretching your legs.'

'I know, I will,' she nodded at the covered carriage. 'Let Efigenia sleep a while longer. If we're lucky, she shan't bother us before breakfast.'

Eucleides watched Alethea get to her feet and begin her excursion towards the heart of the city and the well, two fingers hooked through the handle of one of the *amphorae* they had brought on their journey. Once the crowded streets swallowed her, he set to the task of mending the rein, which was easier said than done considering the fact that he had never before in his life had to mend anything himself. The needle prickled his fingers and the leather was unwieldy in his hands, the simple project requiring his attention in its entirety.

When he was nearly finished, however, he had the creeping sensation of not being alone, and raised his glance.

A broad-shouldered figure approached with the determined strides of a mythical lion hunting. Eucleides squinted, trying to place the face, and as the man came closer, he instantly recognised the unyielding silver eyes: the same kind of eyes he had spent so many hours gazing into, only more intense than Alethea's had ever been, burning cold with hate. Eucleides wiggled back on his heels and stood up, a nasty tickle in his stomach. The more he saw—the glistening skin, the coal-black locks, the linen and bronze cuirass—the higher fear spired in him. *What now? Have I given cause for such a man to pay a visit? Dear Aphrodite, let him be more amiable than he looks*. At the same time, there was that undeniable similarity that he could not quite pinpoint, that odd reminder of the woman he loved.

'Greetings, stranger. Might I be of any service...?'

The Spartan—Eucleides knew his visitor could belong to no other *polis*—clenched his jaw visibly but offered no reply. He took the last stalking steps towards Eucleides. His hands shot out and grabbed the collar of Eucleides' *khitōn*, almost lifting him from his feet, and slung him down on the dusty ground.

Eucleides gasped for air, rubbing his elbows and knees where gravel had carved into his skin leaving red little marks, and stared up at the Spartan who now towered above him. For the first time, he noticed the short bronze sword resting against the man's muscular thigh. Panic hammered in his chest. *If only I knew what I did to offend you—*

A crushing knee pressed against his ribcage, nailing him to the ground. Eucleides kicked and wriggled, stirring up dirt and scraping up his bare feet, but it was futile. 'Why—' he whiffed, the pressure on his chest forcing the air out of his lungs.

'You know why.'

'I don't! Please...'

'I never heeded Athenian squeals for mercy and I've no intentions of starting now.'

'If you only let me go, I'm sure I could explain! This...this animosity has no reason!'

'Reason?' the Spartan hissed. '*Reason?* My sister is enough reason for killing a hundred of your kind.'

Your sister. You mean... Eucleides' thoughts were cut short as the Spartan grabbed both his shoulders and smashed his skull against the rocky plain. The dull sound was nothing like the searing crack Eucleides had expected; the collision had not been hard enough. *Not because he couldn't have done it if he wanted to. Don't, don't, please don't.* The pain was all-consuming, spreading from the back of his head to his temples and forehead, shooting down his neck. It was as if his very brains had been beaten with a club. Dark flickered before his eyes, threatening to claim him, but to his distress, Eucleides remained conscious.

The other man reached for something in his belt—not his sword but a smaller, yet lethal knife. 'This is for all you cost me, all you cost her.'

I never hurt her. Never! Don't, don't— Eucleides wanted to scream but feared he might wake Efigenia, who still lay sleeping in the carriage. If the Spartan found her, there was no way of knowing what he might do.

'I swear...' He only got so far before the knife's cold blade slowly punctured the vulnerable skin just below his jaw. A trickle of warm blood emerged. In a horrified haze, he recalled what Alethea had told him when they had planned Cosimo's death: blood passed through an important vein there. Once it was cut, life would seep away quicker than wine pouring from an *amphora*. He had watched it being done to sacrificial animals time and time again, only now he was not just an onlooker.

The icy pain came in waves, each making him nauseated anew. The Spartan worked slowly, deliberately, though not a trace of enjoyment could be found in his face.

'You...' *You have gotten the wrong man. You must have!* The knife pushed just a little deeper, moved just a little farther, and Eucleides' mouth filled with blood rising from his throat.

A mere heartbeat later, something in the corner of his eye made all the gruesome pain seem insignificant in comparison. Only the scar on her cheek truly set Alethea aside from what had to be her brother—and the softer curve of her shoulders, dearer to Eucleides than any other sight.

'Apolonio! *Apolonio!*' She stumbled on the hem of her *khitōn* as she rushed towards them, cursed, and hiked up the fabric to her thighs.

The Spartan flinched and turned at his sister's voice. The knife slid a fatal hair's-width. Eucleides knew the vein had been severed as soon as the crimson trickle turned to a never-ending stream.

Something gnawed at Alethea's heart, just like the reputed fox who was said to have killed the boy who had tried to hide it underneath his tunic. It would gnaw on and devour the soft, mushy parts, however small those were, until only a hard lump remained. *At least then I won't feel a thing. That's preferable.* She dug her nails into her palms, piercing the skin. There was an incomprehensible torture in losing what had been the single source of light in her life for well over a year. Her chest cramped; vomit rose in her throat. Fate had stretched out its claws and mercilessly torn away the one person with whom she had ever felt Aphrodite's infatuating spell. The blood on her hands—Eucleides blood mixing with her own where her nails had left marks—stared back at her, mocking.

CHAPTER THIRTY-EIGHT

EFIGENIA COULD NOT erase the memory of what she had seen. Woken by Alethea's screams, she had peered through a crack in the wooden carriage. She had watched the two Spartans shout and gesticulate. She had beheld the scene as Alethea dropped to the ground and pressed her palms against Eucleides' throat in a fruitless attempt to stop the little fountain of blood, her hands soaked. Through that narrow crack of light, Efigenia had, for the first time, come to understand what true grief could be. After the initial screams, not a single sound crossed Alethea's lips. Her cheeks were wet with tears and her hands wet with red, yet she said nothing to her brother nor to Eucleides, whose own attempts at speaking only shortened his life, making him choke.

They had been forced to burn the body in a haste, without the chance to build a proper funeral pyre or execute the traditional ceremonies, since a body turned black from flames or better yet crumbled to ash could be claimed to have died a natural death, whilst a bloody corpse was an obvious sign of murder. None of the three living—Efigenia, Alethea, and her brother—had been emotionally fit to take care of the dead young man, but the alternative had been unthinkable. Sparta could be banished from the sacred grounds of Delphi on charge of breaking against the rule that peace be maintained between consultants at all costs. At least, Alethea had said in a voice crackled from crying, there was likely no *miasma*, seeing as Sparta and Athens were still very much at war and the gods might not consider the incident murder in the traditional sense.

Four days had passed since that morning and Efigenia still felt physically sick whenever she thought about it. *One of you belong to Hades. So that's what she meant. There are only two fates left, then... But it seems great misery is for both of us.* Eucleides had shown her more kindness than anyone else since she was a baby, Efigenia realised with a pang of pain. With him gone, she felt more alone than ever, for she was too different from the Spartans who had taken her and Alethea into their camp after the incident. She could never be one of them, never follow them back to their native city, and she knew they secretly loathed her for her fanciful appearance.

Efigenia had, however, quickly developed a fondness for Delphi. Mount Parnassos was as beautiful a scenery as she could have imagined, the striking cliffs and valleys flecked dark green with flourishing nature, the air crisp and somehow light. The city itself was so bustling with life and wealth yet so divinely sedate that no one who saw it could question that it was indeed the centre of the world, as found by Zeus' eagles. It rested between the earthly and the sublime, made irresistible. Indeed, it was a fine place to die—Efigenia did not know whether Eucleides would have preferred Athens— yet an even finer place to live. *And the heart of it all is the temple. Those who lodge there are truly fortunate.*

In that moment, she knew the answer to the question she had been asking ever since her husband died. Her future lay here, here in this pinnacle of wonders. No relative could locate her here; no man could hunt her down if her life was given to serving the god Apollo. If her father was searching for her, returned from his travels, he would never think to look in Delphi, and even if he did, he could do nothing to revoke the holy vows she intended to take. Doing so would be a grave offence against the gods, and Thaddeus was a pious man.

It had been Alethea's plan all along to find shelter for her in some sanctuary or other, Efigenia knew, and here was the ideal hideaway right before her eyes: beautiful, rich, secretive. The Pythias' female attendants lived in simplicity, true, but they lacked nothing, and possessed something far more valuable than any luxury: a privileged position. *Before, I would have wished to serve Hera, goddess of marriage, but what could be more tremendous than to be a priestess of light and of music?* Amidst all the sorrow and horrid images flashing before her eyes, she felt a warm thrill. *If I stay, I can watch over Eucleides' grave. If they'll have me, if they think I look virginal and...and gifted enough, then I shall be happy here. In due time. And I'm not a silly girl for daring to think that.*

'Talk to me. Please,' Apolonio pleaded for the fifth time that day. 'I'd rather you held a flowery oration than...than this.'

I don't care what you want. You know nothing of flowery orations. Eucleides did, he knew so many stupid things and— Alethea refused the barley bread her brother offered her. Neither her silence nor her fasting was really intended as a protest—she did not know what in particular to protest against—but there was something in her that paralyzed her, making it impossible to do anything but sit with her legs pulled up to her chest, chin resting on scraped knees, staring blankly ahead. Her greatest joy had turned into her greatest sorrow; in a matter of heartbeats, the soaring in her chest had switched to an abyss of despair. *If I could turn back time... If I had stayed and explained my abductor was already dead and not here with me, or if I had not gone for water...* The *if* stung her like no other word ever had. *If only, if only.*

Myrrene had once told her daughter of the denial which so often followed great loss, but Alethea found no trace of it. She knew Eucleides was naught but ashes and bones just as she knew the sun would rise in the east. His rose-petal lips would never again touch her skin. His unscathed hands would never again hold a scroll while he recited a favourite passage from a play to her. A million things had been snatched from them both, all in the blink of an eye.

Alethea had once wished she could hate Eucleides. Now, she wished the same of Apolonio, yet it was equally impossible despite his actions. Whichever god presided over these emotions was a cruel deity, cruel and perhaps full of blessings both, steering her mind where she did not want to go. *I should remain here always, until I wither away. I shouldn't go back, not forgive either.*

In that instance Alethea stopped herself. Such a sentiment was the contrary of everything she believed, it was as useless as a cup with a hole in the bottom. She was a firm believer that one had to pass through life not allowing neither sudden loss nor sudden gain to impeach on one's path. What good would it do her *polis* that she sulked away in Delphi? How did her paralyzed state further Sparta's victory?

And Apolonio. I do love him, I do. Didn't he act out of love for me, too? Was it not a twist of fate, or perhaps only coincidence, that dealt the true blow? Alethea could not deny it: had she been in her brother's shoes, she would have given the alleged perpetrator the same punishment.

The following morning, Apolonio delivered the message she had been expecting several days: the Spartan envoy was returning to the Peloponnese, and they had every intention of taking her with them. Sparta could not afford to lose a presumably fertile, native young woman, and he could not afford losing his dearest friend again.

'I told you once, did I not, that you've grown too soft-hearted,' Alethea mumbled.

Apolonio's eyebrows shot up. 'I hear you still have your voice.'

'Of course I do.'

'Don't mock me for my affections, then, when your own has nearly ruined you.'

'Don't you dare.'

'Will you come?'

She stood up and brushed the dirt off her *khitōn*. Her legs were stiffer than wooden poles after sitting in the same position through dawn and dusk many times over. 'I will. I know where I want to go. Home. But you'll have to bear with my mocking like you always have.'

A fragment of a smile twinkled in Apolonio's eyes. 'Gladly. I would have things as they always were.'

'Yes.' *It must be, with the passing of time and the turning of years. One loss already. Two is unnecessary.*

Taking farewell of Efigenia was no easy task. To Alethea's irritability, she had grown fond of the girl, especially during the past month, when Efigenia's vanity and skewed sense of hierarchy had begun to diminish little by little. The bond between them had shifted from acrimony to something almost resembling friendship, and not only because of the crime they had committed together.

'So you'll stay here?' Alethea tucked a strand of hair behind her ear, the wind stubbornly loosening it again. They were standing by the gate to the innermost part of Delphi. People surged forward on both sides of them, caught up in their daily businesses, the clopping of goats' hooves and the creaking of cart wheels mingling with raised voices.

'I will. They have already accepted me—not into the priesthood, yet, but as an attendant.'

'How did you bring that about?'

Efigenia shone, smoothening her new garments. 'I stopped waiting and took action. I went to the temple and sought out one of the priestesses. There are many of them, see, more than there are priests, but they keep out of public sight and assist the Pythia when she's not prophesying.'

Aren't you a bold little thing? Who would have thought? A knot of words struggled up in Alethea's throat. 'Promise me...promise me to...'

'To watch over his grave and see to it that his spirit does not wander in agony? Yes, I will.'

Alethea nodded several times, then shocked herself by clasping Efigenia in an embrace, nearly crushing the frail body in her arms. The scent of lavender oil was still present in the girl's skin; perhaps she had sneaked a bottle into the carriage when they left Athens.

They said nothing more. Alethea released her friend and turned away, joining the remnant of the Spartan envoy, who were impatiently tramping on the spot, eager to return to their polis to deliver whatever counsel they had received from the oracle regarding the war. Like a droplet of blood moving across the ambrosial landscape, the red-clad retinue began their journey.

Alethea's feet stirred up a cloud of dust as she ran, little sharp stones carving into her hardened soles. Her thighs burned, her throat was dry as leaves in autumn, her heart banged in her ears, yet she soared in a way she had not soared for almost two years. Apolonio's steps pounded behind her but she knew he would not win unless she let him. *I was always the fastest. I almost forgot it for some time.*

The chilly air bit her cheeks. When she finally stopped, allowing her brother to catch up, she soaked up the surroundings: her beloved Eurotas valley where the river trickled like a vein of teal. Winter was on the threshold; soon, the racing tracks would be coated in frost and the earth frozen.

'You're a sight for sore eyes, sister,' Apolonio said, panting.

'Now you lie. I'm all flustered.'

'Maybe.'

Alethea laughed and gave him a shove with her shoulder. 'Well. Pretty is not my most valuable quality, is it?'

Apolonio arched an eyebrow. 'Not by any means.'

'Good. Too tired to race back, too?'

'You insult me.'

As they sprinted towards the centre of Sparta, Alethea closed her eyes. In that moment, she did not think of how her heart had been beaten and battered, but only felt the ground beneath her feet.

EPILOGUE

ALETHEA COUNTED THE years under her breath, beholding the weathered gravestone where Eucleides' ashes lay buried. *Thirty-eight*. Yes, the memory of how her brother had helped her erect the first suitable stone they had found to mark the grave was thirty-eight years old, and yet it was as vivid as if it had happened that same morning. Time had dulled the pain until only the faintest trace remained, but it could never make her forget.

The warm breeze brushed against her tanned skin where wrinkles had long since emerged. She filled her lungs with the scent of olive trees and absorbed what lay before her. The city of Delphi was majestically perched on the mountain's slope like a bridge between earth and heaven.

The Pythia was not receiving visitors today—though the month was right, the day was not—but Alethea knew her old friend would welcome her in a less formal guise, just as she had done before being elected oracle from the pool of priestesses.

Efigenia's hair was a cascade of white gold let loose around her face, the colour as rare as the influence she commanded. As much as Alethea had initially hoped that she might be the one to obtain fame extending beyond that of kings and more wealth than queens, that hope had dwindled with every passing year, and she had reconciled with the lot of the miserable. After all, misery was highly temporary.

'I expected you,' Efigenia said, pouring them each a cup of wine. Her rich *khitōn* swayed as she crossed the mosaic floor in the temple's secret back room and sat down next to her guest on the steps by the colonnade. Here, no one would disturb them, yet they had an open view over the city below. She handed Alethea the gold-embossed cup. 'So. You aren't here merely for my sake, are you?'

'Do you know what he told me once, before we visited Eleusis?'

Efigenia leaned back against the sun-basted column and shook her head.

'That if he could, he would live forever.' Alethea sipped on the wine.

'Hm. Forever. We were never meant to—what would set us apart from the gods if we did? We wouldn't be able to stay quite sane.'

'I agree. I did then, too. But a few more years among the living wouldn't have hurt.'

'He would have been touched to see you visit so often. Almost every year, yes? Your husbands have been lenient.'

Alethea chortled and crinkled her nose. 'You still forget we do not play by the same rules in Sparta. Lenient or not, I'd have gone.'

Crysanthos had indeed never cared to interfere with her annual little excursions. They were brief and discrete enough, and he had still been preoccupied with his own reflection as well as with Apolonio's captivating glances. When he was unsuccessful of siring children and Alethea, to her smug delight, was wed to a member of the *krupteía*—

a match resulting in four little contributions to the *polis'* population—she had insisted on maintaining the tradition. After this husband's death in that fateful battle of Amphipolis, which soon brought about the first peace between Sparta and Athens, Alethea had promptly refused every offer of remarrying, though she could still have born children for years to come.

'Do you miss it? Your city of silver?'

Efigenia tilted her head. 'You haven't asked me that in a long time. I'm not so sure Athens is still that... My consultants ask me when it shall regain its glory. I cannot reveal it, since Apollo sends me no sights of it.'

'Well. We were merciful, were we not? We could have burnt it to the ground. The idiots rejected our peace offerings time and time again, if you recall.'

'They did many unwise things, it's true. Yet I would not call them idiots—you cannot deny it's a truly illustrious place.'

Alethea could not suppress the half-smile as she, for the thousandth time, thought of how the Athenians had broken the first peace by launching an expedition to Sicily and ended up with their fleet demolished. *That Alcibiades was never good for much else than drinking and running after* hetairai. *To let him lead an expedition...!* The war had raged on, the wound brutally opened when it had barely begun to heal, continuing for another decade before Sparta with its weapons of bronze at last stood victorious over Athens with its wealth of Laurion silver.

'What...what do you think will become of this Hellas of ours?' Efigenia asked, squinting at the houses and the wide-stretched landscape below.

'Only the gods know that. But I think it will be well remembered.'

AUTHOR'S NOTE

I believe accuracy is key when writing historical fiction. *City of Bronze, City of Silver* largely focuses on real events and several of the minor characters are based on historical figures. However, I have taken liberties with certain details for the benefit of the story.

Historians differ on much regarding the Ancient World and our sources are often biased and fragmentary. Source material which is particularly scarce is that concerning women. Women were, as I have attempted to convey in this novel, thought to be better seen than heard, and sometimes not even that. According to their contemporaries, the ideal Athenian woman should be discreet enough to not be spoken of by men, a sentiment which is clear in, for example, Pericles' famous funeral oration as retold by Thucydides. On the few occasions when women are mentioned in Athenian law court speeches, it is generally not by name but in reference to their male relatives, often their guardian, who exercised complete control over them. Add to this that highly regarded philosophers such as Aristotle and Xenophon considered women to be baser, "failed" versions of men, and it becomes obvious that Ancient Greece was not always as civilized as we tend to imagine.

Sparta was the rare exception. I will refrain from going into great detail on the differences between a woman's standing in Sparta versus in Athens and other parts of Greece since the subject remains a theme throughout this book. What should be noted, though, is that while the otherwise so conservative Sparta was radical in its attitude towards women, it was in no way a feministic utopia per today's definition. Rather, the liberties women enjoyed there were based on the state's simplistic ideals and its need for thriving mothers, not a modern philosophy on gender equality.

There is also the issue of slavery. This institution was considered a natural part of society to the extent that extremely few contemporaries reflected upon it; there was no abolitionist movement that we know of. Many city states' economy was entirely based on slave labour, especially Sparta's, where the relatively small clique of citizens was vastly outnumbered by the suppressed *heílote* population who tended to their fields.

One final thing to note is that sexuality in ancient Gree ce was viewed very differently from how we see it today. People rarely, if ever, identified with being hetero-, homo-, or bisexual, to mention only the most common present-day labels. These terms did not even exist at the time. Rather, sexuality was thought to be fluid and change through life's different phases. The practice of pederasty, in which an older man acted as a mentor, teacher, and lover to an adolescent boy until the boy reached adulthood and could switch to the role of the older party, was widespread, especially in the elite. Of course, we would define it as statutory rape, but ancient Greek societies considered it the purest kind of love, as discussed at length in Plato's *Symposion*. However, homosexual relationships were expected to include an age gap and not occur between two grown men (or women). This was because one party in the relationship would always have to take on the passive, "feminine" role, which in turn was thought humiliating for an adult male, while a boy was already inferior by nature.

The opinions portrayed in *City of Bronze, City of Silver* belong to the characters and are not synonymous with my own.

ABOUT THE AUTHOR

Saga Hillbom is a Swedish author of historical fiction, as well as an avid reader. *City of Bronze, City of Silver* is her third novel; earlier works include *A Generation of Poppies* and *Today Dauphine Tomorrow Nothing*. Saga currently studies history in Lund. To get in touch, you can send an email to @sagahillbom02@gmail.com, send a message on Instagram at @writing_history_, or visit her author website at sagahillbom.blog.